MW00762847

Dream Destinations
Every River Has a Story II

Fly Fishing Fabled Waters

John Mordock

Art by Melody Mordock

This book is dedicated to my wife Melody, who sometimes accompanied me on my trips to Western rivers, and to all my children, Kalay, Kaylin, Marten and Mason, who tolerated the time I spent fishing.

An Invitation to the Reader

Readers who have visited the rivers I discuss are welcome to share their thoughts with the author. On some rivers, especially those subject to riverside development or releases from dams, situations may change and the fish populations may change along with them. Address correspondence to: John B. Mordock, c/o Hidden River Books, 52 Old Farms Road, Poughkeepsie, New York, 12603. All letters are appreciated.

Copyright © 2009 by John B. Mordock

ALL RIGHTS RESERVED: No part of this book may be reproduced or transmitted in any form by any means, electronic or mechanical, including photocopying and recording, or by any information storage and retrieval system without written consent of the author/publisher, except in the case of brief excerpts in critical reviews and articles. All inquiries addressed to

Marson Productions/Hidden River Books
52 Old Farms Road
Poughkeepsie, New York 12603
845-849-1930

Library of Congress Control Number: 2009920763

Mordock, John B.
Dream Destinations: Every River has a Story II
ISBN 978-1-58776-898-9
p.cm
1. Fly Fishing—Western Rivers. I. Title

All photographs are by the author or his wife unless otherwise noted
Art and Illustrations by Melody Mordock
Cover photo: Idaho's Big Wood River courtesy of
Terry Ring of Silver Creek Outfitters
Mountain Man drawing by Marten Robitaille
Cover Photo of Rainbow Trout courtesy of Richard McCombie

675 Dutchess Turnpike, Poughkeepsie, NY 12603
www.hudsonhousepub.com   (800) 724-1100

Contents

Preface

In my first book, *Northeast Trout, Salmon, and Steelhead Streams: Every River Has a Story*, I featured streams in the Northeast. Although a number of Northeastern streams are storied ones, New York's Beaver Kill is the only one fished substantially by out-of-state visitors. Recent creel surveys suggest that anglers from 40 states and 8 countries visit the river each year. Nevertheless, few anglers consider trips to Eastern streams to be "dream trips." More often anglers plan "dream trips" to rivers in the West. Whether they make only one major trip in a lifetime or one every year, it will most likely be to a river discussed in this volume. For example, in 1991 and 1992 anglers from every state but Delaware, and from 11 foreign countries, fished Bighorn River, discussed in Chapter Five, and in 2005, the last good year on the Bighorn before the region's recent droughts, 43,332 nonresident anglers fished the first 13 miles of river.

My angling companions and I make one major fishing trip each year and our choice of rivers to visit follows conversations with other anglers and reading articles in national magazines. With the advent of the Internet, there are now websites featuring every major river in North America. Unfortunately, material on the Internet, or even in national magazines, like *Northwest Fly Fishing,* is not always helpful. Information in these sources is often written by owners of fly shops, lodges, and outfitting companies, and even by fishing guides, and they often stretch the truth. Although the credits under an article may state that the author is a "freelance writer and photographer," often the writer earns his livelihood on the river.

For example, on a website about Red Deer River, located in Red Deer, Canada, pictures of large browns appear and the written material stresses that the pictured fish were caught on dry flies. Drooling over the possibility of fooling 20-inch fish on the surface, we drove from Calgary to Red Deer on one of our trips to Alberta. Unfortunately, the river was high and dirty and although we saw some huge rise-forms in a section too deep to wade, we saw no others rising elsewhere. Working a section, where we'd been advised to go, three of us had no hits in two hours of fishing. In addition, slime covered the shoreline cobblestone and slimy algae stuck to our lines and waders. If I lived nearby, I might find more aesthetically pleasing waters and learn to catch the Red Deer's big fish in them. Nevertheless, talking later with anglers in Alberta, they felt the Red Deer wasn't worth the travel time and that most of its big browns were caught at night on streamers.

The major rivers I discuss in this volume, as well as relate stories about, especially stories about those who lived along them, include a number in national parks, such as: the Madison and Yellowstone in Yellowstone National Park; the North and South Forks of the Flat Head in Glacier National Park; the Snake in Grand Teton National Park, the San Juan in northwestern

New Mexico, near the Four Corners and Mesa Verde National Park; the Bow in Calgary, with headwaters in Banff National Park; and the rivers of Southern Alberta, near Waterton Lakes National Park. Others are located near national monuments or in or near national recreation areas, such as: the Bighorn, in Eastern Montana, adjacent to both Bighorn Canyon National Recreation Area and Little Bighorn Battlefield National Monument; the Green, in northern Utah, near Flaming Gorge National Recreation Area and Dinosaur National Monument; and the Big Wood and Big Lost, as well as Silver Creek, in Idaho's Sun Valley, near the Sawtooth National Recreation Area. Still others are near major tourist centers, such as the Frying Pan and Roaring Fork in the Colorado Rockies near Aspen and Independence Pass.

All these rivers, and those nearby that I discuss, are in vacationlands visited by millions each year. The last chapter highlights the River Itchen and its storied history, a chalk steam in southeastern England where dry fly and nymph fishing was born. Not many anglers plan a "dream trip" to the River Itchen, but some plan a family vacation to Great Britain and those familiar with our sport's history may travel to Winchester to visit this storied river and perhaps even to wet a line in it.

Along with the stories and historical information I present in the text, I weave into my fishing tales lots of technical information about fly fishing. As a result, novice anglers should come away with a host of techniques to help them to fool the most wary of trout. Important to family members who don't fish, is that I suggest places to stay and to dine, sites worth seeing, and activities family members might enjoy near each river.

Perhaps the major feature of this book is that I discuss rivers from the perspective of one who fishes to capture the memories and emotions each river environment generates. While hooking and landing fish is exhilarating, more important are the pleasures one gets from a specific river, pleasures I try and relate throughout the book. A quote from George Mendoza's 1977 book, *Secret Places of Trout Fishermen*, sums up what I try to capture.

> When I wade into a river fishing for trout I feel as though I am entering another part of my soul. And as I watch the early lights flower in the shadows, I know I have come to the river seeking more, much more than the catching of trout.

I would like to acknowledge: Terry Ring, of Silver Creek Outfitters, for the use of his photographs, with one appearing on the cover, another in the color inserts, and still others in Chapter Four; Hal Harris, of Bighorn Fly Shop and Jeremy Gilbertson, of Big Sky Fly Fishers, for photographs that appear in Chapter Five; and Scott Daniels, Richard McCombie, Harold McMillan, Jr., Tom Royster, and Mike Zelie for the use of their photographs.

Chapter One

Putting It Into Perspective

Like my first volume, *Northeast Trout, Salmon and Steelhead Streams: Every River Has a Story*, this volume describes my experiences on rivers that many fly fishermen only dream of fishing, others visit at least once during their lifetime, and the well-healed visit regularly. All of the rivers but one, Great Britain's River Itchen, are located in North America's West and all but several have been featured in outdoor publications.

Most of the days of my life pass by without leaving even a trace, but every so often, a day stands out so sharp and clear that everything else in my past fades into oblivion. Fishing has provided me with many such days. The book features days that stand out in my memory. Memories of blue-ribbon rivers I've traveled to fish and perfect moments on them, and memories of people who fished them with me. These memories enriched my knowledge of those who took substance from these rivers and those who gave substance back. Stories about the rivers will include those about early pioneers, horse thieves, Native Americans, river keepers, and river characters. Hopefully, my stories will provide readers with a mental picture of each river, because with meaningful imagery, a visit to a river is more enjoyable. English River Keeper, Frank Sawyer, in his 1958 book, *Nymphs and the Trout*, remarked:

> It is very fascinating to peer into the water, for even as the sky changes when the sun or moon passes from east to west, so changes a running stream. What is seen any hour of study must forever remain only as a picture imprinted on the plate of memory and if sufficiently interesting it will never be forgotten.

I also hope my stories will add to the reader's personal geographies and enlarge their sense of possibilities.

Each of the Western rivers I discuss flows through a matchless environment, but common among them is the weather. Each day begins with the faint light of dawn and if a cloud or two are on the horizon, the backdrop turns pink, and then red, and then silver. Later, the rising sun sends streaks of gold across the river valley. As the sun creeps higher, a soft haze forms and the shades of the surrounding cliffs change colors and sizes. Warmth, mixed with the crisp morning air, follows and the distant haze vanishes.

About midmorning, single clouds have come together to form patches and a warm breeze sweeps across the valley grasses and sings through the foliage of riverside trees. Then the patches multiply, casting shadows across the river valley that hide the wandering course of the river.

By late afternoon, the clouds become dark, towering castles and rain showers appear on the horizon. Then it grows dark as the castles gather and flashes of lightening plummet from their midst to the valley floor. I leave the river to seek shelter and, as the clouds move closer, I brace myself against the accompanying winds. The heavy rain peppers the river with giant drops, making heavier splashes than rising fish. Just as quickly as the threatening storm arrives, it departs, the sun reappears, and I'm casting to rising trout once again.

Other mornings are cold and bleak and dark gray skies suggest that heavy rains will spoil the fishing, but the clouds separate by mid-morning and when the sun's warmth breaks through, the landscape becomes a colored mosaic. I begin each morning clothed in a sweatshirt and raincoat, but, before long, the sun warms my back and I strip down to my short-sleeved shirt and dip my hat in the river to cool my sweating forehead. A prairie breeze, or a light afternoon thundershower, is welcomed. Occasionally, a cold front moves in and hailstones fall from the clouds. I hastily put on my sweatshirt and raincoat. Within a short time, however, the dark clouds move on and the afternoon sun reappears and I strip down again.

Toward evening, cool air, dropping from higher elevations, accompanied by a brisk wind blowing softly through the cottonwoods and ruffling the meadow grasses, prompts me to, once again, don my sweatshirt, and sometimes my raincoat to beak the wind, but the cold is a welcome change from the late afternoon sun. At dusk, the clouds begin to break up and by the time I'm at my car, disassembling my equipment, they've disappeared and bright stars illuminate the entire sky.

For weeks after I return East from fishing a brawling, open Western river, I feel closed in, confined, restricted; I miss standing on a riverside knoll, seeing the distant mountain peaks, the vastness of the lowland valleys, and the clear skies at night and I begin planning my next trip almost immediately. More than 100 years ago Viscount Grey of Fallodon, best described my feelings in his 1899 book, *Fly Fishing*:

There come times when the beauty of the day or of the place seems to possess us, so that the thought of angling afterwards becomes full of beautiful associations of delightful meadows and woods, of light upon water, of the sounds of streams, till the recollections of days that are past, the vision of these things, perpetually rises up and fills us with joy.

Life holds many promises and we set numerous goals in keeping with them. Nevertheless, after each goal is reached, most of us feel a little lost and, after a time, experience new longings. Eventually, we learn that life is full of longings never quite realized, causing the philosophers among us to contemplate the meaning of life. Nevertheless, listening to a rushing stream and watching the shadows of clouds moving across a river valley, animals drinking along a riverbank, birds of pray drifting in wind currents high overhead, wild flowers rustling in prairie winds, and trout rising steadily to hatching mayflies, causes all longings, as well as philosophical dilemmas, to be forgotten and life experienced in its fullest; nowhere is it experienced fuller than in the vast open spaces and high mountains of the West.

The Roots of This Book

I once submitted to an outdoor magazine an article describing my fishing experiences in northern Wisconsin, where I'd spent a summer as a visiting professor at the University of Wisconsin at Green Bay. I thought my angling adventures in this popular vacationland might benefit fishermen who thought the area worth a visit. Green Bay is Wisconsin's limestone thumb that juts northward into lake Michigan, often compared to Cape Cod, but with a Midwest atmosphere.

As a boy, I'd fished the waters of Lake Michigan and Green Bay for warm-water fish, with my mother cooking perch as fast as we caught them. My father was in the Navy Reserve and he kept a boat at the Great Lakes Naval Station. Each summer, after sanding and varnishing its weathered mahogany interior, and sometimes repainting its old wooded hull, we would cruise up the Lake Michigan shoreline, catching and cooking our meals on our way to Green Bay. Nevertheless, I'd never fished any of Green Bay's inland rivers and was looking forward to this opportunity after 35 years away from this magnificent country.

Maps of the area weren't much help. The Wisconsin Department of Natural Resources published a 100-page guide, *Wisconsin Trout Streams,* which classified streams into three categories. Nevertheless, all the streams were drawn the same size on the state map. Similarly, the county maps purchased from the Department of Transportation failed to adequately distinguish their size. I wasted hours exploring blind alleys, hiking along creeks, expecting them to widen as they approached the lakes, but instead finding them deeper and narrower and impossible to cast into. Working

Tom Royster on a small mountain stream in the Canadian Rockies

upstream, hoping to find open wetlands, I ended up in mosquito-invested, half dead, mucky forestland.

After a summer of exploring the region's streams, with 196 streams listed as trout waters for Marinette County and 104 for Oconto County, only two in Marinette County, the Pike and Middle Inlet, and two in Oconto County, the Oconto, and the upper North Branch of the Thunder, contained some fly fishing waters. Middle Inlet was a creek-lovers delight, but from the highway, it was indistinguishable from the others. I discovered that browns travel up Middle Inlet from Lake Noquebay, a 2,000-acre lake, to occupy its cool waters during the summer months, unwilling to share the lake's cool depths with pike and muskellunge. I describe my experiences on Middle Inlet in my book *Capturing Rogue Trout: Strategies of a Third Generation Fly Fisherman.*

I also wasted time on the Pestigo River's fly-fishing-only section, located below a power plant. An article in a national magazine touted it as an excellent tail-water fishery. In the morning, I could walk across the river in rubber boots, but not long after a siren sounded, I would need a John Boat with a heavy anchor. The article said 20-inch holdovers inhabit the river, but I saw neither fish nor another fisherman. There wasn't a dimple when a hatch began, nor did my streamer produce any hits; the place was dead! Either the stocked fish were taken earlier or washed downstream. Stocked trout often die of exhaustion in tail-waters with large releases and my bet is that many Pestigo River trout did just that! Years later, studies on the river revealed that browns travel up to 12 miles to reach tributaries where high releases can be avoided. One brown moved downstream 10 miles in four days, but did it move or was it flushed downstream?

The Wolf River, a river protected by the Wildlife Scenic Rivers Act in

1968, which runs the length of nearby Menominee County, and Langlade County above it, was a major body of water and an article in *Field and Stream* said that big trout haunted its upper waters. The state classified it as a Class II stream, meaning it contained some native trout, but required moderately heavy stocking to maintain the fishing. On my one trip to the Wolf, it looked like it belonged in a class by itself. If this was a wild and scenic river, than the Chicago River should be similarly classified. The water was extremely muddy, refuse formed much of the structure, the rocks were covered with slime, and the backwaters were thick with algae. In addition, a local Native American tribe was involved in major disputes over property and river rights.

In the article I wrote about the area, I described my efforts to separate productive from unproductive streams. I mentioned the long hikes required to locate fishable spots that held trout, but emphasized that once a big trout was located, it was a challenge to fool it underneath the overhanging bushes where it fed, as the big fish spooked easily and retreated to places where only proficient casters could reach them. The magazine editor rejected the article, claiming that readers were not interested in negative experiences. Perhaps so, but trout fishermen considering a trip to Green Bay might have benefited from the article and saved hours of wasted efforts.

Years later, in October of 2004, I planned a trip to Northern California's Sacramento River after reading several intriguing articles about it. The first article, on the upper Sac, appeared in the Spring 1999 issue of *Northwest Fly Fishing* and the second, on the lower Sacramento, appeared in the September 1999 issue of *Fly Fishermen*. Both articles are misleading, as they suggest that large rainbows can be easily taken in the river by visiting anglers. Unfortunately, this isn't true. Time and patience are required to learn the river's secrets and certain water conditions are needed to apply them. In addition, the river environment leaves much to be desired.

I first learned to fly fish for trout in Northern California, but not in its major rivers, but in the streams and lakes in the High Sierra. My Uncle Jim invited me when I was a boy to accompany him and my cousins on a pack trip that began from the floor of Yosemite Park and went up into what is now called the Ansel Adams Wilderness, named after the famous photographer who extensively photographed Yosemite Park. I remember both the beautiful Merced River that meandered through the Park and the Tuolumne River that ran through meadows by the same name. I asked Uncle Jim why we didn't fish them and he remarked that the rivers in the valley were heavily stocked and crowded with anglers. He claimed, and he was right, that we wouldn't see another fisherman in the high-lakes region.

I remember well my mule, named Fly. She liked to look over the edge of the cliffs as she walked along the steep trails winding our way up the mountains. I was sure I would die, but the guide assured me that Fly had been gazing into the valleys for years and hadn't fallen yet. Fly also liked to stop when she gazed, holding up the other mules. The guide got annoyed at me because it wasn't easy for me to get Fly to move again. I asked him if he would like to exchange his horse for Fly, as I had ridden some stubborn horses, but he assured me that Fly was more sure-footed and that only an experienced trail rider could handle a horse on this terrain. When we came to a wide section in the trail, the guide singled me to stop so the others could pass me by. Fly and I were now second to last in the convoy. The guide was afraid that if I went last I would never be heard from again.

I was surprised to learn that meadows exist in the high mountains: meadows towered over by iridescent granite domes. Our base camp was alongside a clear stream winding through a meadow laced with wild flowers. The stream, like others in the area, was so small I could straddle it in places. Yet, it contained trout up to 15 inches. I didn't catch any, however, until my Cousin Becky showed me how to approach them from the bank. Much of what I learned from my cousin and uncle, I later read in Ray Bergman's classic book, *Trout*. For example:

> I approached the bank with great caution, crawling on my hands and knees for the last twenty feet. Then on reaching the water I cautiously peeked upstream. The best way to fish this stretch was to crawl along the bank and cast carefully some distance upstream (*Trout*, pg. 237).

The High Sierra's biggest fish occupied the clear, glacial lakes above the tree line—Red Devil Lake, Edna Lake, and others. No scrubs grew around their shores and they contained no vegetation; they were simply granite bowls. If strong winds blew, and they often did, the long hike from base-camp up to a lake was immediately followed by a long hike elsewhere.

I had planed to return to the High Sierra, but trout may no longer occupy the high mountain lakes I fished as a boy. The introduction of trout into waters normally without them had unforeseen consequences on the biological habitat. The mountain yellow-legged frog, once the most common amphibian in the High Sierra, may become listed under the Endangered Species Act. Unlike other tadpoles that turn into frogs within several months, the yellow-legged frog lingers in the tadpole stage from two to four years in the deep lakes. As a result, trout have feasted on them to near extinction. If only the frog was endangered, most environmentalists wouldn't care, but introducing trout into the high lakes produced other problems as well. Fish waste spurs excessive growth of algae, which, in turn, pushes out certain aquatic creatures and causes a decline in terrestrial predators, like the mountain garter snake; no snakes results in more small animals! The result is a ripple effect that travels up and down the food chain.

Ralph Cutter, owner of the California School of Fly Fishing, argues that trout shouldn't be stocked in waters in which they never existed. He remarks, "These fisheries are entirely artificial. It's like a peewee golf course for fishermen." I would agree with his position on biodiversity, but I would strongly disagree that fishing these high lakes is like fishing stocked ponds. I can assure you they were not; catching trout in these lakes was as tough, if not tougher, than catching them elsewhere, an experience I describe briefly in *Capturing Rogue Trout.*

Arriving at Redding around four o'clock, I left Melody at the motel and went to fish for California's "Hot Sac" rainbows in the lower Sacramento, a tail-water river where one author wrote, in the September 1999 issue of *Fly Fisherman,* that "football shaped rainbows" will "run you into your backing." Although I doubted the author's statement that "the prospect of hooking as many as 50 fierce-fighting rainbows in a day is good," I was intrigued by his belief that "Sacramento's football shaped rainbows are the hardest fighting rainbows I've ever encountered anywhere in North America."

Unlike the Bighorn, Green and San Juan, where very cold water either limits or prevents rainbows from spawning, rainbows can successfully spawn in the lower Sac because releases from Shasta Dam, America's second highest dam at 602 feet, are not bottom releases, but releases from portals located at different levels on the dam. There also is a water-cooling facility at Shasta Dam that helps make the water more suitable for spawning salmon. The released water then travels through a seven-mile channel where it's released from Keswick Dam into the lower river. Many rainbows are stocked, however, because the high water conditions limit the spawning areas.

One author wrote that the river has good public wade-in spots at the Knighton Road access and at Anderson River Park in the town of Anderson, eight miles south of Redding. I headed to the closer of the two, the Knighton Road access. Nevertheless, access to the river is actually along River Road, reached by taking the Knighton Road exit from Hwy. 5, south of Redding, and turning at the first left. Driving along this road, I located only three small pull offs. Two were full, and at the third, the river was too deep to wade. I then drove downstream to his second suggested spot, Anderson Park, but the river was even deeper and motorboats were anchored off the park.

I went back toward Redding and attempted to access the river at the launch site at South Bonnyview Road. It was too deep. Two guides were retrieving drift boats from the water and I asked them where I could wade the river. They directed me to where I'd already been—River Road, off the Knighton Road exit—suggesting that I park next to the first gate I came to, called "Blackberries Gate," and then take the trail running from the gate north to the river. Having already been there, I knew there was just enough space for the two cars currently parked at the gate, where three dead Chinook salmon were on the ground, taken by poachers who must've had second thoughts and left them. I then asked one of the four anglers how their group did and he reported that they each hooked three fish. I asked if they'd been on a full or a half-day float. One responded indignantly, "A full-days float, of course!" I left thinking that three fish in a day's float were a far cry from the numbers reported by one writer.

I returned to River Road and parked at a pull-off past Blackberries Gate.

Two anglers, a man and his wife, were leaving the river. I asked them how they did and they reported "zilch" for their first day's effort. They, too, had been attracted to the river by a magazine article. They were from Pennsylvania and had fished for trout throughout America. Like myself, they'd been intrigued by the claim that "Sac" rainbows fought harder than comparably sized Alaskan rainbows and since they'd both fished in Alaska, they were anxious to test this assertion.

They fished upriver from Turtle Bay in Redding in the morning and at River Road in the evening, working "Glow-Bugs" (imitation salmon eggs), behind spawning salmon, a technique recommended by one author who wrote, "If you can find spawning salmon, you can often find rainbows behind them feeding on eggs." Neither had hooked a fish nor had they seen trout caught by others. As it was now growing dark, and the trail from Blackberries Gate to the river was long, I decided to wait until tomorrow to begin fishing.

On my way back to the motel, I stopped at The Fly Shop, located on Churn Creek Road, and got free maps of the area. After examining the maps and talking with the shop manager, I decided to fish at the islands off Girvan Road. When I awoke the next morning, rain was pouring down and the wind was howling. Melody had already made plans and insisted I go fishing. I ate a leisurely breakfast and when the wind died down, about eleven o'clock, I went to the Girvan Road access.

Three fishermen were rigging up when I arrived. One was familiar with the river and was helping his companions to rig up properly, telling them their Glow Bugs had to be right on the bottom, with the proper amount of weight the key to hook ups. I asked the leader about the fight of the fish and he said that the wild fish, usually those shaped like a football, were good fighters, but they fought no better than those in many other California rivers. In fact, he mentioned a river I'd never heard of where he thought rainbows fought exceptionally hard.

I rigged up in the rain, thankful that my no-sweat waders would allow my rained-soaked pants to dry while I fished. After working my way along the islands and over rocks covered with yellow slime, I found the main channel where the three anglers had begun fishing. The river was at its lowest level, with a release of 5,000 cubic feet per second (cfs), and all but the main channel were too shallow to hold fish. Nevertheless, if it were summer, when releases are between 8,000-cfs and 15,000-cfs, these channels would be too deep to wade. The river can be waded only when the release is around 5,000-cfs, usually between October and April.

Wading out to cast up into the seam bordering the fast water in the main channel required finding spots where rocks were free from yellow slime because footing was difficult, even with studded boots. Well-spaced along the bank, and slinging well-weighted Glow Bugs below yarn indicators, we all caught nothing in the 90 minutes I fished. I left the three to their solitude as about 90 minutes of unproductive slinging is about all I can tolerate.

In the afternoon, Melody and I drove above Shasta Lake, the largest reservoir in California, to fish the upper Sac, 38 miles of freestone water enclosed by dams creating Lake Siskiyou to the north and Shasta Lake to the south. I'd forgotten about the morning's rainstorm, however, and the upper Sac was a torrent of brown water that would take several days to clear up, suggesting that scheduling a short fishing trip to the upper Sac is not advisable. In contrast, such a rainstorm would make little impact on most of the rivers featured in this book. Even when the river is clear, however, it's primarily deep-pocket water fishing, not may favorite activity.

In the evening, I fished the lower Sac above Turtle Bay in a section called "Posse Grounds." All of the anglers, including one drift boat, were casting along the seam adjacent to the fastest water (called "power water") in the main channel, where waves were breaking, reached by wading across wide flats occupied by spawning salmon. Unfamiliar with the flats, I was reluctant to wade across them under low light conditions and instead fished riffles on the park side of the river.

Salmon were spawning in these waters and, considering the recommendation to fish behind spawning salmon, I wondered why all the anglers were fishing the power water instead of the flats, where salmon were spawning. Once in a while a salmon in the power water would catapult out of the water several times, making huge splashes on each return. I was told that these were females trying to shake the row loose from their inner skins.

There was one other angler beside myself on the park side of the river. He was wheelchair bound and was spin casting with a Glow-Bug below a bobber. This was the first time he'd fished the river, but he'd also read the suggestion to fish behind spawning salmon and could easily reach some from this spot. Neither the Glow-Bug nor the Woolly-Bugger I threw, when I became board slinging a weighted rig, resulted in a single hit, nor did those cast by the physically challenged angler. I inadvertently snagged several salmon, but they were intent on spawning and not on escaping, and I had to jerk the fly loose.

Salmon in the Sac have swum through the Golden Gate, traveled northwest through San Francisco Bay and into the delta, and moved upriver to their spawning beds. The river also has a winter run of Chinook that spawn in the spring, the only population, or subspecies, of Chinook that do so, but because of the highly fluctuating winter water releases from the dam, this unique population faces extinction.

I caught the ancestors of these salmon in the Pacific Ocean as a teenager. My second cousin, George Rust, and I would take his small boat out under the Golden Gate and fish for salmon in the waters just north of the bridge. George got seasick every time we went, but his love of fishing enabled him to tolerate it until it passed. Forty-eight years later, my daughter, Kaylin, caught a 20-lb. salmon in these same waters. She currently lives a stone's throw from where my Uncle Jim and Aunt Kay lived. As a special treat, her employer chartered a boat and took his staff salmon fishing.

George lived in New York for a short time and during this period he and I fly fished together on several occasions. His first love, however, was going after big salmon. His daughter caught a 60-lb. fish at the mouth of Alaska's Kenai River. Before a stroke in 1999 left him handicapped, George told me his goal was to watch his daughter catch an 80-pound salmon. The world record Chinook was captured from the waters where he and his daughter fished. It was caught in 1985 and it weighed 97 pounds.

Sadly, the salmon population has declined so much on the Sac that if I visited the river today, I would see few salmon spawning. Some attribute the decline to water diversion and others to changes at sea resulting from Global Warming. In any case, a moratorium has been placed on fishing for them.

Although beyond this book's scope to discuss the efforts to counteract the negative affects of dams on Pacific salmon, let me mention that they've involved 50 years of efforts. These efforts have included: building a hatchery downstream from the dams (and later a hatchery for winter run salmon); designating Chinook as an endangered species; closing the commercial salmon fishery; establishing Salmon Unlimited, an advocacy organization; creating a Salmon Stamp program; establishing a 200 mile fishing limit in the ocean; lifting the gates of downstream diversion dams during spawning runs; screening openings to hundreds of irrigation channels; and releasing cold water from the base of dams to create downstream spawning habitat.

While watching the spawning salmon, I kept my eye on the anglers across the river. I did see several wading anglers into fish. Each rainbow hooked jumped high out of the water as it raced down the river, quickly followed by the angler, as well as a companion who netted the fish if it didn't escape. Each time a fish was netted, each angler spent considerable time re-rigging, and I couldn't figure out why this process took so long.

The first two anglers to return at dark were fly fishermen and one of them reported hooking and losing one fish in the 90 minutes he fished. The other had no hits. The next two fishermen to return were spin fishermen and they each landed three fish, the biggest weighing about two pounds, and lost several others. They each had long handled, relatively stiff, nine-foot spinning rods and a weight rig with which I was unfamiliar. The rig featured weight-packs that were attached to a break-off swivel. Now, I realized why it took so long to rig up after each fish. When I saw how many weights each used, I realized that I couldn't successfully fish this water.

The anglers told me that they out-fished fly fishermen throughout the year because fly fishermen couldn't put on enough weights to stay on the bottom and, for this reason, the river was primarily a spin fisherman's river. They said that anglers using fly rods had a better chance in drift boats because they could drift more weights or work to rising fish, but emphasized that they would still catch significantly more fish on their rigs, perhaps five to one if the fly fisherman was experienced on the river and ten to one if he wasn't. They also said that the Glow-Bugs I'd bought in Eureka were tied on too large a hook and one angler gave me several he tied on #16 hooks. I thanked him for his generosity, but knew I was through fishing this river.

I guess I'll never learn if Sac rainbows fight as hard as claimed. I'll admit that I've never seen two-pound rainbows jump as high as those I saw above Turtle Bay, but, then again, I've never hooked two-pound rainbows on 4# test spin-line free from weights. I do know, however, that if I used the amount of weight on my leader that these spin fishermen used, any trout I hooked would be unlikely to jump at all!

Local Sac fly fishermen will undoubtedly resent my rebuke of their river, but they need to remember that it's directed at the traveling angler who plans only a brief visit to a river—the angler familiar with the river needs no assistance from a book. Since I fished the river, I've come earlier articles about it that I missed. The first, by Brad Jackson, featured the lower Sac. It appeared in the December 1990 issue of *Fly Fisherman*. Jackson made it clear that it took him some time to learn the river, commenting, "My early efforts to learn the river yielded little success." The second, by Chip O'Brian, in the Fall 2002 issue of *Northwest Fly Fishing*, perhaps the best article on the river, emphasizes that, "Lower Sac trout are not easy."

The third and fourth articles were on the upper Sac and both supported my observations that this narrow, steep-gradient river typically runs fast and high. Van Nostran, in the February 1996 issue of *Fly Fisherman*, suggested using fast sinking shooting tapers in order to hug the bottom in the river's deep holes and fast-moving runs Ted Leeson described the river, in the January 2001 issue of *Field and Stream*, as one requiring, "short line nymphing and boulder scrabbling," tactics required to fish successfully Taylor River, mentioned in Chapter Two.

Ted Leeson also wrote that the upper Sac was not for men "dressed in tweed." I don't think I would distinguish in this fashion those who prefer floating a dry fly through riffled water from those who guide weighted flies through swift currents, but I think the upper Sac is unlikely to be friendly to the first time visitor regardless of what cloths are worn, even if the visitor prefers, what Leeson calls, "blue collar fishing."

Many years ago, Duncan Hines, a sales representative for a number of companies, kept a notebook on the restaurants he visited when traveling on business. When friends asked him to recommend a restaurant, he would show them his notes. The more trips he took, the bigger his notebook became. His friends found the notebook information so valuable that they suggested he publish it. He did, publishing *Adventures in Good Eating* at his own expense. Not long thereafter travelers would see signs on restaurants saying, "Recommended by Duncan Hines." This book is about adventures in good fishing; perhaps it can serve the same purpose as Hines's efforts.

Brad Jackson wrote an article for *Fly Fisherman*, in February of 1993, entitled, "Planning Dream Trips." Although few of my trips have been nightmares, I did waste time on some rivers, with several examples already discussed. Although I won't dwell on negative experiences, I will honestly describe my success on the "Dream Rivers" that many fly fishermen make plans to visit. Not only do I try to describe the unique features of each river, but I also list places to stay near them and nearby activities that should interest family members who don't fish, as they should enjoy trips as much as the anglers in the family.

Outdoor magazines have featured most of the rivers I discuss. Some of the articles are grossly misleading and others exaggerate the successes achieved. The "honest" articles usually differ from mine in several ways. First, the writers usually stress the technical aspects of fishing the featured river. I include such material, but, in contrast to most articles, I use each river as a jumping off place to tell a story, either about an angling experience or about historical figures that lived near their waters.

I also try and describe the mood of each river, how I was affected by the swirling currents and surrounding countryside; how I changed as a result of fishing it; what I took home from it. I also compare and contrast the rivers as I move along in the book. I include photographs of most of the major rivers discussed, but outstanding ones can be seen on the Internet by simply "Googling" a river's name and searching websites until they're found.

Some readers might question whether my visits to these rivers were typical, but rest assured, as I checked my experiences with other visitors to the same waters. Local anglers, who regularly fish these rivers, may have different experiences, but the purpose of this book is to inform readers about what they can expect from their first visit. We all learn how to catch fish on our home rivers; such learning takes time—a luxury that visitors don't have!

The Rivers

In addition to the rivers I cover in this book, I've had both good and bad luck on other Western rivers, but my experiences on them may have been atypical and other anglers could not be found to corroborate them. For example, I caught nothing but small trout on the Bitterroot in its scenic sections above Darby, as did several others who floated five miles on the same day. More recent information, however, suggests that the river has significantly improved since I fished it.

The rivers I fished on the West Coast were fished so long ago that my experiences on them are out of date, although Mike Zelie and I recently fished California's Trinity River on separate occasions. He caught one "half-ponder" (a term used for small steelhead that migrate up the river) in its upper waters and I caught nothing in its lower waters. To be fair to such rivers, except for the comments already made about Sacramento River, my experiences on them will go unshared.

I also discuss River Itchen in England, a river I lived near for seven weeks and observed extensively, but never actually fished. How could I have lived near River Itchen, the birthplace of fly fishing, and not fished it? You'll have to wait for the last chapter for that story!

All of the rivers featured contain wild trout. The Bighorn, Bow, Castle, Crowsnest, Elk, Livingston, Oldman, River Itchen, Kootenai, the Flatheads, Silver Creek, and the rivers in Yellowstone and Teton national parks contain only wild trout. The Green, Frying Pan, Big Lost, and Big Wood have a healthy mixture of wild and stocked trout throughout their waters. The

Roaring Fork contains wild trout above the Woody Creek Bridge and predominately stocked trout below the bridge. Colorado's White River contains mostly stocked rainbows in its lower sections and native cutthroats in its upper sections. The San Juan has stocked rainbows in the trophy section and wild browns in the lower sections.

Scott and Tom on Alberta's upper Castle River

My Angling Companions

Although I introduced my angling companions, Scott Daniels, Tom Royster, Bob Young, and Mike Zelie, in my earlier book, I'll re-introduce them here because at least one of them has either fished with me, or fished without me, on the rivers I discuss. Tom, with whom I fish the most, is 200 plus pounds, and over six feet. In addition to his good looks, he is warm, unassuming, and modest. He also read the manuscript before it was published to keep me honest. Bob, who died recently of heart failure, would fish all day if we let him; the perfectionist in him was unwilling to make one last cast. This same persistence, if not stubbornness, made him a good psychotherapist, a superb coach of child soccer players, a par golfer, and a man determined to keep all the stuff in our rental car organized.

Scott loved to get away with the guys, relished his Manhattan Perfects, and was keen on the card game of hearts, refusing to let any of us avoid playing. Although he enjoyed fishing, bonding was his thing. Often, over our objections, he would keep the game going well into the night, but he would be the first to awake in the morning and get us to the river early; he was the manager among us. Mike, who fishes with us in the East, has traveled to many of the rivers discussed and his experiences were included. My wife, Melody, has also fished with me, but you will learn about her later in the book

A Word About Guides

I first fished the rivers discussed without the help of guides. Scott and I hired a guide for an afternoon on the Bighorn before drift boats were available to rent. I hired one on a family trip to Snake River because I wanted my loved ones to experience a day's float trip on this scenic river. I hired another for a morning on the San Juan to demonstrate the best way to fish midge pupae in the shallow flats below the dam, a spot we'd unsuccessfully fished on three previous mornings. Clark D'Ambrosio, in an article in *Hooked on the Outdoors* (April, 2003), best expresses why I don't hire guides when fishing a new river:

> I don't like to hand over any more of my life to experts than necessary. With fishing in particular, I prefer the costs of a few extra days—days used to make mistakes and accumulate failures and, by a strange process, come closer to the place, to the river and the fish, then having all these things handed to me by a guide. With a guide, you're buying a lifetime, but there's something wrong with it, something slightly off— it isn't your life. You aren't in your life and you aren't on the river in quite the same way. It lacks valor.

Accommodations and Other Activities

Many anglers travel with family members who don't fish. Even if some do, like my wife and children, they have the patience to do so only for short periods. Bored family members can spoil the experience for others. Consequently, after listing places to stay, I discuss other activities near each river that family members might enjoy.

Chapter Two

Yellowstone Waters
Where Beauty and Death Blurs

The first time I made a pilgrimage to nature's sacred place, a place Native Americans identify by many names—"place of hot water and many smoke," "buffalo country," "the summit of the world," I didn't grasp its true nature; I didn't realize that beneath the beauty of Yellowstone Park was an ongoing melodrama of sex and death and of mother love and mayhem; a place where beauty and death blurs. I didn't understand that my experience there could cause conflict between my mind and my heart.

I'd read articles about Yellowstone Park's rivers in outdoor publications and found appealing the idea of fishing with geysers erupting around me. Nevertheless, my goal at that time was to catch big trout, not to appreciate experiences wild places can offer. I'd been to the Park as a boy and had seen Old Faithful and other Park attractions. Touring the Park was not on my agenda. I wanted to catch large trout on a fly. I read *Fishing Yellowstone Waters* and *Nymph Fishing for Large Trout,* both by the late Charles E Brooks, to learn about the Park's rivers and how to catch big fish in them.

In the early 1980s, I went with Bob and Tom, who'd never been to the Park, and who, like me, had never caught large trout. The great tail-water fisheries, like Utah's Green, New Mexico's San Juan, or Arkansas's White, were either unheralded or not yet created, and the Bighorn was not yet open to the general public. In the lower forty-eight states, Yellowstone Park was the place to catch big wild trout and that was where I wanted to go.

I didn't fish the park's streams as a boy. My family didn't hold in high esteem the park's fishing in those days. Large numbers of fish, many not native to the rivers, were stocked and quickly harvested before they could attain any size. Sport fishing was managed for the greatest possible harvest. Under this philosophy, the fish population suffered under increasing fishing pressure and by 1949, when I first visited it, it was in terrible shape.

My parents brought me to the Park to see its major attractions. I particularly remember lines of cars stopped along the road with black bears standing erect and leaning on the cars in hopes of receiving some tasty morsel. Deer and other animals could be fed by hand. Later, under a new Park philosophy, the dumps were cleaned up, the feeding of animals prohibited, and the bears relocated away from populated areas. But it wasn't wildlife that I'd come to see on this trip; it was the park's reputation for big trout that drew me to its rivers.

The presence of large trout in the park's rivers followed changes in Park management policies. A "fly-fishing-only" section was created on Firehole River in 1950, hatcheries were closed in 1957, fish were no longer stocked after 1959, and limits were placed on fish harvests. No-kill sections were established in 1973 and the Fishing Bridge, in Hayden Valley, above Buffalo Ford, where dozens of anglers use to gather, was closed to fishing to protect downstream spawning runs of cutthroat from Yellowstone Lake.

Several of my friends had fished the Madison and the Lamar rivers in the Park and had fooled two-foot browns from the former and two-foot cutthroats from the later. I also wanted to catch big trout in the Madison-Firehole-Gibbon drainage, where lush meadows, erupting geysers, and bubbling hot springs would surround me. While I would be fishing near the parks famous hot springs, biologists would be harvesting a microbe from the springs that enables them to create the perfect enzyme for the mass-production of DNA.

Jim Bridger, the famous trapper and guide, once remarked about Yellowstone Country, "A fellow can catch a fish in an icy river, pull it into a boiling pool, and cook his fish without ever taking it off a hook." Bridger's many tales about the area stimulated a prominent Montana resident, Nathaniel P. Langford, to gather a group of distinguished local leaders, including the Surveyor General of Montana, to visit the area in 1870. Camping on the Madison River at the junction of Firehole and Gibbon Rivers, which create the Madison, these local citizens plotted a campaign that eventually saved this magical place from private ownership and exploitation. Langford kept a journal of the trip that was later published as *Diary of the Washburn Expedition of the Yellowstone and Firehole Rivers in the Year 1870.*

At the urging of this distinguished group, the government mounted an official study of the area. Accompanying the exploration party was Thomas Moran, a renowned artist and William Henry Jackson, a famous landscape photographer. Their photographs and paintings accompanied the 500-page land survey presented to Congress and, in 1872, it members voted to set aside more than two million acres as Yellowstone National Park.

Because of his vision, Langford was appointed to serve, without compensation, as the park's first superintendent. Langford displayed his leadership abilities when he came to Montana during the gold rush. The town of Bannack, where Langford prospected, swelled beyond its ability to cope with thieves, particularly those willing to kill for gold. In response, Langford organized a volunteer committee of vigilantes to enforce the law and punish offenders. His *Vigilante Days and Ways*, published in 1890, remains one of the best accounts of frontier justice.

On my first trip to the park, my companions and I stayed in West Yellowstone, the fly-fishing Mecca at the time. Bob Jacklin's and Bud Lilly's fly shops were located there and we hoped the wisdom of their employees would rub off on us. We quickly learned, however, that we faced several obstacles that Charles Brooks neglected to mention in his books. When the Firehole, Gibbon, and Madison rivers warm up from thermal runoff, their resident brown trout travel downstream to Hebgen Lake, a man-made reservoir. By August no browns are left in these rivers. Rainbows tolerate heat better than browns and stay in the rivers until the water approaches 80 degrees, but we didn't see any in the sections we searched.

Fly-shop employees suggested we rent float tubes and fish Hebgen Lake for "gulpers," large, surface feeding browns that gulp down the tremendous spinner falls for which the lake is famous. Nevertheless, "gulper" fishing is primarily an early morning activity because the wind makes the lake inhospitable most of the day. Besides, still-water fishing wasn't what attracted us to the Park. Shop staff told us that to catch large river trout, we should fish

This magnificent stretch of Madison River in the Park was without browns during our August visit (Photo by James Blank, Courtesy of Hank Roberts)

the Madison River below Hebgen Lake, waters outside of the Park.

When we asked about the large cutthroats in the Buffalo Ford section of Yellowstone River, in Hayden Valley, shop employees looked disdainful, remarking that cutthroats in the valley were not sporting to catch because many of them have been caught repeatedly, perhaps as much as 15 times each since opening day on July 15. They emphasized that cutthroats were poor fighters, and their fight was even poorer after being caught so often.

Madison River

Shop employees insisted that the true angler swings weighted stonefly nymphs in the pocket water, or plops grasshopper imitations, along the banks of Madison River below Quake Lake, relating that coldwater releases from Hebgen Lake Dam, warmed to optimal feeding temperatures by Quake Lake, two miles below, keep the fishery good during the summer. Although few flies hatch in August, the river holds considerable subsurface food. The browns were said to hold only several feet from the banks, while the rainbows stayed out in the fast water.

We were told to expect either an early morning or late evening hatch. Actually, mornings and evenings were the only times you could work dry flies because strong winds between 10:00 A.M. and 4:00 P.M. made casting extremely difficult, another fact Brooks failed to mention. I later learned, from an angler who camps each summer at one of the five riverside public campsites below Quake Lake, that he has good luck using caddis patterns in the mornings and evenings. Between these two periods, while the winds howl across the river valley, he catches up on his reading.

Many anglers regard August as the low point in the Yellowstone angling season. Nevertheless, fly shop staff emphasized that big fish could be caught in the summer's heat where they suggested we fish. With nymphs in hand, we left the Park and drove northwest to fish the recommended section between Lyon and Grizzly Bar, located several miles below Quake Lake, a lake formed in 1959 when an earthquake tumbled half a mountain down into the river to create a natural dam. Twenty-eight people died in the quake. Quake Lake is 140 feet deep in its deepest spot, with remains of submerged trees still visible and two cabins, removed from their foundations by the quake, lying just above the lake as confirmation of this natural disaster.

The lower Madison is a big, rapidly flowing river, essentially a continuous riffle all the way north to the town of Ennis, Montana. It's noted for its "Salmon Fly" hatch from mid-June to early July. Pale Morning Duns, Western Black Quills, and Western Quill Gordons also hatch in large numbers in June and July. The section we fished had fast rapids in the middle and pocket water on each side. Earlier in the summer, I would've placed a dry fly behind every rock, but August called for different tactics, so I waded out from the shore and slung my weighted nymph into each pocket.

Wading was extremely difficult, the wind was howling, and my nymph kept getting caught on the rocks. At a buck a nymph, the fly-shop price in those days, I lost $10 quicker to the rocks than to Las Vegas slot machines, but we were told that if we weren't getting hung up, we weren't getting deep enough. I persevered until I could no longer stand it. I clipped off the big nymph and I put on a #12 Royal Wulff and, with the wind behind me, cast it into the river's middle and onto a two-foot wave that washed over a large boulder. I did this not because I thought I'd catch anything, but because I felt like stretching muscles stiffened by slinging weights and tensely watching for strikes that never came.

As the large fly floated down the back of the wave, the head of the biggest fish I'd ever seen appeared and sucked the fly under. Most likely, it was a rainbow, but I'll never know because the fly popped to the surface an instant later. Needless to say, I cast and cast again, but the fish never repeated its earlier effort; wild trout never do!

Pondering my fate, I walked upriver to find Bob and Tom to ask if they were hungry for lunch. From a distance, I could see them engaged in an activity that looked like they were ready for the "men in white coats." The sequence of their activities was as follows: They would scramble up a little knoll, crawl around on their hands and knees, run down the knoll, return to the river's edge, and stand along it for a brief period. They then repeated this strange sequence of frenzied activity.

When I finally reached them, they both yelled, "Come and look at this!" Tom took a live grasshopper from his closed fist and tossed it into the water.

A braided stretch of Madison River where Mike Zelie landed a large brown during his 2006 trip to the Park (Mike Zelie Photo)

It floated along the bank unmolested.

I said, "So what."

He replied, "Wait a moment." Just after he spoke, the bug was gulped down by a large brown holding no more than a foot from the bank. The fish simply rose up, inhaled the hopper, and eased back down into the water. I stared down into the relatively shallow water, but I couldn't see this fish or any other.

"There are large fish all along this bank," Bob asserted. "In fact, that grasshopper floated over two other big trout before the third one took it."

"How do you know that?" I asked.

"Because we've been throwing grasshoppers at them for the last half hour and know where most of them are," Tom replied.

"So why aren't you fishing grasshoppers?" I asked.

"We were, but we didn't even get a rejection," answered Bob.

"Watch this grasshopper closely," said Tom, as he threw another into the water.

Again, it floated for a brief moment before another large trout sucked it in. They were right about the number of fish along the bank because the trout that now took it was upstream from the first hungry trout.

"Did you see what happened? "Tom asked me.

"Of course," I said. "The trout took the bug."

"That's not what I mean; did you see when it took the bug? Go catch your own, throw it in, and watch what happens."

I felt foolish crawling around on my hands and knees on the little knoll above the river, but I finally managed to catch a hopper. I discovered that catching them, like catching fish, required a special set of skills. After mastering them, I returned to the river and threw the bug in the water. Disappointed, I watched it float down the stream and out of sight. Puzzled, I asked why no fish took it.

"For the same reason none took our imitations," answered Bob.

"And what reason is that," I asked.

"Because it never twitched its leg," they both replied in unison. "Watch again" and Tom promptly tossed another grasshopper into the water. Sure enough, it floated over the two earlier feeders, but as soon as it twitched its leg, it was eaten by a third.

"The leg has to move before the trout will take the hopper," they both said emphatically. "We tried dancing, twitching, and smacking our hopper imitations, but nothing worked. We even tried smacking live ones on the surface, but none were taken until their legs twitched."

"We'll have to get IBM to install a computer chip in our hoppers and with a remote, signal them to move their legs," I remarked.

That drove us into hysterical laughter, and we clutched our bellies and rolled around on the ground. An angler, across the river, who'd been equally unsuccessful working a hopper pattern along the bank, had stopped fishing to view our sequence of activities. When he got home, I'm sure he recounted his experiences beginning with, "You should've seen the nuts I saw today!"

These large browns were sucking down live hoppers in an "artificial-lure-only" section of the river. But here was a chance for a huge fish. As a member of Trout Unlimited, the Sierra Club, Catskill Waters, Save the Whales, and the Nature Conservatory, could I stoop so low as to violate the conservation laws I believed in? You bet I could! With a knowing nod to my friends, we striped our hooks clean of fur and feathers, scrambled up the knoll, caught some hoppers, and cast the little buggers into the river.

We caught only two fish before we quit. First, guilt overcame us, second, the scornful eye of the angler across the river was upon us, and, third, most of the grasshoppers would not move their legs when impaled on a hook. To this day, I'm not much of a grasshopper man. When I do use one, I retrieve it shortly after slapping it on the surface so I can slap it again elsewhere. Rarely have I caught a trout on its quiet float up or downstream.

So much for Madison River—we left it never to return again. In spite of its fame and fortune, it was too much for us. Since our trip to the river, many of its rainbows have died of Whirling Disease, but I understand, from those who visit the river regularly, that it still harbors many large browns. Bert Darrow, author of *Fly Fishing with Bert Arrow*, took a two-foot brown on a Montana Stone Fly from the very section we fished. Every fall my friend Howard Weldon visits the Madison and he and his companions fool browns, primarily on streamers, up to 20 inches when they make their run out of Hebgen Lake and up the Madison to spawn. Mike Zelie got an early runner during a brief stop at the river on his September 2006 trip.

Yellowstone River at Buffalo Ford

I love Buffalo Ford; a section where Joe Brooks disparagingly says even the beginner can catch fish. Although that may be true right after opening day on July 15, it certainly isn't true in late August. It's an easy section to wade, but it can also be fished from the bank. In fact, it can be fished from a wheelchair if a friend pushes the disabled angler to the bank. There are several long riffles where trout can be fooled by casting either upstream, while wading, or across the stream from the bank. In the morning, we caught cutthroats up to 18 inches in the riffles and in the pools above them.

The shop employees were right, however, as cutthroats less than 17 inches simply flopped around on the surface, but several bigger ones took me into my backing. At night, there were so many fish feeding in the riffles it was unbelievable, but I couldn't catch a single one, either on a high floating fly or on a nymph. Looking back years later, I suspect they were feeding on freshwater shrimp that had washed down from Yellowstone Lake.

Most of the day at Buffalo Ford I cast over pods of fish easily spotted from the bank. I repeatedly cast a #22 green midge nymph (as cutthroat

Buffalo Ford when most anglers are still in bed

sometimes eat algae) so that it floated through the pod. It might float through 20 times before a fish would open its mouth and suck it in. Why one fish in a pod, having seen the same fly drift past its nose many times, would suddenly inhale it was unknown to me, and perhaps even to the fish.

I always tried to float the fly by the largest cutthroat in the pod and I hooked and landed several pushing 19 inches. I lost one well over 20 that screamed across the river twice before the hook straightened. Although locals may speak disparagingly about cutthroats in Hayden Valley, I found fooling them in late August to be challenging.

What I enjoyed most about Buffalo Ford was Buffalo Ford itself. It was a marvelous place to be; no wonder it's so heavily fished! I would go there once a year if I could. We didn't realize the import of this section's name; it should have been obvious, but we never gave it any thought. We'd been there for about an hour when we heard a growling noise in the distance, a noise that got increasingly louder. Was a bear coming to the river? We soon realized that the "growl" was actually a "symphony of snorts" because we saw the small herd of buffalo, which were making the strange noises, traveling along a bluff across the river from us.

They continued along the bluff, slid down its banks, and entered the water directly across the river from where Tom was fishing. When he realized these large animals were crossing the river directly in his path, fighting the fish he had on was no longer a priority. Moving well away from the bank where the buffalo would depart from the river, the three of us watched them in awe. The herd then dispersed and began grazing in the meadow behind us.

After a time, we went back to fishing and forgot about our buffalo companions grazing at our rears. Once, fixated on a trout along a steep bank, I was startled by a loud snort behind me. I'd lost track of each animal's whereabouts and one had ambled along until it was right behind me. I forgot about the trout and made a hasty retreat down the bank. The Journals of Lewis and Clark record their experience of the Buffalo. Lewis states:

> The Buffaloe, Elk, and Antelope are so gentle that we pass near them while feeding, without appearing to excite any alarm among them; and when we attract their attention, they frequently approached us more nearly to discover what we are, and, in some instances, pursue us a considerable distance apparently with that view.

Park rangers support these early observations of Lewis, stating that buffalo are not aggressive if left alone, but caution Park visitors to keep a safe distance from them, especially when they're escorting their young or rutting, as they are in August. No one had to tell me that. But I'm always surprised by the brazenness, and ignorance, of some of our youth. One teenager was gored to death when we were at the park. He had tried to mount the animal to impress his friends! Crazy Horse was an *Ongloge Un*, or "shirt wearer" before he was 13 years old. Four councilors were elected by their peers to help their chief lead the tribe. Upon investment in office, each was given a special form of a hair-fringed shirt. The recipient was lectured about his responsibilities of office. "Though you now wear the shirt, be a big-hearted man. This shirt here means that you have been chosen as a big-heart. You are always to help your friends. These rules are hard to comply with, but we have given you this shirt." I can't imagine American teenagers in such a leadership role.

Bob Young taking a picture of buffalo crossing the river at Buffalo Ford

Black Canyon of the Yellowstone

On my first trip with my companions, upon the advice of fly shop employees, we hiked down into Black Canyon to fish Yellowstone River below the falls. Here we caught numerous small cutthroats, but none were more than 14 inches and all were poor fighters. Mike Zelie hiked down into the canyon in September 2006 and, other than one 17-inch fish that didn't fight well, he also caught only small fish. Unfortunately, steep cliffs and fast waters in the section that greeted us prevented our walking very far either up or down the river

Black Canyon (Mike Zelie Photo)

Charles Brooks speaks of big fish in this water, but we saw none in this short section. Nevertheless, the hike was pleasant and coming back uphill not that strenuous.

Gallatin River

We finished the Gallatin River at Milepost 22, off U.S. 191. Charles Brooks was correct when he said, "On those days when you wish to pleasantly relax and enjoy the out-of-doors, some lovely, restful scenery, and fish a friendly stream with light tackle, fish this section of the Gallatin." We caught numerous rainbows and browns up to 14 inches in the riffles and heads of pools and thoroughly enjoyed ourselves, an experienced repeated on future trips to the river.

The Gallatin has been featured in two articles, one in the Winter 2000 issue of *Trout* and the other in the Fall 2000 issue of *Northwest Fly Fishing,* where Paolo Marchesi wrote, "The Gallatin is a perfect river for the traveling angler. It has easy access, diversity, and abundance of trout—this Montana river has it all."

Slough Creek

In the evenings, I enjoyed Slough Creek. Charles Brooks wrote that the cutthroats in the creek "are not as simple to fool as their more numerous kin of the Yellowstone." He also says they're "*very* difficult to catch in the larger sizes (twenty inches and up)." although he neglects to add that 20-inch

Slough Creek at First Meadow (Mike Zelie Photo)

cutthroat are rare, so the difficulty of catching them may be more a function of their scarcity than of their cunningness.

The unique creek has three spring-creek-like stretches flowing through open meadows, with pocket water and boulder strewn sections in between. The in-between waters look fishy, but most of their occupants are small fish. I fish the easily reached First Meadows below the campground, but Mike Zelie hikes five miles upstream to the Second Meadows, where he landed a 21-inch rainbow and an 18-inch cutthroat during his September 2006 trip. The creek's meadow sections have pools, runs, and riffles, one after another, as the creek meanders along.

I landed a cutthroat pushing 20 inches in the First Meadows. It took my fly just before dark at the end of a riffle above a small pool, with Bob and Tom yelling from the parking lot that it was time to leave. They couldn't hear my reply, that I was fighting a large fish, and kept shouting throughout my struggles. The big fish confined its efforts to the shallow pool and this was its undoing and my salvation. When I returned to the car, all Bob and Tom could say was that I'd made them miss dinner because the restaurants would be closed by the time we returned to West Yellowstone.

Unless I wanted to concentrate my efforts on waters west of the Park, I wouldn't return to West Yellowstone; its too far from spots I liked to fish.

A Trip with My Family

Earlier, I wrote that I didn't grasp the essential nature of the Park during my first fishing trip to it. My failure to get a 20-inch trout was not my only failure. My quest for big fish interfered with grasping the full significance of the Park. Yes, I enjoyed the spectacular scenery, enhanced by fishing alongside grazing buffalos and mule deer, but these experiences were secondary to catching fish. Certain experiences you couldn't avoid—the Park thrust them on you. Nevertheless, I failed to value the total Park environment. On this trip with my family, I took in the whole Park, or better said, I let the whole Park take me in. Chief Seattle put it even better when he said. "The earth doesn't belong to us, we belong to the earth."

Considerable drama unfolds in the wilds, particularly the relationship between predator and pray, some seen, but others unseen, like the protozoa that creates whirling disease in rainbow trout. Every death in the Park affects every life. When wolves kill coyotes, more mice survive for fox to eat, and fewer mice for hawks results in their capturing more trout. A merganser weighing three pounds can swallow a trout half its weight and the swift otter can eat five adult trout a day The Park allows us to see the ancient relationships between animals and to realize that Nature is far from benign. I always cherished the beauty of running waters, but didn't grasp that trout streams are actually violent places, that every splash is a death—the splash of rising trout, the death of a caddis fly; the splash of diving osprey, the death of a trout. The trout's overwhelming desire to reproduce renders it vulnerable to predators, both from above and below.

Since cutthroats in the Yellowstone River spawn in early July, visitors can easily observe nature at work, at least they could until recently, when lake trout became established in Yellowstone Lake and decimated the lake's cutthroat population, most of which spawned downstream in Hayden Valley and could be seen from the Fishing Bridge.

We drove the scenic route up to the Northeast Entrance of the park, not stopping at the Clark's Fork, as its tumbling waters looked too difficult for my sons to successfully fish, but I did fish Soda Butte Creek in Cook City, accompanied by our son Marten, where I fooled some small cutthroats.

Lamar River

The next day we fished Lamar River in Lamar Valley, a river looking like "chocolate milk" during my trip with Bob and Tom. In the summer, heavy rains bring flash floods to the upper Lamar and the rain is followed by a torrent of mud that immediately dirties the lower river. Since it had not rained recently, it was relatively clear. Nevertheless, we didn't see a single fish. Several years earlier, past president of the Mid-Hudson Chapter of Trout Unlimited, Jan Wiedo, had exceptional luck on the Lamar in a section just above the valley, where he fooled several cutthroat close to two feet long.

Charles Brooks writes that Lamar cutthroats cruise the river and anglers must walk the banks to find where they're holding. Unfortunately, I didn't read that chapter until after our trip and I probably hadn't walked far enough in my brief exploration of the river. As a result, my family fruitlessly fished good-looking holding water, but it probably didn't contain a single fish!

Buffalo Ford and Slough Creek Revisited

I took Marten and Mason to Buffalo Ford after the first dinner seating in the lodge where we were staying. After taking what seemed like an eternity to suit up, we finally entered the river. By then the boys were hungry again. It was now getting dark and the fish were rising at our feet. We cast and cast to them, but none struck. "Why can't we catch them?" the boys cried.

"Darned if I know," I replied. They immediately lost faith in my fishing ability and I'm sure that when they returned home, they stopped bragging to their friends about their father's fishing skills.

We saw a fish flopping oddly along on an island bank. We waded over to the bank, where we saw a 16-inch cutthroat attached to a leader that had parted from the line and tangled around a downed tree limb. The flops were the fish's fruitless efforts to escape. My oldest son proclaimed, "Let's see what the angler who lost it hooked it on." Out of the mouths of babes!

After unhooking and releasing the fish, I saw that the fly was a Green Sedge. The boys chimed together, "Do you have any of those?" I replied that I did, but added that the fish weren't feeding on caddis emergers at this moment, adding that the fish must have been hooked earlier today. This view was immediately unpopular, so I gave them each a Green Sedge. I wish I could report that I was mistaken, but neither son caught a fish. Someday I would like to return to Buffalo Ford and try shrimp imitations because the trout might have been feeding on freshwater shrimp that washed down from Yellowstone Lake. This vexing experience certainly didn't spark either son's interest in fly fishing; both are spin fishermen today. Charles Brooks, shame on you for saying it was so easy! .

Slough Creek between meadows
(Mike Zelie Photo)

At Buffalo Ford, we enjoyed watching the animals at sunset—bald eagles, elk, deer, coyotes, foxes, rabbits, otters, and others. The boys loved the buffalo; they could watch them graze and move about for hours. During the day, we hiked the various trails overlooking the Grand Canyon of the Yellowstone.

I began to enjoy fishing in the Park as a unique opportunity. Catching big fish was still a goal, but it mattered less. The Park operates differently from when I was a child—it's no longer managed like a zoo. The mission is to maintain the Park in its natural state and to protect all animals. Natural fires are allowed to burn in order to replenish the earth. Park rangers enjoy pointing out the environment's unique features, such as trout from the lakes moving downstream to spawn or rainbows in the Firehole spawning in the winter, when the water conditions are more favorable.

At one time, less than two-dozen Bison remained in our West. Their introduction into the park, a harsh habitat compared to the plains, saved them from extinction. Forty-five years ago there were few ospreys, elk herds were dramatically depleted, and wolves and mountain lions were absent; park practices resulted in these conditions. With the change in practices, wolves were reintroduced in 1995 and nearby mountain lions wandered in and stayed. There are now eight large elk herds in the "larger park," which extends from the Tetons to the Beartooth Mountains.

In the past, Park managers killed large predators; now they're left alone to become both predator and pray, resulting in the return of life and death

struggles between the park's larger animals. The balance of nature has been restored because man has let nature take its natural course; allowed it to become truly wild once again.

Nature's power to inspire depends upon its wildness and the Park has returned to that wondrous state. Watching wild nature express itself has a magical power like no other observation. Nature doesn't just take place "out there" in national parks. It's all around us, but protected places like Yellowstone Park deepen our connection with nature, enabling us to bring it back and keep it

Gallatin River (Mike Zelie Photo)

with us always. Wild lands also cause us to ask ourselves tough questions, like, "What type of world do we want to live in?"

Nevertheless, fishing isn't just about being in the great outdoors or we'd all be hikers or mountain bikers. It's also about trout. Robert Haig Brown put it best when he wrote in *Fisherman's Fall*:

> In the last analysis, though, it must be the fish themselves that make fishing—the strangeness and beauty of fish, their ease in another world, the mystery of their movements and habits and whims . . . their appeal is more nearly that of hidden treasure, except that this treasure has life and movement and uncertainty beyond anything inanimate . . . Perhaps it adds up to nothing more than a primitive curiosity, but if so it remains powerful and lasting.

Yellowstone River in Paradise Valley

Before we left the Park through the North Gate at Gardiner, I stopped briefly at Park's Fly Shop, operated by Richard Parks, and first opened in 1953 by Richard's father, Metton Parks. Parks asked me which river I enjoyed the most and I included Slough Creek in a list of two. He informed me that the Slough was one of the last bastions of large purebred native Yellowstone cutthroats, fish significantly smarter than those at Buffalo Ford.

I told Richard that I'd fooled a large cutthroat in Slough Creek on my last trip to the park, but found the big ones difficult to catch at Buffalo Ford. He laughed and said they were difficult because they were weary from being caught repeatedly. I forget to ask him what the Ford cutthroats were gorging themselves on in the evening, clearly the most difficult time to catch them.

We left Gardiner and drove to Chico Hot Springs, where we would end our vacation. I looked forward to fishing in Paradise Valley, near the famous Hot Springs Lodge where we had reservations. This picturesque valley is bordered in the west by the rolling hills of the Gallatin Range, made of shale and sandstone billions of years old, originally formed on the bottom of primeval seas. To the east, it's bordered by the rugged North Absaroka Mountains, built up from voluminous lava flows and explosions, one of the most beautiful mountain ranges in the continental United States.

Yellowstone River, the last large free-flowing river in the lower forty-eight states, was named by the French, *la Roche Jaune*, or "The Yellow Rock," although the Dakota called it, *Mi-tsi-a-da-zi*, or "Rock Yellow Water." The Crow, however, knew the river as Elk River. When Clark, of the Lewis and Clark Expedition, traveled the river, he saw many elk, as well as yellow rocks along the way. Because the Crow name for elk and the French name for yellow rock sounded alike, members of the Crow tribe believe Clark became confused and mistakenly adopted the French name.

Paradise Valley is such spectacular country that it could easily serve as a source for creations myths, of which there are many, but the one told by the

Arikara, a native American prairie tribe, is similar to those told by Eastern Woodland tribes:

> Wakonda, the Great Ski Spirit, looked down below his sky at his two ducks swimming eternally at peace in a limitless lake. He directed Wolf-Man and Lucky-Man to instruct the ducks to dive and bring up mud to make the earth. From this mud, Wolf-Man made a great prairie for the animals to live in. Lucky man made undulating ground with hills and valleys where in the future the people could hunt and seek shelter. Between the two regions the great river began to run as it still does.

We saw no place to access the river along the scenic drive from Gardiner to Chico Hot Springs. Talking with lodge staff, I learned that few public access cites exist along the Yellowstone below Gardiner. The river must be floated to fish it. Nevertheless, I was directed to one close by, but was told it gets heavy pressure from both guests and staff, although many guests traveled north to fish Armstrong, DePuy's, and Nelson's creeks, located just south of Livingston, pay-to-fish spring creeks that require advance reservations for a day, or a half-day, on them.

In the afternoon, while my family rode horses in Gallatin National Forest, I tried the river at the site. Unfortunately, wading was restricted to a short stretch because the power water ran along steep banks in both directions not far from the site. I fished the short stretch for several hours, catching some small fish and losing one that stripped out my line and then broke off. I returned with my family after supper and we fished until dark, catching some whitefish, but no trout. We enjoyed the Lodge, inappropriately described by

Yellowstone River in Paradise Valley (Mike Zelie Photo)

the *Wall Street Journal* as the "Elaine's of Montana," referring to a Manhattan restaurant where New York's elite gather.

After leaving Chico Hot Springs, we stopped at Dan Bailey's Fly Shop in Livingston, operated by his son, John. I got carried away at the bargain box, lost track of the time, and had to drive 85 miles an hour for two hours to get to Billings in time to make our flight. Speeding along in the car, I saw no fishermen on the Yellowstone flowing below the highway. Yet, I learned later that the 43-mile stretch from Livingston to Caprella has 11 public cites, where anglers can assess the river and fish for its large brown trout.

Dan Bailey died in 1982, after many years as an advocate for the river. A former physics professor at Brooklyn Polytechnic Institute and an avid fly tier, it was he who insisted that Lee Wulff name his Gray Wulff pattern after himself, rather than the Ausable Gray, as Lee was going to call it, and the Wulff series of flies were born. Dan invented several Wulff flies, most notably the Black and Grizzle. Dan left New York, where he had a cottage on a stream I regularly fish, and started his tackle business in Livingston in 1938.

Dan was an ardent conservationist, starting a local chapter of the Izaak Walton League and later helping to start Trout Unlimited. The first struggle of these conservationists was to limit sheep grazing in the Yellowstone High Country, followed by struggles with sterilization by mine tailings, sewage from settlements in and around the park, mountain runoff from timber clear-cutting, poisoning by pesticides, and the use of car bodies as rip-rap for banks.

Dan's major contribution to the free flowing river was to help stop the proposed dam at Allenspur, a narrow notch several miles upriver from Livingston. The dam's purpose was to store water for a proposed coal gasification plant, to be located hundreds of miles downstream, part of a plan

Yellowstone River in Paradise Valley (Courtesy of Harold McMillan, Jr.)

to make Montana the "boiler room of the nation." In the 1970s, Dan, and other river supporters, halted the last effort to build the dam, refusing to allow degradation of this prized resource. Hopefully, a dam at the spot is now a dead issue. When Dan died, the Montana Fish and Game Commission declared August 14 as "Dan Bailey Fishing Day" in Montana.

Accommodations and Other Activities

With the exception of the South Entrance, where one nearby ranch rents rooms, motels are present near a Park entrance. The Park also has a number of lodges. I planned my family trip during the winter and learned that I should've started planning in the fall. I couldn't make reservations anywhere in the park—all accommodations were full. I wanted to stay at both Roosevelt Lodge, near Slough Creek, and Grant Village, at West Thumb, near the geyser fields. My second choices were Canyon Lodge and Cabins, a reasonable drive to both Slough Creek and Buffalo Ford, and Yellowstone Lake Village, not far from the geyser fields along the Firehole.

I was put on a waiting list; in the meantime, I booked motel reservations at Cody, close to the East Entrance, near both the North and South Branches of the Shoshone rivers, and at Gardiner, near Slough Creek. I then waited to hear from the Reservations Department of TW Recreational Services, the organization that books all Park reservations. About a month later, I received confirmed reservations at both Canyon Lodge and Lake Yellowstone Hotel and canceled my backup reservations; fishing the Shoshone rivers would have to await another trip. Canyon Lodge was half the price of the cabin at Yellowstone Lake Hotel. Had I known that, I would have stayed there the whole trip, as its location was close to all Park events.

To learn about Park activities, anglers can study guidebooks prior to arrival or wait for the weekly calendar of events published at the park. Films and lectures occur at the park's amphitheaters, but we were usually tired from hiking and went to bed early.

Chapter Three

Frying Pan, Roaring Fork and White Rivers
Northwestern Colorado's Varied Fishing Opportunities

I gave the lead in this chapter's title to the Frying Pan, not because I prefer the Frying Pan to the other rivers, but because a trip to fish near Aspen can result in the Frying Pan being the only river that can be fished. I also fancy how the Pan got its name. The tale is told that Ute Indians attacked two mountain men trapping on the river. The unharmed member of the pair left his seriously injured partner in a nearby cave while he went for help. He hung a frying pan in a tree to mark the entrance to the cave. When he returned with soldiers, the frying pan helped him to relocate his fallen partner, who, it turns out, did not survive his wounds.

When I brought my daughters to visit their grandparents and cousins who lived in Colorado, I visited the Colorado, Crystal, Eagle, Frying Pan, Roaring Fork and White rivers. I say visited because the Eagle was always orange from sludge washed from the former Gilman Mine site, the Roaring Fork and Colorado were high and muddy many summers, and the Frying Pan often was clear only above Seven Castles, a cliff formation adjacent to the river. Even after brief thundershowers, the creek from Seven Castles brings red clay into the river and the Pan runs bright red downstream for four miles to its confluence with the Roaring Fork at Basalt. One day of heavy rain and the Roaring Fork can also be too discolored to fly fish. The Crystal River, a fast-flowing, turbulent stream that feeds the Roaring Fork, and which is stocked with hatchery-reared fish, was murky on all of my summer trips and, therefore, I never fished it.

The first time I fished these rivers with Bob and Tom was in July of 1980. I borrowed my father in law's camper van, hitched his jeep to the back, and drove from Arvada to Basalt, where the Frying Pan joins the Roaring Fork. At Basalt, we stocked up on groceries and then drove the 14 miles from Basalt to a campsite on the reservoir near the dam. Along the way, we were impressed with the striking scenery in the river valley. The valley is cut into red beds of sandstone and shale that contrast strikingly with the surrounding green hillsides. We were particularly taken with the red sandstone formations, suitably named "Seven Castles" The campsite was convenient for fishing the Pan, but not for visiting nearby Aspen or fishing the Roaring Fork. On our next trip we stayed at the Best Western in Basalt.

Frying Pan River

When construction began on the Ruedi Dam in the 1960s, fishermen opposed the dam, not only because miles of good trout water would be lost, but also because they believed bottom releases from the dam would be too cold to support insect life and, therefore, trout life. Shortly after the dam was completed in 1969, articles appeared complaining that the Pan had been ruined and that nothing lived in the cold water below Ruedi Reservoir. Maybe so, but very shortly thereafter big fish appeared in the Pan.

Nobody anticipated that prolific hatches of midges would occur below the dam, that fresh water shrimp would be flushed from the reservoir, or that the water would warm quickly in this shallow and narrow river, making for prolific fly hatches throughout most of the lower Pan's 14-mile length. Within several years, fishing below the reservoir dramatically improved; trout biomass quadrupled, growth rates dramatically increased, and the result was a 1,000 pounds per surface acre of trout. A respectable mountain trout stream turned into Colorado's premier river. With normal snow pack and controlled releases from the dam, the Pan can be fished all year long.

Lines in white are pubic water

I vividly remember the first time I fished the flats below the dam. It was before sunup on our first morning and the river was covered with fog so thick we couldn't see each other in this 100-yard stretch. Using a Mickey Fin streamer, I caught three fat 16-inch rainbows and four 14-inch brookies, the biggest stream brookies I've ever caught. When the fog lifted, the action stopped!

In the early afternoon, the Green Drake hatch began and the number of fish rising to it was phenomenal. Each of us caught and released more than a dozen trout, including at least one of each species: brook, brown, cutthroat, rainbow, and cutbow (a cutthroat-rainbow hybrid), with the largest exceeding 17 inches, all strong fish that fought well. Because the river's rainbows have difficulty spawning during high spring flows, many of the rainbows we caught were stocked fish.

In my book, *Capturing Rogue Trout*, I discuss the huge trout, trout I call "Hogs," that dwell in a short section directly below Ruedi Dam and I'll repeat some of the story here. I first learned about these monsters from two Colorado anglers who took us to the bend pool below the dam and gave us each some 6X tippet and several #24 nymphs tied with white latex wound with fine copper wire. They called the fly "Miracle Nymph," remarking that we'd quickly learn how the fly got its name.

We were instructed to put several small weights just above the blood knot connecting the 18-inch tippet to the leader, flip the leader and fly into the head of the pool, and hold the rod out over the water so that only the leader, and not the line, drifted downstream with the fly. When the leader hesitated, we were to set the hook. They called this technique "straight-line" or "short-stick-nymphing." This was the first time I'd used this technique. I went first and on

Tom on a spring-creek-like stretch

my first drift, the leader hesitated, I raised the rod tip, and a trout around six pounds catapulted out of the water downstream from where I stood. The two anglers both laughed and declared that the fish had been on my line, but the force of its movement had broken my 6X tippet (1# test in those days) before it cleared the water. Mouth wide open, I turned to my two instructors, who proclaimed, "There are plenty more like that one in this pool and even some much larger. We don't know what the Miracle Nymph imitates, but it sure works miracles! Have fun, but we guarantee that if you switch to a larger tippet or another fly you won't get a single strike."

With this proclamation, they left to fish downstream. We lost three more mammoth fish before the resulting commotion turned off the pool. At dusk, some of these enormous fish moved up from the pool into the flat water above it to feed on what we now know are Mysis shrimp. The shrimp become active at dark in the reservoir above and are washed down the sluesway into the river. To capture them, the trout stacked up like cordwood in this stretch and in several below it.

The two different Colorado angling guides I purchased later, both written in 1985, failed to mention that Pan trout feed on shrimp or that there were huge fish in the river. Tim Kelly's 1985 guide said fish "run to 18 inches" and Chuck Fothergill and Bob Sterling's 1985 guide declared, "12 to 16 inch fish are common." Yet, those in the know in the 1970s used the Miracle Nymph to hook huge trout. Maybe the pattern's originator knew what it imitated, but those using it for many years thereafter did not. It wasn't until 1988, when the Colorado Division of Wildlife published a free pamphlet, entitled *Fishing the Three Rivers*, that I saw anything in writing about the Pan's monsters. In it they described the catch-and-release section of the Pan as a "football freak show" of trophy rainbow up to 15 pounds that reach these weights by feeding on freshwater shrimp.

I'd caught good size fish during the Green Drake hatch in August, but never any of the monsters in the Bend Pool. In fact, I've not fished this pool since my 1980 experience, primarily because of the crowds in this catch-and-release section below the dam. Much of the land along the lower 14 miles of the river is now posted, forcing more fishermen into smaller stretches, especially pocket waters better fished with weighted nymphs, a technique I'm not crazy about. If the water is discolored below Seven Castles, the river upstream becomes congested in the summer.

The three of us took a second trip to the Pan in 1985. On this trip, our early morning visits to the flats below the dam resulted in no fish. Although we caught many fish on both dry flies and nymphs, we caught no brook trout. I'd tied up some Miracle Nymphs for use in the Bend Pool, but other anglers always occupied this water. I saw none hooking any big fish, however, and upon questioning them learned they were using Hairs Ears and 4x tippets. When I showed them a Miracle Nymph and suggested they use it with a 6X tippet, I was greeted with laughter.

A Trip With Melody

I took Melody to the Pan in August of 1991. I fished upstream from the Taylor Creek Fly Shop, while Melody took a casting lesson from the shop manger. The shop was named after a feeder creek to the Pan because its first owner, Bill Fitzsimmons, started out by selling flies from a small cabin by the little creek. When I returned an hour later, Melody told me she'd been a witness at a wedding. She'd remained on the water after her lesson to practice casting when a couple arrived with a justice of the peace, waded into the river by her, and asked her if she'd stand with them as a witness. They said their wedding-vows in midstream and Melody drank Champaign with them after the ceremony. Neither partner fished.

I then took her to a section of stream just above Seven Castles Creek. Melody liked to cast, but didn't like to hook fish because "It was a cruel trick to play on such lovely creatures." I gave her some flies with barbless hooks, to help alleviate her concerns, and found a fine-pebbled bottom, where she could concentrate on casting without worrying about her footing. After watching her successfully wading, I left to avoid "hovering over" her.

I glanced upstream and saw her trying to reach a fish rising just out of her casting range. I stopped fishing and walked upstream, thinking I might help her to cast just a bit farther. She was dropping the rod on her back cast and as, a result, her casts fell short. Holding onto her arm, I hoped she would get the feel of a better cast. Unfortunately, when we cast together, the fly hit the water just ahead of the rising trout and the fish took it as it floated by. Boy, was she angry! "You hooked my fish!" But I didn't mind because I was pleased by her enthusiasm.

On this visit with Melody, most of the rainbows I hooked simply gave up; few jumped and none screamed out the line. Even the 17-inch rainbow I inadvertently caught that angered Melody simply flopped around. The Pan's increasing popularity had resulted in many of its stocked rainbows caught and released throughout the season. Only the wild browns fought well, especially in waters bordering the Dart property managed by Taylor Creek Fly Shop, where several anglers could fish the property at designated times.

One late afternoon, Melody and I were returning from fishing near the dam and, as we approached the managed stretch, it began to drizzle. Although I hadn't reserved a spot, it was deserted. I put on a Blue-Winged Olive and looked for rising fish. While Melody waited in the car, I hooked and landed four browns

Good dry fly water above Seven Castles

between 14 and 16 inches and they were all strong, hard fighting fish. Fortunately, for Melody, who had nothing to do in the car, the drizzle became a steady rain and the fish stopped rising. On the way home, a rainbow shimmered over Seven Castles, and after it faded, the sunset tipped the surrounding cliffs with gold, a fitting end to the day. Unfortunately, the Dart property was sold, but anglers can still fish 1,100 feet of river along the roadside bank across from it. Unfortunately, the good pools are along the other bank.

Melody and I retuned to the Pan in May of 2004 after attending our son's college graduation in Denver. Howie Garber, a professional photographer, joined us and took photos of us fishing the Pan, several of which appear in *Capturing Rogue Trout*. Blue Winged Olives hatch in May, but the hatch never materialized during our visit. I caught some fish on midges, especially in the stretch just downstream from the dam, but not nearly as many as we fooled during the marvelous Green Drake hatch in late July.

Only trickles were flowing from the dam and fly shop staff said that shrimp pass though the outlet only during high flows. They also remarked that fish fooled by shrimp imitations are caught primarily in the pool directly below the dam outlet, now open to fishermen, who stand on the concrete abutment lining the pool and cast down into the deep, swirling water; not my kind of fishing.

Unfortunately, some of the Pan's best dry fly water is now posted and repairs to the road following floods resulted in numerous slab rocks along the banks. One new owner, who bought and posted a long stretch of good dry fly water, created pools by building V- and Wing-Dams on his stretch. Although the pools may attract and hold fish, unless he feeds them, they'll have to go elsewhere to find hatching flies.

When I visit the Pan again, I'll do so in the off-season. Although fishing is outstanding during major hatches, it's difficult to find spots free of anglers and guides working with clients, with the latter expecting you to stay well away from them. One time, I crossed over the river well behind a guide and his client, walked 25 yards upstream, and started casting. The guide rapidly crossed the stream, walked up to me, and asked me, not so politely, to leave because I was in "his waters." I remarked that fish were rising everywhere and I was well away from his client. He indignantly replied that, over the course of the day, they would be working their way up to where I stood! This guy could never survive on New York's crowded Beaver Kill!

Roaring Fork River

On our first trip to the area in 1980, Bob, Tom, and I fished the Fork one afternoon in a wide and relatively shallow riffled section just above Carbondale. The water was cloudy, so we worked dark colored nymphs down through the faster sections. On this stretch, two Colorado Division of Wildlife conservation officers, who floated the river in a Drift Boat, asked to see our licenses. We heard them coming because their boat's bottom occasionally scraped the riverbed. My brother-in-law, who lived in Silt, west of Glenwood Springs, joined us, although we never saw him after he took off downstream, working his worm through riffles and into eddies below them. When he returned at dusk, he had two fat 18-inch browns for his evening meal. All we caught on nymphs were several small ones!

The first time we seriously fished the Roaring Fork was in 1985. We accessed it by climbing down, and later up, the steep shale bluffs through which the river flows below State Rt. 82. Shortly thereafter, we reached this section by walking a level trail from Upper Woody Creek Bridge—it pays to get a fishing map or to ask directions before you fish!

One late afternoon, I worked the river below Upper Woody Creek Bridge, while Bob and Tom worked the long deep pool just above it. I caught and released three 17-inch rainbows that merely flopped around in the shallow step pools that characterize this stretch. Walking back upstream, I watched Bob and Tom taking turns fishing.

At the pool's head, Bob would hook a rainbow that jumped and raced downstream, requiring him to follow it along the gravel bank. Tom would move into the spot vacated by Bob and, within several casts, he, too, would be into a fish that would jump and race downstream. After landing his fish, Bob

Roaring Fork River

would return to the pool's head, now vacated by Tom, who was following his fish downstream. They each hooked four or five rainbows at the head of the pool, with the biggest about 17 inches. Why did their trout fight better that those I caught? I couldn't answer this question until I learned that trout are stocked downstream from Upper Woody Creek Bridge. Bob and Tom had been hooking wild fish while I'd been hooking hatchery raised ones!

The Roaring Fork, unlike the Frying Pan, is tough to fish because hatches of mayflies and caddisflies are infrequent in its turbulent waters. Heavily populated with stoneflies, it's a pocket water fisherman's paradise, especially when not filled with whitewater kayakers. Most of the time, we cast attractor patterns into the few riffled sections we located. Because the Fork is so tough, fewer fish are caught and released. As a result, the wild fish put up a great fight, with 14-inch fish taking us into our backing when hooked in fast water. I vividly remember Tom fooling a rainbow in a long, boulder-strewn section that required careful wading to follow the fish 50 yards downstream. I thought he'd finally caught the illusive "20-incher" we sought. Tom knew better, however, because he saw the fish jump and estimated it to be about 14 inches.

Arkansas and Taylor Rivers

On our second trip to Aspen, we drove over the Continental Divide and paralleled Arkansas River as it tumbled down from Leadville on its way to Canyon City. Like the Eagle, the upper section suffered from the toxic discharges of abandoned mining operations in the gulches near Leadville and it looked burnt orange as we drove along it. Most of the land along the river was fenced and those sections without fencing were subject to marked flow changes. Extremely low flows occurred where water was diverted from Turquoise to Twin Lakes and extremely high flows occurred below Twin Lakes, where water was needed for irrigation. Today, the headwaters are clear and the river throughout its length fishes much better, with the most popular stretch the 75 miles of water between Buena Vista and Canyon City, with

Roaring Fork above Aspen

many anglers focusing their efforts in Salina, where special regulation sections are located nearby.

After arriving at Poncha Springs, near Salina, we discovered that much of Arkansas River was posted and what wasn't posted wasn't productive. As a result, we headed for Taylor River, a tributary to the Gunnison, about 60 miles west. We discovered, however, that the Taylor was a continuous current of tumbling white water throughout its 25-mile length and, worse, it contained masses of large angular rocks and deep holes. The small public section downstream from the dam looked hazardous and it required short-line nymphing. The only place where we dared to stand and cast was the flat section between Lottis Creek and the base of the dam that created Taylor Park Reservoir, a short stretch crossed by Ct. Rd. 306. Huge fish were rising in the pool below the dam outlet, but this section was posted. We returned to our motel in Poncha Springs. Early the next morning, we left for Basalt and when we arrived, we realized we'd driven 300 miles without wetting a line.

Recently, several stretches of Taylor River have opened to the public, including the short, level stretch, less than a half-mile long, below the dam, where huge fish are caught with some regularity. Like trout in Montana's Kootenai, Taylor River trout in this stretch become enormous feeding on Kokanee salmon fry and Mysis shrimp that wash down from the Taylor Park Reservoir. Most are probably stocked fish, as the state stocks large numbers of 10-inch rainbows, and those in this small catch-and-release stretch have the best chance of survival.

Below this short section are several public stretches, where the fish are much smaller. To warn anglers about the hazards of wading in these stretches, a trout organization has posted signs saying, "Voluntary No-Wading Zones." The signs also state that fishing from the riverbanks is productive, but I would wait for the fall when the flows diminish.

Colorado River Between Glenwood Springs and Riffle

I have fished the Colorado in its upper reaches near Hot Sulphur Springs. Private clubs have posted most of it and the short stretches that are open to the public contain mostly stocked trout. But the Colorado between Glenwood Springs and Grand Junction, 60 miles of water, is another story. It contains some of the biggest river trout in the nation, but its usually bait fishermen's water. It's deep, fast, usually discolored, most of the bordering land is private, and most anglers fish it from a boat, although boats can spook the larger trout.

When I fished it with my brother-in-law, Ron, years ago, we fished it from its high grassy banks between Glenwood Springs and Rifle. Ron fed his family with trout he caught in the Colorado. When I speak about big trout, I speak about those just over 20 inches; when Ron spoke about big trout, he spoke about those over six pounds.

Enhancing the walls of several bars in downtown Aspen are the toothy jaws of huge brown trout caught in the upper Roaring Fork. Engraved plaques give the sizes of these immense fish and the nymphs that fooled them. Those who believe these fish were once residents of the Roaring Fork would be mistaken. The Fork is home to some good size browns near Carbondale, but the mounted jaws in the Aspen bars were those from fish that swam upstream from the Colorado. Their teeth looked like pike's teeth and they grew to this size ingesting fish that inhabit the Colorado. No mater what Roaring Fork enthusiasts tell you, even those caught in April were Colorado River browns that wintered over in the Fork.

Elk Creek

Although Ron was a meat fisherman, who believed fly fishing was casting a chunk of meat covered with flies, he knew the activities my friends and I would enjoy and suggested we fish Elk Creek, a small creek flowing out of the mountains north of his home and into the Colorado River. Bob, Tom, and I drove up the canyon road, parked at a pull off, went through a trail gate in a cattle fence, and walked up a steep trail that paralleled the creek. Rod told us not to worry about the trickle of water we would first see, because water in the Elk's lower sections was diverted through pipes for irrigation. He said the creek would be deeper in its higher elevations about a mile or more upstream.

The hike, although not difficult, was not for the faint hearted. I fell behind when I stopped several times to catch my breath and take a drink. On one stop, I found myself by a relatively deep pool. There were no fish in it, but it looked inviting for another reason. I took off my clothes, waded in, and took a dip in the waist-deep water. When sufficiently cooled off, I climbed out and went to retrieve my clothes. To my dismay, I discovered a swarm of ground hornets all around them. Evidently, my discarded clothes had covered their nest entrance. Several stung me as I tried to grab my belongings. Being stark naked, further stings were to be avoided. Finding no sturdy stick to move my clothes, I sunned myself on the rock and took a nap.

I lay on the rock until the sun went behind the mountain and I shivered in the cold. I decided that hornet stings were better than hypothermia and I carefully approached my clothes. I was in luck. The hornets eventually found a way under my things and entered their nest and, with the sun now behind the hills, they were inactive. I dressed and started up the trail. I hadn't gone far when I saw Bob and Tom returning. They reported that the creek contained considerably more water about a mile further upstream, where it leveled out and flowed through a deep, red-walled canyon. They both caught and released about 20 cutbows, from 10 to 11 inches in length, in pristine conditions. They said it was well worth the four-mile round trip. They asked how I did and I reported that I had a good swim and a nice nap.

White River and the Flat Tops Wilderness Area

The White and its tributaries flow out of the Flat Tops Wilderness Area, located in White River National Forest, a plateau region of Western Colorado, north of Glenwood Springs. A series of mesas, or plateaus, declines gradually in step-like intervals to the western border of the state. The North and South Forks of White River cut deep and rugged canyons through the upland ranges of these plateaus, meet in the valley at Buford and together, as one, wind their way through the valley to join Green River at Ouray, Utah.

The first time I fished White River was during a ten-day vacation in August of 1978. My family and I stayed at a ranch in the Flat Tops

Wilderness Area, about 35 miles from my relatives in Silt. When my first wife and daughters rode horses, the ranch owner, Norm, or his son, drove me down to the river each day around noon and returned for me five hours later. The snows were heavy in Colorado in the winter of 1978 and the river had been high throughout July. Now the water level was perfect and hatches occurred throughout the day.

Even in August, weather in the Flat Tops Wilderness Area is predictably unpredictable. Clear and sunny mornings were followed by dark and overcast afternoons. Thundershowers were as short as the fight of a 10-inch fish or as long as a boring day at work. Even when no clouds were in the sky, Norm always reminded me to take my raincoat. In keeping with Norm's cautions, around two o'clock each day a thunderstorm would roll in and it would rain for about a half hour while I sought cover under bushes that lined the banks. One time it even snowed! After each brief storm, I returned to fishing and my catch rate was as good as it had been earlier.

On morning, the whole sky was black from a rapidly approaching storm closing in from three compass points. I asked if it would pass over, like so many did in this area. Norm's son doubted it, stating that it looked like the big front the weatherman said was coming from Oregon, where it snowed the day before.

On a trail ride to the South Fork of the White, the previous day, we were caught in a brief hail shower and had fearfully watched lightening strike an adjoining ridge, as the storm moved rapidly toward us. Fresh from this experience, I didn't want to be in the river during a big thunderstorm. The storm came by, but within an hour the sky was clear. The next evening the expected storm arrived and with it hail the size of salmon flies. During our 10-

The White near Buford below Flats Top's Primitive Area

day August stay, the temperature ranged from 28 to 80 degrees, it hailed twice, and snowed lightly once.

The White River was a pleasant and relaxing river and I never shared it with another angler during my entire stay, although I took Bob and Tom there years later. The water was crystal clear, the hatches were abundant, and the air crisp and cool. It was a perfect place. When it got hot in the late afternoon, cool breezes, seemingly from the river bottom, served to renew my efforts. Only the breezes and the flowing water disturbed the quiet of this desolate place, a place where the mind can make deep adjustments and where comfort can be taken in the ordinary earth.

The White is neither a Gold Metal River nor a state designated wild-trout-river, but it contained some wild rainbows and cutbows among its stocked fish and native cutthroat in its two wild branches. All the fish I caught took a surface fly. I particularly remember one wild rainbow that jumped four times and ran the width of the river three times before I finally brought it to the net. It was only 14 inches, but it put up a memorable fight.

A River Threatened

I've wonderful memories of the White, a river threatened by a proposed shale-oil mining operation during the oil shortages in the 1970s. It may be threatened again by the high price of oil in 2008 and the promises of politicians to free us from reliance on foreign oil by finding alternative energy sources. The stratified plateaus in Garfield and Rio Blanco Counties contain

the largest reserves of shale oil in the United States. I wondered at the time whether White River trout would go the way of the Ute. "The Utes have gone" was the cry of pleased settlers after these Native Americans were forced to leave their White River homeland for reservations in Utah. Encroaching civilization drove the last of the red men from their beloved "Mothering Mountains," spirited men, who refused to abandon their rugged mountain wilderness for valley living and agricultural pursuits.

Nathan C. Meeker accepted the job as White River Indian Agent in the spring of 1878. He

The upper White—West Slope Cutthroat   wanted the Ute to stop their migratory hunting activities and adopt the plow. He plowed under the Ute's favorite pastures and ordered an irrigation channel built through a field where the Ute raced their horses. When his favorite Ute, Chief Johnson, protested the project, Meeker suggested sarcastically that some of the Ute's ponies be killed to free up more farmland. Johnson responded to Meeker's insensitivity by throwing him up against the wall. Realizing he was in trouble, Meeker requested help from the army and a detachment of soldiers was sent from a nearby fort.

Captain Jack, the chief leader of the Northern Ute, intercepted the military on its march to the reservation and urged the troop commander, Major Thomas T. Thornburgh, to travel alone with him to the agency and negotiate a peaceful settlement. The military leader refused, resulting in the last Indian war in America when the detachment was ambushed at Milk Creek by a small band of Ute. Angered by Meeker's use of the army to enforce his regulations, the small band raided the agency, burned it to the ground, and killed Meeker and 10 of his employees. The event was later referred to as the "Meeker Massacre" of 1879. Eventually, the Ute were banished to a reservation south of Venal, Utah, a desolate section discussed in Chapter Six.

Prior to their defeat, the Ute were elusive foes, safely retreating to their mountain hiding places. So, too, must the fisherman go high into the White Mountains, former home of the vanquished Ute, to catch the remaining native Colorado cutthroat that reside in the upper branches of the White and its main tributaries, Miller, North Elk, Ute, Marvine, and Big Fish creeks.

From Trapper's Lake, the White River flows for six miles down to Himes Peak Campground, below which it runs through private property until it reaches the North Fork Campground, where the public has access to its clear waters. Twenty miles from Buford, the main branch of the White passes through Meeker, but west of Meeker, the trout fishing is poor

Flat Tops Ponds

In my chapter on coldwater lakes in *Capturing Rogue Trout*, I discuss my experiences on Flat Tops ponds, but only some of that information, and none of the technical material, will be repeated in this chapter. Ray Bergman fished the largest of the ponds, Trappers Lake, and he called it "one of the best ponds for fly fishing that I ever fished." Unlike the lakes in the High Sierra, which I fished as a boy, clear glacial lakes with barren shorelines, these ponds looked like bass lakes back home. Although high in the mountains (Trappers Lake is 9,000 feet above sea level), the ponds had gradual sloping bottoms that allowed for considerable weed and shoreline growth. As a result, fresh-water shrimp, nymphs of all types, dragonflies and damselflies, grasshoppers, and countless minnows helped the trout grow fat. Fish could be seen feeding almost any time of day.

I learned to love these mountain ponds, nestled in the highlands where

Teddy Roosevelt used to hunt. During the mornings, when the air was cooler than the water, the ponds would reflect the fog in gray tones. Later, when the sky was blue, the ponds would turn blue. Long strands of dew drops in the morning midst draped the leaves of the thistles and cat tails along the banks, turning them into diamonds and emeralds in the early morning light.

I often took a break from fishing and let nature entertain me. I watched the shadows and subtle moments, the color and striking contrasts as the sky changed from one phase to another, each producing differing lights and colors. I watched the subtle changes in the shading of the grasses, as the sun moved higher and higher in the sky. I watched the hawks ride the air currents and gazed even higher at the clouds as they drifted across the imperceptible paths of the wind. Even when it rained, I enjoyed the splat of raindrops on the brim of my hat and the dry air sucking the moisture from my cloths and leaving me refreshed. The Native Americans say when we've been in a place of perfection, it will live forever in our spirit. No photographs are needed to keep the images of these ponds alive in my mind.

My youngest daughter, Kaylin, was my constant companion on the ponds. She used a spin rod with a bobber and weighted damsel-fly-nymph attached several feet below it. She would cast, using a small, closed-faced spin reel, near rising fish, gently retrieve the bobber, and the fish would chase the nymph that was pulled along behind it until the most aggressive one grabbed it. On the smaller ponds, we would walk the shoreline until we spotted fish. She out-fished me on these little ponds, until I learned to keep my back cast unusually high to avoid the tall thistle weed that took over the surrounding fields. My oldest daughter, Kalay, fished with me several times, but, more often, she accompanied her mother on trail rides.

Anglers who hike into accessible ponds and lakes in the Flat Tops Wilderness Area need a compass. We bumped into several lost fishermen who walked for hours trying to find lakes less than a mile from the road. Looking for a 10-acre pond is not as easy at it may seem. Open grazing is allowed in White River National Forest and the cattle make many trails that crisscross one another. Following a trail through the forest can lead to a big open space, but the space can be filled with cows and grass instead of water.

As strange as it may seem, a Flat Tops angler invented the San Juan Worm, a pattern now tied to imitate the aquatic worms found in many tail-water rivers. When I first fished the Bighorn, discussed in Chapter Five, I examined a clump of floating river grass and found embedded within it red worms about two inches in length and a quarter inch in width, a worm the San Juan Worm easily imitates. Nevertheless, the fly evolved from one tied to imitate fresh water shrimp in Flat Tops waters.

In the 1950s, Jim Aubrey, of Grand Junction, wrapped a hook with orange chenille over lead wire, interwoven with red floss, to make a red band. After Aubrey moved from Colorado to Albuquerque, he gave some of these flies to his cousin. After going fishless during a 1968 trip to the San Juan, his cousin tried Aubrey's orange invention. To his surprise, he began catching fish! Other tiers then modified the pattern, particularly Chuck Rizuto, a San Juan River guide mentioned in Chapter Nine, who tied them in Ultra Chenille.

I enjoyed fishing the Flat Tops ponds for the fat 14- and 15-inch fish they contained, as well as fishing for native cutthroat on the White River's South Fork. The better parts of the South Fork are reached by horseback and provide the ultimate in wilderness stream fishing.

Accommodations and Other Activities

Interstate 70 parallels the Eagle River for quite a distance and over the years, the river has cleared up considerably and is now an excellent rainbow fishery, with drift boats concentrating on the waters below the Village of Eagle. It's worth a stop to wet your line on your way to Basalt. Basalt, originally a railroad town supporting nearby Aspen's silver mining activities, provides for all the basic needs of the traveler: lodging, a supermarket, two fly shops, and several nice restaurants, as well as a good breakfast cafe. We stayed at the Best Western Aspenalt Lodge (303-927-3191), where trout swim in the Pan right behind it and where their outdoor whirlpool can be enjoyed at the end of the day. There's also a Days Inn and a four room bed-and-breakfast inn, the Shenandoah Inn (970-927-9466).

Four inexpensive campgrounds are located on Ruedi Reservoir: Mollie B, with 26 sites; Little Maud, with 22 sites; Little Mattie, with 20 sites; and Deerhammer, with 13 sites. Several miles above the reservoir are: Elk Wallow, a free 8-site campground, and Chapman, with 42 sites.

The Rainbow Grill, overlooking the Pan, serves 125 different bottled beers. Its corrugated scrap tin ceiling, walls of barn wood from Texas, and a bar constructed from Aspen Times printing plates create a unique dining

Spawning tributary at its junction with the Roaring Fork

ambiance. Chefys, just south of Besalt, is a small restaurant with an outside deck that makes for pleasant summer dining. Unfortunately, the dining rooms in both these restaurants stop serving before the evening hatch ends—Chefys at nine-thirty and the Rainbow Grill at ten. Roaring Fork anglers can dine at Woody Creek Tavern, made famous in the 1970s by Rolling Stone writer, Hunter Thompson. It's right by the river and serves until ten. Wind surfing is popular in Ruedi Reservoir and several hiking trails start near Basalt.

Aspen, a noted resort community, is only 18 miles upstream from Besalt. Summer visitors can play golf or tennis, enjoy concerts, plays, music festivals, ballet, and rodeos, ride on chair lifts or in hot air balloons, and take nature tours. In addition, numerous educational seminars and workshops are held throughout the summer. Those who inquire about the price of lodging in Aspen shouldn't stay in Aspen. Nevertheless, budget minded anglers could call Affordable Aspen (800-243-9466), a small group dedicated to locating value priced lodging.

Prospectors founded Aspen in 1879 and named it "Ute City." Shortly after, two railroads started serving the area and the town became the world's richest silver producing community. When silver was demonetized, most residents left to find work in the gold camps. From a population of 15,000 in 1892, Aspen's population dropped to 700 in the 1920s. After World War II, members of the army's Tenth Mountain Division returned to Aspen and started the ski industry for which Aspen is famous.

In the Maroon Bells-Snowmass Wilderness Area, there are more than 100 miles of trails at elevations from 9,000 to 12,000 feet. The trip to Maroon Bells, itself, was our favorite. Although the darling of photographers, and usually crowded with tourists, we loved it anyway. We also enjoyed the drive up to Independence Pass on the Continental Divide. The drive passes the decaying ruins of several log homes, attesting to the tenacity of our forefathers and serving as fodder for our imagination.

In Glenwood Springs, raft tours and white water trips on the Colorado

Author on a Roaring Fork tributary (Howie Garber Photo)

River can be arranged. For a modest fee, less robust family members can soak all day long in the hot springs pool and anglers who skip the evening hatch can join them until it closes at ten o'clock. The pool is two city blocks long, making it the largest warm water mineral pool in the world. Many believe, like the Ute years ago, that the waters cure one of various ills. The Ute also believed the waters made them more skillful warriors and hunters. John "Doc" Holiday, the famous gun fighter, is buried in Glenwood Springs. Perhaps if he'd spent more time in the springs, rather than fighting at the O.K. Corral, he would've lived longer than age 35. On weekends, couples can dance to live music at Buffalo Valley, a tavern; otherwise, there's not much to do in the evenings.

Anglers trying for the monster trout in Taylor River can stay at the Best Western Tomiedo Village or the less expensive ABC Motel (970-641-2400), both located in Gunnison, or at the Waunita Hot Springs Ranch (970-641-1266), located 27 miles north east of Gunnison at an altitude of 9,000 feet. In addition to the services offered by most guest ranches, it has a hot springs pool, but a two-night minimum stay is required.

Budget minded anglers fishing the White River could rent one of 14 rustic cabins at Trappers Lake Lodge (970-878-3336) or one of 21 cabins with small kitchens at the Sleepy Cat Guest Ranch (970-878-4413). A drawback of the Sleepy Cat is its location near the main highway. Two hotels in Meeker are the White River Inn (970-878-5031) and Meeker Hotel (970-878-5255), an 1896 refurbished inn and restaurant.

The Meeker Cafe, next to Meeker Hotel, and the restaurant attached to the Sleepy Cat, provide alternatives to hotel food. I stayed once at Seven Lakes Ranch (800-809-4772), now listed in guidebooks as an expensive guest ranch. Orvis also discovered the area and endorses Elk Creek Lodge (970-878-5454), located 18 miles east of Meeker. Guests have access to six miles of private water on White River and Marvine Creek, plus 100 pools along the lodge's three-mile stretch of the North Slope's Elk Creek.

Campgrounds along the White include the South Fork, East Marvine, Marvine, North Fork, and Himes Peak campgrounds. At Trappers Lake, campgrounds include the Bucks, Shepherds, Rim, Trapline, and Cutthroat campgrounds, all located past Trappers Lake Lodge. RV hookups are available at Rim Rock campground (970-878-4486), a private campground in Meeker. There are many hiking tails in White River National Forest. The most popular trails are: the Chinese Wall, Marvine, Mirror Lake, Peltier Lake, Skinny Fish Lake, McGinnis Lake, Shut Cave, and Trappers Lake.

Chapter Four
Big Wood River, Big Lost River and Silver Creek
Three Unique Settings

Take a freestone stream flowing through hardwoods and pines, take another flowing through desert and sagebrush, and add a spring creek flowing through high grasses, then put them in close proximity to each other, and you have options for fishermen who travel together, but who have different tastes, or for one fisherman who likes them all.

For those unfamiliar with spring creeks, they're streams fed primarily by ground water rather than runoff. As a result, they maintain a fairly constant temperature around 57 degrees F. throughout the year, the optimal level for trout growth. Spring creeks are usually rich in aquatic life, with a variety of insects, as well as crustaceans, dwelling in their weedy riverbeds. Their fly hatches are unusually thick and bring up the biggest fish in the river. Since the fish are visible in the gin-clear, slow moving waters, anglers can pick and choose among them and cast to the largest fish or to those in the most easily reached lies.

On this trip west, our usual group of three was a bit larger. Scott and his father, Chuck, met myself, Bob, and Tom in Sun Valley in the second week of August, where we all stayed in a condominium that Chuck rented, a style to which we were unaccustomed. In fact, Tom liked it so much that he was torn between fishing and relaxing around the condo pool. "I can always fish," he said, "but when do I ever get an opportunity to live like this?" I could see that the good life appealed to him. Chuck was not a stranger to our group, having fished with us for many years in New York's Thousand Islands and New Hampshire's Lake Winnipesaukee.

Chuck, a highly successful IBM salesman, retired early to enjoy life, but after becoming bored, directed his energies into running the small oil company his second wife inherited from her first husband. Each year, Chuck treated his oil delivery men to an annual fishing trip to the Thousand Islands for pike or to Lake Winnipesaukee for landlocked salmon and smallmouth. Our group joined his group and stayed in an adjoining cabin. We brought hot dogs and beans and Chuck brought prime rib, but he brought enough for us all, so we took most of our meals with his group. We got to know Chuck's drivers quite well and looked forward to seeing them each year.

Chuck eventually retired from the oil business, but, being an entrepreneur, he didn't stay idle long. Having repeated troubles renting a limo to take friends into New York City, he bought one and rented it to friends when not using it. Before long, he had a fleet of limos. In appreciation for his generosity, I made him an 8-ft. fly rod, for 5-wt. lines, out of the finest fiberglass available at the time. It was as thin and light as any graphite rod made until just recently. I wish I had it today.

Big Wood River

On our first day in Idaho, we fished Big Wood River, a small river by western standards, but one touted as the best wild rainbow stream in the state before anglers gained access to Silver Creek. John Glen, Charlton Heston, Steve McQueen, and members of the Kennedy family fished the river for its wild fish. Since then, like most rivers, development and flood control efforts degraded its habitat and its wild rainbows have less structure along the river in which to dwell and, as a result, their numbers have decreased accordingly.

In most freestone rivers, 10 times as many trout inhabit unaltered reaches, such as banks lined with heavy woody debris—root balls, root clusters, tree stumps, and fallen trees—compared to banks covered with grass or rock revetments, such as riprap. As a result, when we first fished the river in 1985, the state stocked about 28,000 rainbow yearlings in 25 miles of the river throughout the season, about 1,120 per mile, but like most stocked fish, many died or were quickly caught and kept, so that, at any given time, greater numbers of wild than stocked fish inhabited the river, about 700 per mile, so the bigger fish we caught were wild ones.

In 2001, to improve the wild trout fishery, the state started stocking triploid rainbows, which are sterile and, therefore, cannot spawn with wild fish and dilute the strain. In 2001 they socked about 10,000 fish in 25 miles of the river and then gradually reduced the stocking numbers to 5,500 fish in 2008. The state now stocks triploid rainbows in all of its wild trout waters.

The Big Wood flows from the heights west of Galena Peak, over 11,000 feet high, southeast and then south through the wooded valley lands of Sun

Woody debris on the banks of Big Wood River
(Courtesy of Terry Ring, Silver Creek Outfitters)

Valley. From Sun Valley, it flows southeast past Ketchum, Hailey and Bellevue, and then into Magic Reservoir, also a decent trout fishery. Below Magic Reservoir, a short tail-water section can sometimes produce quality fishing. Below the reservoir, the river is joined by Little Wood River, fed by Silver Creek, and then empties into Snake River at the bottom of Malad Gorge. State Rt. 75 parallels the Big Wood and there are numerous access points between Ketchum and Bellevue.

Most anglers fish the river from its junction with its North Fork, about 10 miles north of Sun Valley, down to Bellevue, approximately 25 miles of water with beautiful pools, riffles, and runs throughout its length. Several miles below Bellevue, a diversion dam removes water and during years of heavy irrigation, the river from Bellevue to Magic Reservoir can be too low to hold trout, but when levels are higher, this stretch holds some relatively large browns. We fished the no-kill section near where it flows under Rt. 75 in Ketchum. Viscount Grey of Fallodon could have been describing the Big Wood, when he wrote in his 1899 book, *Fly Fishing*:

> An ideal piece of water would be one with broad shallows here and there, but with plenty of deep stretches, not stagnant, but with a good current all down through: its breadth in the deeper parts should be about as much as can be cast across by a single-handed rod, and considerably more in the shallows where wading is possible.

Fly hatches on the Big Wood are typical of those on Western freestone streams, although in mid-August, a moth, called the "Spruce Fly," best imitated by a #10 caddis, visits the river to drink, lighting on the surface and floating for short distances, an activity bringing up the river's biggest trout. In September, a Red Quill hatch lasts for several weeks. Small *Baetis* and Little Yellow Craneflies also hatch during this season.

In stretches near Ketchum, the Big Wood can be 100 feet wide, but in many sections, it's no wider than 40 feet. The gradient is gentle; the riffles are short; the clean bottom is easily waded; and the pools are deep, but not too deep. You could be waist deep in most pools and easily reach fish rising on the opposite bank. When fish weren't rising, they could be fooled by casting a nymph upstream into riffles, so clear you could see the fish flash as they inhaled the nymph, but if your line wasn't tight, their flash was all you'd see.

Most of the time, however, fish were rising, making it difficult to break for lunch. It was easy for Tom, because he couldn't wait to swim in the condo pool and relax on the its large wooded deck, but Bob, well Bob could never make a last cast. One our first day, I drove Tom back to the condo, had a quick bite, and made a sandwich to bring back to Bob. When I arrived, he was still in the same spot! He even had a hard time stopping to eat the sandwich.

The fish were all hearty rainbows, ranging in size from 12 to 16 inches. At dusk, we caught slightly bigger fish, with Bob and Tom sticking with dry flies and I switching to streamers. Some of the fish we caught didn't fight very well, but most likely they were stocked holdovers.

I enjoyed the Big Wood, perhaps better than any Western river I've fished, with the exception of Colorado's White, preferred because of feelings connected with having the White all to myself for 10 days. Strong rainbows challenge you in both rivers, where wading is relaxing, the water is clear, and the sun shins through cloud cover, making the summer's heat less overwhelming. I saw only several rainbows in the Big Wood that looked

Typical Big Wood riffle (Courtesy of Terry Ring of Silver Creek Outfitters)

larger than 17 inches. Bigger browns can be caught, both above and below Magic Reservoir, especially in the fall, but big rainbows are scarce. Fly shop staff claimed that plenty of 20-inch rainbows inhabited the Big Wood, but I doubt if visitors will catch any larger than those we caught; but they'll catch them in superb surroundings.

In the Winter 2003 issue of *Northwest Fly Fishing*, Greg Thomas writes that he spent dozens of days on the Big Wood, during all seasons, and never caught or witnessed one rainbow "stretching an honest twenty inches" until he encountered one during a Green Drake hatch, a hatch which begins in late June and extends into July and brings up the river's biggest fish. If after big rainbows, spend time on Silver Creek, the home of many big fish.

Silver Creek

Let me say right off, that, in spite of its marvelous fishing, I've spent only one morning on Silver Creek, a river with the highest density of wild trout for its size in North America. Armstrong, DePuy's, and Nelson's creeks, mentioned in Chapter Three, tributaries to Yellowstone River above Livingston, Montana, are other famous Western spring creeks, but they're smaller pay-to-fish waters that flow through private lands. The slow moving, flat water and the surrounding environment of Silver Creek in the Conservatory stretch didn't move me—although its quiet openness suggested that different weather patterns would create different moods—and neither did its fish. I didn't like their domesticity and, after I hooked one, I didn't like the way they fought. Stocked rainbows in New Mexico's San Juan River, discussed in Chapter Nine, were more fun to catch, even though I typically prefer fooling wild trout.

With the help of Ernest Hemingway's son, Jack, the Nature Conservatory bought the former Sun Valley Ranch, marshy plains just south of Gannet (a hamlet southeast of Hailey) at the creek's headwaters, and created conservation easements for several miles downstream, where, in partnership with landowners, fencing was erected to keep grazing cattle away from the banks. In addition, the State of Idaho owns a large section of the creek. Like the Big Wood, the creek can be fished all year.

Anglers can fish the headwaters section, a fly-fishing-only, catch-and-release section, called Cabin Reach, by registering at the preserve headquarters (the cabin) and then walking a trail to the creek that slowly winds its way through tall meadow grasses. Greg Thomas writes that Silver Creek is a technical river, "where anglers go to test their ability against some of the wariest large trout in the West." Although I enjoy challenges as much as the next guy, as my book *Capturing Rogue Trout* demonstrates, Silver Creek's Cabin Reach is not where I'd choose to hunt for them; other sections of the creek are more appealing.

Let me add that I also didn't like Letort Creek in Carlisle, Pennsylvania, a

Matching the evening hatch on Silver Creek
(Courtesy of Terry Ring of Silver Creek Outfitters)

limestone stream featured in writings by its patron saints, Charlie Fox and Vince Marino, with Marino's *In the Ring of the Rise* now a classic. Theodore Gordon learned to tie flies along its banks before moving to the Catskills. I'd been looking forward to fishing the creek for years. After a day on the Yellow Breaches, another river I dislike because it contains only stocked trout, I walked the banks of the Letort behind two stone monuments honoring Fox and Marino. The creek was no wider than a single-lane road and when I visited it in 2001, it was choked with weeds and flowed through overgrown fields behind small wood lots. It was not attractive and the few trout I saw barely fit into the few open spaces among the thick water plants.

The creek needed either a river keeper (a man whose job includes "mowing" river weeds) or a powerful spring flow to flush it clean. I didn't even rig up my fly rod! I guess I'll always be a freestone freak; I love the sound of water rushing over rocks. Freestone creeks capture my imagination, especially forest-lined ones, where my back cast can gets caught in trees, so tall they block the sunlight, rather than in grasses and sagebrush. Andrienne Rich would not have written the following poem had she seen only spring creeks.

> Sport like water molded by unseen stone, sandbar, pleats and funnels
> according to its own submerged necessity —
> to the indolent eye pure willfulness,
> to the stray pine needle boiling in that cascade-bent pool a random fury:
> Law, if that's what's wanted, lies asking to be read in the dried brook bed.

Hooking Silver Creek fish requires a drag-free float, made difficult by the creek's many different currents and by the floating algae that gets caught on the fly and on leader knots; forget knotted leaders! If you arrive before 10:30 A. M., the predictable time of the Trico hatch in August, the rainbows are congregated in deep holes, waiting to move up into shallow water to feed on the hatch. The situation reminded me of when Tom and I saw barracuda swimming anxiously around among small fish in the deep water just off the flats in the Florida Keys, waiting for the incoming tide, so they could move up onto the shallow flats and more easily capture prey. But the trout in Silver Creek's holes weren't moving; they sat perfectly still in their chosen hole.

I stood over one hole, watching the fish in their hypnotic state, and dropped a weighted nymph by the nose of several, but nary a one moved. I then stuck my rod tip down and tapped one on the nose. It casually moved away. None could be spooked from the hole—my efforts were only a minor annoyance. That's when I decided I didn't care for this stretch of the creek! Nevertheless, hooking its trout was quite a challenge.

Exactly at 10:30 all the rainbows, like a trained army of soldiers, marched off to take a position on the flat, sandy-bottomed sections of the creek. These sojourners then rose everywhere in knee-deep water. Catching them required selecting the one desired, moving upstream from it, and floating a #22 Trico spinner imitation downstream on 6X tippet into its feeding lane. When a drag- and algae-free float was made, and the fly seen in the atrocious glare, fish could be hooked, but keeping them on the barbless hook was another matter!

They were big fat fish, and their initial spurt of energy often tore the fly from their mouth; if it didn't, then the hook usually worked lose after they dashed into the streambed's aquatic vegetation. Unlike San Juan River rainbows, that jumped and dashed across the flats like hooked bonefish, these rainbows headed for the nearest weed beds. Because most visitors are wading anglers, Cabin Reach is heavily fished. I suspect that many of its fish were hooked before and learned to escape in the waterweeds.

Another thing I didn't like about Cabin Reach was that only about half of the short stretch could be waded; it became too deep to do so not far downstream, where the creek remained pretty much a float tuber's river until it joined Little Wood River miles downstream. Were I to visit the creek again, I would rent a float tube so I could fish its more challenging sections.

Today the creek can be accessed at 11 other spots, 9 of them along unpaved roads below Cabin Reach. They are as follows: Stalker Creek Fishing Access, above the preserve property, where Stalker and Marsh creeks join to form Silver Creek; The "S" Turns; Kilpatrick's Bridge (also called Pond Access), below which catch-and-releases spin fishing is allowed; Federal Hwy. 20 Bridge, below which two fish can be kept between 12 and 16 inches, except between December 1 and February 30; Silver Creek-West Access; Silver Creek-East Access (Idaho Fish and Game Point of Rock Access); the Old Larkin Ranch; Picabo Bridge Access, which enables a long float through private property down to the last access, Fish and Game Public

A windy day at Silver Creek (Courtesy of Terry Ring of Silver Creek Outfitters)

Access, located just above Federal Hwy. 93 and accessed from an unpaved road between Hwy. 20 and Hwy. 93. For the exact location of access sites, a map can be downloaded from the website of Silver Creek Outfitters.

At the last site, bait fishing is allowed and general rules apply, except between December 1 and February 30, when fish can't be harvested. In the stretch below the Hwy. 93 Bridge to the creek's junction with Little Wood River, fish can be harvested all season, but the creek flows through private property and isn't readily accessible. Below Kilpatrick Bridge, only a short distance downstream from Cabin Reach, anglers in float tubes can best fish the creek (rafts and boats are not allowed). In fact, the creek widens into large ponds just below the bridge, but even below the ponds the creek is deep. I've talked to anglers who've found spots to wade in these stretches and they relate that their resident fish are more challenging to hook and more fun to land than those in the preserve, but that spots much be found that can be either waded or successfully fished from the banks.

When I fished the creek, rainbows dominated Cabin Reach, the section with the highest density of trout, with browns more numerous downstream. Browns now share the reach with rainbows in equal numbers and will probably outnumber them in future years. Very few rainbows in the creek live longer than three years and few exceed 18 inches. In contrast, browns, which mature later and live longer, can easily reach two feet. Silver Creek is not the only river to experience brown trout encroachment, as it's taking place on both the Green and Bighorn and on other waters throughout the country.

After catching and loosing a few rainbows to the weeds, I walked downstream to watch Chuck working with his guide. Chuck, whose ego

Silver Creek in the fall (Courtesy of Terry Ring of Silver Creek Outfitters)

wasn't invested in his fishing success, always hired a guide to shortcut the learning process and to make fishing easier. The guide would tie on the correct tippet, attach it to the correct fly, spot a big fish away from competing whitefish, position Chuck upstream from it, walk downstream to the fish, and yell back instructions that helped Chuck to float his fly over the trout instead of over the nearby whitefish. Chuck hooked several rainbows about 18 inches long while I watched, but his biggest was a 23-inch brown he fooled on a grasshopper when he returned that afternoon

The rise of whitefish could be distinguished from those of trout by the barely visible tails of whitefish breaking the surface. If only a dimple was seen, it was usually a trout; if a "double-dimple" was seen, it was usually a whitefish.

Not much activity occurred when the Trico hatch finished. By noon the swarm of Trico spinners and corresponding rises were replaced with empty air and unruffled surfaces. A few of the fish returned to their holes, but most disappeared elsewhere, perhaps positioning themselves for grasshoppers that might blow into the creek with the afternoon winds. Sometimes the creek's browns will take a hopper imitation, but fooling its biggest ones is not easy. Many feed at night, chasing and engorging half asleep young rainbows in the shallows. They also eat mice and voles and are sometimes fooled by deer hair mouse imitations.

Some anglers weren't satisfied with the slow current of the creek and sought even slower waters; perhaps they were aficionados of pond fishing. Within the Conservatory property, are two large sloughs where spring water seeps into the creek. I watched one fisherman cast a scud pattern into one of the sloughs and catch a large, fat trout cruising in search of food

As we ate our sandwiches by the creek, Bob, Tom, and I agreed that something was objectionable about Cabin Reach. The trout were stream-born rather than stocked, but they didn't act like the wild fish we were accustomed to catching. We considered the experience worthwhile, as a one-time venture; it was interesting, but not worth repeating. If we ever returned, we'd fish lower stretches. Consequently, we didn't join Chuck and his guide for the afternoon "hopper-hatch," but instead returned to the Big Wood, where, once again, we caught lots of fish. The next day we fished Big Lost River.

Big Lost River

I've never fished, and probably never will fish, a river like the Big Lost. It begins in a high desert valley, called Copper Basin, below the Lost River Range, and flows in the shadow of Borch Peak, Idaho's highest mountain. It's a small river above Mackay Reservoir, no bigger than the Catskill's small streams, but it flows fast, has some deep holes, and contains some large fish, some wild and others stocked.

We assessed the Big Lost by taking a gravel road from Sun Valley that went up and over Trail Creek Pass and put us into Cooper Basin, where the river begins. We fished the river's East Fork above MacKay Reservoir. Below the reservoir, the river parallels Hwy. 93 and is a bigger body of water. We were the only anglers on the East Fork. In fact, not a single car passed us while we fished. We had a ball and returned the next day.

The Big Lost, and the Little Lost, north of it, got their names because they both get lost—they disappear into the desert. Both flow into lava beds, near Butte, and reappear more than 120 miles southwest at Thousands Springs on the Snake River in Hagerman Valley. The two rivers filter through the lava,

East Fork Big Lost River

more than a mile thick in some spots, and end up in an enormous aquifer. When the water flows out of this subterranean reservoir, it may be thousands of years old, making the water older than that flowing out of England's chalk beds into their famous chalk streams, discussed in Chapter Twelve.

When we first fished the East Fork, it was stocked throughout the angling season with 6,800 rainbows, with stockings reduced to 2,200 triploid rainbows in 2008. More than 10,000 cutthroats were stocked in 2001 and again in 2007, in an effort to return the fishery to its natural state, but a cutbow fishery is more likely to be the result. Similar efforts are being made on its North Fork, with annual stockings of cutthroats since 2005. In addition to rainbow stocking, huge numbers of brown trout fingerlings were stocked below the reservoir in the 1980s, but a tail-water fishery for browns never materialized, to the fishery's benefit because the lower river has substantial numbers of wild rainbows.

Most of the whitefish we tried not to catch approached 19 inches. We all caught rainbows up to 17 inches and I lost one close to 19. Tom also caught a small golden trout. When Tom went to net my big one, the net got caught on a submerged branch, Tom stumbled, and the fish broke off. Tom also failed to net the biggest northern pike I've ever hooked in New York's Thousand

East Fork Big Lost (Tom Royster Photo)

Islands. He forgot to check the net for holes!

Greg Tomas describes the fishing on all three streams in the July 1998 issue of *Fly Fisherman*. Thomas also discusses the Little Wood and Salmon rivers. We didn't fish the Little Wood in 1985, a year-round fishery stocked annually in the fall with about 6,500 browns, because it was bone-dry. The dam on Little Wood Reservoir was being repaired and no water was being released. When you see the lava rock and stunted sagebrush lining the empty riverbed, it's hard to imagine the Little Wood as anything more than a gully. Nevertheless, when it's full of water, good-sized trout are caught in it.

Salmon River

Thomas's article includes a discussion of steelhead fishing on Salmon River, most of which occurs in March and April. We saw no trout in the Salmon during our trip; even though more than 50,000 rainbows were stocked that season. Staff in Silver Creek Outfitters, formerly Dick Alfs Fly Shop, didn't recommend the river, adding that small numbers of both Chinook salmon and steelhead were still in the river and often spook the trout into feeder streams, although I suspected that few of the stocked fish survived the harsh winters, but that didn't explain the absence of wild fish.

Dick Alfs, and his friend, Ruel Stayner, who owned Stayner's Sporting Goods, in Twin Falls, where Alfs hung out before opening his own store, kept fly fishing alive in the area during the 1950s, when spin fishing became popular. Alfs began his career as a waiter at Ram Restaurant, a four-star restaurant in Sun Valley Village, still serving food today, and he solicited orders for his hand-tied flies from customers, tying them all night and delivering them the following morning. Terry Ring, who allowed me to use his photos in this book, is the current owner of Silver Creek Outfitters. Terry's photos capture rich colors and converting them to back and whites doesn't do them justice.

The scenery along Salmon River, rather than its fishery, was what attracted our fancy. We took time off from serious fishing and drove north from Ketchum on Rt. 75 to view the Sawtooth Mountains northwest of Ketchum in the Sawtooth National Recreation Area. And how marvelous our American Alps are, with their 42 chiseled peaks jutting up 10,000 feet into the sky. We stopped to admire the river at Stanley, where the snowfall averages eight feet per year, and to visit the Redfish Lake Visitor Center. Early settlers gave the lake its name after seeing it colored red by thousands of sockeye dead after spawning.

After sitting in Sun Beam Hot Springs, we drove north as far as Challis, where, behind the interpretative center of the Yankee Fork Historic Area, towers a 60-foot cliff used by Shoshone tribes to drive Bison over the precipice to their deaths. Unlike European hunters, who killed them by the millions, first for their hides and later just for fun, the Shoshone, like other

Bob looking without success or rising fish

Native Americans, found a use for every part of this noble animal.

Along Rt. 75, the Salmon River, easily seen from the road, was crystal clear, like the three branches of Northwest Montana's Flathead River, discussed in Chapter Seven. From the highway, we could look down into the deep pools of the storied "River of No Return" and see the river bottom, even in pools 10 feet deep. We stopped at several places and saw no trout, even though aquatic flies were hatching sporadically.

On our third stop, Scott shouted, "Look at these huge fish!" Sure enough, when we looked to where he pointed, two large, dark creatures were visible; both motionless in the deep pool directly below, casting shadows making it look like there were four. They remained still for a long time, causing us to question our perceptions, but when they finally moved to the head of the pool, we knew our eyes hadn't deceived us. They were Chinook salmon and, like the steelhead that arrive in the spring, they'd traveled nearly 900 miles, struggling up the fish ladders of eight Army Corps of Engineer dams on Washington's Columbia and Snake rivers, along the Oregon/Idaho border, and then up the Salmon to this spot.

Excited by our observation, we stopped several more times along the road, but these two salmon were all we saw, reminders of a time when the river teemed with these silver fish, although they're far from silver by the time they reach this section of river. Idaho's rivers were once temporary homes to millions of Chinook, Coho, and Sockeye salmon, as well as steelhead. Coho were declared extinct in Salmon River in 1986 and, in 1996, only one Sockeye made it back to the Sawtooth Hatchery near Redfish Lake.

Wild Chinook are an endangered species, with only small numbers of redds spotted recently along Marsh Creek, a major spawning cite on the upper Salmon River. Relatively few Chinook enter the river to spawn and only the strongest make it to their spawning sites. Runs of wild steelhead had also decreased considerably.

The diminished return of salmon from the sea, a topic briefly discussed in Chapter One, is only a part of the problem. The fish ladders didn't help the salmon fry in their efforts to get downstream to the sea. Many died when their swim bladders exploded after they were sucked through powerhouses at high pressures and high speeds. Others died of disease exacerbated by high water temperatures below the dams or were eaten by predators during their downstream journey through slow-moving waters. Death was estimated at 15 percent per dam and 20 percent per pool. With eight sets of dams and pools, 95 percent of upper Snake River fry died before reaching the sea. Before the dams, wild fry made it to the sea in 7 to 10 days. After the dams, the few who made it took more than a month. In fact, after 15 days, a fry's focus on swimming downstream is lost and it's less able to switch from fresh to salt water, its "smolt" stage of development.

Man's efforts haven't really helped the beleaguered salmon, efforts including raising millions of fry in hatcheries and trucking, or barging, them to the sea. Barging fry to the sea in the mid-1970s resulted in a 98 percent survival rate, but less than two percent returned as adults. Stocked trout experience extreme difficulty surviving in streams; why would we expect stocked salmon to do any better in an ocean?

North of Stanley is Yankee Fork of the Salmon River, a river that experienced rough going in the early 1950s. Droves of gold mines along the river's banks, near the mining towns of Custer and Bonanza, damaged the river in the 1890s, but the damage they caused was nothing compared to that inflicted between 1940 and 1952. A huge floating dredge, weighing almost a half-ton, put into the river just below Bonanza and slowly moved downstream to the Fork's junction with the Salmon. The barge lurched along, night and day, every day, dredging out the riverbed from beneath its bow, extracting gold from more than six million cubic yards of gravel, and spewing out the reminder from its rear end to form huge, ugly tailings along the riverbed.

The barge operated until the gold ran out, some 13 years later. Its owners, extracting only a million dollars worth of gold, simply abandoned the barge and made no effort to clean up the destruction left in its wake. When finally asked to remove it, the owners had the gall to donate the barge, where it stood, to the Forest Service, who accepted the ridiculous gift and turned it into a museum. The General Mining Act of 1872, which to this day makes mining a preferred use of federal lands, is silent on environmental protection issues and, therefore, requires no clean-up efforts. Since the river's natural rebound, it's been stocked annually with rainbows, with about 4,000 triploids in 2007.

Ruins enthusiasts can take Yankee Fork Road, a gravel road, and travel 10 miles north to Bonanza and Custer, both ghost towns. Actually, Custer is not technically a ghost town because it contains a small museum, housed in a former one-room school, and a general store. Custer was noted for the General Custer Stamp Mill, which stamped over twelve million dollars worth of gold bars, an opera house, a minor's union hall, a large hotel, a China Town, and its own newspaper. Bonanza is empty, except for a small graveyard and crumbled building

Salmon River

foundations. At one time, both Bonanza and Custer were booming mining towns, each with more than 600 residents.

Considering that cowboys terrorized the Chinese in our western towns, I can understand why some gravitated to this remote place. Cowboys chased them through the streets, tied them up, cut off their pigtails, stripped them, and often shot off their toes and fingers to prevent them from taking jobs from white laborers. In addition, when Chinese discovered gold and tried to stake a claim, claim officers wouldn't recognize their claims and alerted white men to their whereabouts so they could claim them. The saying "Not a Chinaman's Chance" originated from this practice.

Today, Bonanza is the more famous of the two towns because a legend about it lives on. It's the story of the unhappy fate of Lizzie King. Lizzie and her first husband, Richard, arrived at Bonanza by stagecoach when it was a bustling mining town. Richard came to prospect for gold and Lizzie to start a saloon. Shortly, thereafter, Richard was killed in a gunfight. From this point, there are two different versions of Lizzie's fate. The first is that she left Bonanza after Richard's death and moved to Butte, Montana, where she met prospector Bob Hawthorne. The two moved back to Bonanza, where they ran the Yankee Fork Dance Hall and Saloon and married in 1880. Their adjustment was marred, however, because Hawthorne bragged that he was rich and owned a castle in England. When residents learned that he was actually dirt poor, the humiliation and shame drove him to shoot and kill Lizzie and then to shoot himself.

The second version of the tale is that Charles Franklin, a founding father of the town and owner of its only hotel, was smitten by the penniless widow and helped her with Richard's funeral arrangements, followed by supporting her operation of the dance hall and salon, courting her, and eventually proposing marriage. Nevertheless, after the flamboyant Bob Hawthorne came to Bonanza, she married him instead. Both Lizzie and Bob were found shot to death shortly after their wedding, but neither the murder weapon nor the murderer's identity was ever discovered. The forsaken hotel owner buried both victims next to Richard, but refused to acknowledge Lizzie's new surname on her gravestone. He became depressed and disheveled, neglected his hotel, and retreated to an isolated cabin in the mountains. In 1892, two prospectors stumbled upon his hut and found his decomposed body. In his clenched fist was the locket containing a photo of Lizzie King Hawthorne.

I prefer the second story because it kindles my imagination. If I were a betting man, with apologies to Franklin's descendants, I'd bet that the distraught Franklin, feeling exploited by his Lizzie, killed them both. Perhaps smitten by her when she first arrived, he created events that resulted in her husband loosing a gunfight to a better man. In any case, Lizzie and her two husbands rest in Boot Hill Cemetery, located west of the town.

The jewel of the area is the Middle Fork of the Salmon, one of the first rivers to receive the designation "Wild and Scenic River," and one flowing

Snake River in Idaho, Sec. 2 (Courtesy of Harold McMillan, Jr.)

throughout its length through a spectacular canyon of towering granite cliffs. It's been a renowned cutthroat fishery since 1973, when catch-and-release and single-hook, artificial-lures-only regulations were first established on it. We didn't fish it, however, because it's use is strictly managed. Access is only by drift boat and permits available only through a lottery system. Nonresidents typically book a six-day float trip with an outfitter.

Since we first visited Salmon River in 1985, large numbers of triploid rainbows have been stocked in it and, for reasons known only to Mother Nature, trout fishing has significantly improved in some of its stretches. In addition, the steelhead and salmon runs have increased significantly. In fact, salmon fishing, outlawed since the mid-1970s, has been permitted in certain stretches since 1996, although most of the migrating fish are stocked and only they can be kept. Although the salmon run deceased dramatically in 2008, 230,000 steelhead entered Columbia River that year, the most steelhead over Bonneville Dam since records were first kept in 1938, and many found their way to Salmon River.

On our drive along Interstate 84, to and from Sun Valley, sections of the road paralleled the rim of Snake River Canyon, with the Snake River visible far below. The Snake is now stocked annually with close to 180,000 triploid rainbow fingerlings in the section immediately south of Magic Reservoir, but the river is best known for its smallmouth bass fishery.

Accommodations

In addition to numerous motels and lodges, two Best Western motels serve the valley, Kentwood and Tyrolean lodges. For bed and breakfast lovers, Provey Pensione (208-788-8781) will suit the budget minded and Knob Hill Inn (208-726-8010) will appeal to those with deep pockets. Anglers with families, or in small groups, can stay in one of the eight rustic log cabins at the Ketchum Korral Motor Lodge (208-726-3510) and those with recreational vehicles can stay at the Sun Valley RV Resort (208-726-3429), located right on Wood River. Groups can rent condos through Premier Resorts (800-635-4444), while single anglers can rent rooms at Lift Tower Lodge (208-726-5163). Campers can select from hundreds of U. S. Forest Service Campsites (800-280-CAMP). Within Ketchum and Sun Valley, they include the Meadows RV Park (866-305-0408), on Rt. 75, three miles south of Ketchum, and one of the free campsites at the Ketchum Ranger District (208-622-5371).

Ketchum has many excellent restaurants, but we ate all our meals at the Pioneer Saloon Restaurant, a permanent fixture on Maine Street. The steak house is an old landmark, with pioneer artifacts adorning its walls. It's a relatively busy and noisy place with excellent prime rib.

Other Activities

The resort complex of Sun Valley was established in 1936, the first winter sports resort in Western North America, created long before Colorado's famous ski slopes. A vanguard of recreational development and wilderness preservation, its popularity was instrumental in getting the State to set aside four million acres of wilderness lands near the valley. In addition, when Idaho was admitted to the Union, the federal government retained more than two-thirds of the state.

W. Averell Harriman, Chief of the Union Pacific Railroad, and future Governor of New York, was a ski buff and he hired Felix Schaffgotsch, an Austrian, to search America's West for terrain similar to the Austrian Alps. Lands above Ketchum were chosen and Harriman wrote a check for $34,000, resulting in the railroad owning almost 4,000 acres of mountain and valley land. A lodge was built and plans were made for ski slopes.

Disliking rope tows, Harriman challenged his railroad engineers to invent a better system. In response, James Curran, who'd invented a method to hoist bananas onto ships in South America, put chairs in place of the banana hooks and the chairlift was born. The railroad maintained ownership of the resort until it was sold to an investment group in 1964.

The Sun Valley Center for Arts and Humanities, Sun Valley Music Festival, Sun Valley Summer Symphony, and Northern Rockies Folk Festival provide summer guests with cultural activities. Within the resort complex, the Sun Valley Ice Show (208-622-2135) performs each Saturday from mid-June to mid-September. Anglers with active family members can make arrangements for white water rafting, glider flights, and wilderness pack trips.

Horseback riders can book trail rides at the Galena Stage Stop Corrals (208-726-1735), located 25 miles north of Ketchum on Rt. 75.

Following the first silver strike in the United States in 1880, the Wood River towns of Ketchum and Hailey became boomtowns. On display at the Ketchum Ore Wagon Museum are ore wagons that hauled the precious ore from outlying mines to Wood River Valley. The mining wealth around Ketchum and Hailey helped boost Idaho to statehood in 1890, but the boom didn't last and Hailey was virtually deserted by 1893. Ketchum went on to become a lead mining center. Later, it became the state's second largest sheep ranching community and when sheep ranching gave way to the resort industry, the town became a gateway to the State's mountains, rivers, and forests. Investors, interested in revitalizing Hailey, brought it back to life.

Ernest Hemingway wrote *For Whom the Bell Tolls* when living in Ketchum. A member of a volunteer ambulance crew in Italy during World War I, he took a job there after recuperating from a severe wound. He moved to France, where he came under the influence of a group of expatriate artists and writers, whose members included Gertrude Stein and the controversial poet, Ezra Pound. His association with Pound, born in Hailey, probably motivated him to settle in Ketchum after returning from Europe. Later, he moved to Cuba, where he wrote *The Old Man and the Sea*, the Pulitzer Prize winning story of the fruitless efforts of an aged Cuban to bring a captured marlin bigger than his boat back to the harbor. After 20 years in Cuba, Hemmingway left following Fidel Castro's takeover and resettled in Ketchum, where, in 1961, he eventually shot himself, as did his father before him. Hemingway is buried in the Ketchum Cemetery, but his Memorial overlooks Trail Creek, one of his favorite trout streams.

Tom enjoying the view of Sawtooth National Recreation Area

Chapter Five

Bighorn River
Steeped in Native American History

Deception, dishonesty, and disheartenment, Sitting Bull and Crazy Horse, Custer's Last Stand—you feel it in the air. The Delaware River, one I fish every year, is named after a Native American tribe, but the Native American spirit no longer lingers over its waters. In sharp contrast, when driving from Harden, Montana, you pass the stark homes of Native Americans, purchase food in their markets, or even rent drift boats from them, or from others whose lands are checker boarded within their lands. More importantly, the river passes through their reservation, a reservation of more than two and one-half million acres; a river the Native Americans fished exclusively from 1976 until a decision by the United States Supreme Court reopen it to the public in 1982.

The Yellowtail Dam on Bighorn River was named after Robert Yellowtail, the leader of the Crow when the dam was completed in 1967. The dam, 525 feet high and 1,400 feet long, was built for flood control, electric power generation, and irrigation. Designed to produce 250 megawatts of power per day, in the recent dry years, it's produced only about 80 megawatts a day, which powers about 80,000 homes. Water uses for irrigation have minimal impact on the first 13 miles below the dam, the section with the highest number of trout per mile.

After Bay Lake, two miles of water formed by low-head After Bay Dam, evens out the highs and lows of dam releases and warms up the water slightly before it's released into the river.

Bighorn Lake, the name for the reservoir created by the dam, is 71 miles long and 55 of these miles are within spectacular Bighorn Canyon. The dam creating the lake significantly altered the lower Bighorn. Formerly, it was a warm river, heavy with silt, with meandering and braided channels, spotted with many islands and gravel bars. Bighorn Lake trapped sediment in its southern end and discharges from the dam's lower levels were clear, cold, and regulated. The result was an absence of souring spring flows to push up islands or lay down gravel beds. The braided channels gradually became a single meandering river, with long runs, rapids, pools, and lush beds of aquatic vegetation that produced abundant aquatic foods to fatten the trout.

Wind River flows out of Boysen Reservoir, on the eastern border of Wind River Indian Reservation in Wyoming, and after flowing through Wind River Canyon, its name changes to Bighorn River. It then flows through 150 miles of farmland on the western edge of the high plains until it enters Bighorn Lake. Both the lake and the river below the dam are part of Bighorn Canyon National Recreation Area.

Below the dam, at Fort Smith, the Bighorn flows through an open, isolated landscape, with riverbanks that are a mix of grass, alfalfa, brush, and cottonwoods. Small rock cliffs with sparse forests dot the riverbanks along the middle section of the first 13 miles of river below After Bay Dam. The Pryor, and the smaller Big Horn mountains, are visible in the south and west rising from the prairies.

About 20 miles below the dam, the river enters the Crow Indian Reservation, flows through it for about 28 miles, and eventually joins the Yellowstone River, north of the Town of Hardin, as its largest and most significant tributary. The Bighorn clearly is "A Horn of Plenty" and the creation of its bounty is similar to the origin of this popular phrase.

Achelous was a river in Greece that overflowed its banks during seasons of high rains. A Greek fable relates that the river god, Achelous, loved Dejanira, whom Hercules was courting, and sought a union with her. Unfortunately, the river didn't flow through Dejanira's kingdom, so the river god couldn't woo her. The river was thought of as a bull because it made a brawling, or roaring, noise as it ran along its course.

When the river swelled, it made itself another channel. Thus, its head was horned and when the horn flowed through Dejanira's kingdom, the river god could now court her. To keep the river channels from Dejanira's property, Hercules prevented the periodic overflows by building dams and channels. By doing so, Hercules vanquished the river god and cut off his horn. The lands formerly subject to overflow were redeemed and subsequently became fertile—the meaning of the phrase "A Horn of Plenty."

Fisherman familiar with woodland valley streams may initially be uncomfortable in the Bighorn's environment. Few birds circle above the river, feeding on its prolific hatches. No shade trees line its banks, although cottonwoods are relatively thick in the lower section above Hardin. In fact, the direct sunlight on its cool waters is what creates its abundant aquatic growth. The river runs through "wide-open spaces" and great distances can be seen when standing on its banks. Zitkala-Sa, the first Dakota to test tradition and write down Native American stories, describes the feeling in her story "The Great Spirit," written in the late 1800s:

> When the spirit dwells in my breast I love to roam leisurely among the green hills . . . I marvel at the great blue overhead. With half-closed eyes, I watch the huge cloud shadows in their noiseless play upon the high bluffs opposite me, while into my ears ripple the sweet, soft cadences of the river's song. Folded hands lie in my lap, for the time forgot. My heart and I lie small upon the earth like a grain of throbbing sand. Rifting clouds and tinkling waters, together with the warmth of a genial summer day, bespeak with eloquence the loving Mystery around us.

The river will challenge the experienced angler, but, at the same time, family members can easily fish it. Many of its trout can be caught without casting. Youngsters and inexperienced wives can simply toss a line from the boat, hold the rod out over the water, and their nymph, scud, or San Juan Worm will drift, drag free, along with the boat in the river's current. The bright orange strike indicator will hesitate for a moment and, if the rod tip is sharply raised, the family member may be into the trout of a lifetime.

When I first fished the river in 1988, the section had about 10,000 trout per mile, but after years of drought and low flows, the trout population significantly deceased, but with less fish per mile those remaining grew bigger. In 2007, brown trout populations were down to an estimated 2,000 per mile, and the rainbow population, which has trouble spawning successfully,

Floating the Bighorn (Courtesy of Hale Harris of Bighorn Trout Shop)

even less, although the total trout population has fluctuated up and down over the years, with about 9,000 per mile in the late 1970s, 6,000 in the early 1980s, and 11,000 in the mid-1990s. Nevertheless, about 2,500 trout per mile is still a respectable number of fish and should the long dry spell end, the population could rebound to former levels.

Trout grow about eight inches per year in the river, making the capture of 16- to 18-inch, two-year, relatively unsophisticated fish, fairly easy to fool on artificial offerings. The biggest rainbow caught to date weighed 16 plus pounds, and the biggest brown, 13 pounds, but fish exceeding 20 inches, the river's older, smarter fish, are rarely caught by the average visitor regardless of what you hear "through the grapevine."

In the early 2000s, a rumor spread that the river had become so rich with crustaceans and aquatic worms that fish stopped rising to the prolific dry fly hatches for which it was famous. Nevertheless, that rumor resulted from both increasing numbers of unsophisticated visitors with expectations that hatches would occur all day long, rather then at scheduled times, and from diminished hatches following relatively low water releases over the past seven or eight years. Many anglers also had trouble creating drag free drifts because the low water levels resulted in increased algae growth and both their flies and lines would become coated with the stuff with the slightest amount of drag. It was much easier to hook fish floating a weighted shrimp, scud, sow bug, or water worm imitation below a colorful strike indicator.

Nevertheless, hatches still occur with regularity. During mid-day, from April to early June, *Baetis* hatch, imitated best by a Blue Winged Olive. In July, little yellow stoneflies flutter over the surface and from July to the middle of August, Pale Morning Duns hatch toward evening, increasing at dusk. Black Caddis hatch from mid-August into September and Tricos hatch in the fall. Smaller numbers of other mayflies hatch throughout the season and midges hatch all year long. Artificial baits can be used in the deep water in the first 600 feet below After Bay Dam, and then only artificial lures for 13 miles downstream to Bighorn Assess.

Wading at Three Mile Access

When Scott and I first fished the river we stayed in Hardin, a 45-minute drive along Ct. Rd. 313 from Fort Smith. During most of our trip, we fished upriver from Three Mile Access, but a few wading anglers hike the trail that starts at the launch site at After Bay Dam and runs along the river's west bank. Unlike Northern Montana's Kootenai or Colorado's Taylor, where fish become huge by feeding on Kokanee salmon fry washed through the dam's outlet, or Colorado's Frying Pan, where they gorge on fresh water shrimp and midges below the dam spillway, good fly fishing on the Bighorn doesn't begin until you get a mile or more downstream from After Bay Dam. The water is simply too cold, as well as too deep, and the fish feed less on midges than they do on the Frying Pan or San Juan. It was a long walk from After Bay Dam downstream to the first good spot for two anglers, the reason we worked waters immediately above Three Mile Access. Anglers staying at the Cottonwood Camp, a stone's throw a way, fish it heavily, but it usually lacked anglers early in the morning.

After losing a huge fish on a San Juan Worm in a small side channel, I put on a scud imitation and worked my way upriver along an island, making long upstream casts along the bank, watching the line and keeping it straight by rapidly stripping it in as it drifted back toward me. If my fly line hesitated a moment on its downstream drift, I set the hook; sometimes it was an algae clump, other times it was a fish.

When I reached the upriver end of the island, I walked back downriver and started over. Since the fish were feeding on scuds and not on rising flies, downstream scudding would be unproductive. Besides, even if I cast downstream on my way back, I could lose the section to another angler who might be working his way up. Consequently, my walks downstream were brisk to prevent this occurrence. On the Bighorn, you can repeatedly work the same stretch, not only because many fish fail to see your fly on an earlier run, but also because new fish move up from the main channel into the shallow waters along the bank.

By the time I'd made several trips fishing up and walking down the length of "my island," other fishermen had taken spots both above and below me, which was alright with me because I'd become bored with my island stretch. Consequently, I started downstream to look for Scott and to watch him fish. As I crossed the shallow tail of a run between two islands, another angler, crossing from the other side, waved me off. He stopped and began short-casting, more like dapping, his fly into the water not far from his feet. He was

The Bighorn (Courtesy of Hale Harris of Bighorn Trout Shop)

instantly into a fish. After landing it, he carefully moved several feet and began dapping again. I watched him catch three large fish from this ankle-deep water and I can assure you he was not shuffling to stir up nymphs to attract fish from the pool below.

Later, he told me that you didn't need to cast far on the Bighorn on overcast days, or at dusk, because fish move continually into the shallow heads and tails of runs to feed. He said to just wade slowly and carefully wherever you go and look for fish working the bottom. Earlier, I'd stood in this water and cast my fly down into the pool below. Although I took two browns from the pool, I unknowingly spooked equally big fish from the water where I was standing. I learned never to walk aimlessly across a stretch of shallow water in the Bighorn because it can be full of feeding fish, especially at dusk!

I never saw anyone using streamers, probably because Bighorn fish get their fill on nymphs, shrimp, scuds, and water worms. Ninety-six percent of the trout, including those up to 20 inches, feed exclusively on aquatic life that is seldom more than one-quarter of an inch long. Nevertheless, bored with fishing them all day, one evening I worked the faster riffles across and downstream with a Black Zonker and took several good fish.

All the browns we caught fought hard, but on occasion, one fought like the young Mike Tyson. None rolled over and lay down like they do on other heavily fished waters. The poorer fighters probably included those caught recently, but some were simply better fighters than others. The rainbows were another story, as many didn't fight well. We learned later that, unlike the browns, able to reproduce naturally, rainbows weren't spawning successfully. The water was too cold for the eggs to hatch rapidly and too high in the early spring for them to stay anchored. Those fry that did hatch found it hard to locate shallow waters in which to safely dwell. As a result, we were catching rainbows that were stocked

When fish rise in the afternoon, the sun's glare on the water made it hard to see both your dry fly and the rising fish. Often we had to walk to spots where glare was less of a problem. On one afternoon, all I caught were giant thistles on the bank behind me. In addition, a flotilla of algae kept drowning my fly, a common occurrence on the Horn, particularly in the first three miles.

After a while, I looked like a beginner, constantly scampering up the bank behind me to free my fly from thistle weed and stripping in line to free it from algae. I switched from the knotted leader I preferred to a knot-less one to minimize algae hook-ups. Even then, the fly floated free of algae on about one of six casts. Although I cursed at the algae when it stuck to my fly, without it the river would be less rich in aquatic life. Biologists tell us that algae are the most important ingredients in the energy of a river ecosystem.

In 2008, the region saw an exceptional snow pack, with twice as much snow as in average years, and with the heavy spring rains that occurred, the reservoir overflowed during the spring flush and 9,500-cfs of water flowed in the river during the last week in June. In August of that year, the flows were 2,500-cfs, compared to 1,500-cfs in the recent past, with water temperatures from 55 to 60 degrees, resulting in more aquatic plant growth. In addition, the river hugs the banks and good "hopper" fishing results.

The Bighorn's Problems

Unfortunately, tail-waters, like the Bighorn, are not without their troubles. Since the river has no feeder creeks in the trout waters, trout spawn in the river. When the river is low and there are no side channels, they spawn in the margins of riffles and the edges of rapids, both of which become torrents when flows reach 4,500-cfs. High spring flows flush trout eggs and alevin (hatched fry that fed on their egg sac while remaining in their redd) from the river's spawning beds and pushes fry that have left the redds into waters where they become vulnerable prey.

The high flows not only affect the rainbow population, whose members spawn in late winter and early spring before the spring flush, but also the brown trout population whose members spawn in late fall and early winter, but whose eggs incubate during the winter when temperatures are near freezing. In addition, the cold water flowing out of the dam prolongs the gestation period of trout eggs and they may not hatch, and the alevins may not emerge from the redds, until late May or early June.

Even when water doesn't flow over the spillway in the spring, dam operators, to control levels in Bighorn Lake during anticipated spring runoffs, increase releases toward the end of May from 1,500-cfs to 2,000-cfs, and then incrementally to 4,500-cfs (the maximum bottom release) over a three-day period and these increases create the same adverse effects as high spring flows.

The river's rainbows have difficulty spawning in the cold water, regardless of flow levels, as egg mortality increases with decreases in water temperatures below 45 degrees, At 39 degrees, the typical temperature of bottom water releases, no rainbow eggs hatch (although a species of rainbow in Colorado's high mountain streams lay eggs that hatch in temperatures less than 39 degrees).

Consequently, rainbows can spawn successfully only when the dam doesn't overflow and spring releases around 2,500-cfs fill the side channels, which warm more quickly, and they remain full until at least early summer, a situation that hasn't occurred in recent years. Consequently, much like Utah Green's River below Flaming Gorge Dam, discussed in Chapter Six, where rainbows have never spawned successfully and don't do well when stocked, the river is rapidly becoming a brown trout stream.

Another problem has resulted from the recent long dry spell. To keep adequate water in Bighorn Lake, the minimum release of 1,500-cfs has been strictly followed, causing many of the river's back channels, where fish

Fighting a big one (Courtesy of Hale Harris of Bighorn Trout Shop)

typically spawn, to empty in the in the winter. In low waters, algae growth increases and water levels rise over the summer and fill some of the back channels, where browns spawn in the fall. When the algae dies in the winter and water releases remain constant, the water level recedes, the back channels dry up, and the brown trout eggs are left high and dry. Water levels need to be increased to a last 2,000-cfs to maintain water in the back channels.

State biologists have established that Bighorn trout survive best in flows around 2,500-cfs and, therefore, river advocates are calling for an increase in the minimum release to that amount. Unfortunately, during long dry spells, the water levels in Bighorn Lake become so low that boat docks are left high and dry at Big Bend, just outside of Lovell, Wyoming, a premier destination for recreational boaters and lake anglers.

In addition, the silt accumulation in the lake's southern end has increased dramatically and the spawning habitats of warm water fish have been degraded, especially walleye habitat that has completely disappeared. The result is that reservoir users from both states, mostly residents of nearby townships, who greatly outnumber river residents serving primarily out-of-state visitors, strongly advocate for decreases in the minimum release.

Governmental officials of both states realize that even when the lake fishing was outstanding, three times as many people used the river and its average user spent three times the money spent by the reservoir user. Consequently, state officials strive for compromise between the two factions.

Adding to the problem is that both Boysen and Buffalo Bill reservoirs in Wyoming can retain water in dry years and further reduce the amount entering Bighorn Lake. Buffalo Bill Reservoir is on North Fork Shoshone River, near Cody, Wyoming, a river flowing into Bighorn Lake.

Native Americans in Bighorn Country

At one time, the Crow tribes considered taking over management of the river. Anglers were concerned that fishing privileges would be curtailed if this happened; afraid they'd be cheated. Yet, we cheated Native Americans for years, driving them from promised lands, forcing their relocation, confiscating foods and goods earmarked for their use, reneging on treaties, and deliberately wiping out their native languages and culture. The agency created on their behalf, the Bureau of Indian Affairs, left a legacy of racism and inhumanity. Sitting Bull put it succinctly when he said, "I would have more confidence in the Grandfather at Washington if there were not so many bald headed thieves working for him."

When you fish one of the best trout streams in America, as a guest of the Native Americans, you owe them some understanding of their history. Although the Crow Reservation borders the lower river, it was the Dakota, or the Sioux, as the English called them, that made the area famous.

Our frontier history speaks at length of the Indian Wars on the Great Plains. Yet, relatively few Native American tribes occupied the western plains before Europeans arrived. The Shoshone lived on the high western plains, along the Saskatchewan River in Canada, long before the birth of Christ, and occupied the fringes of our western plains during the 18th century. The Cree shared land with them in present day Alberta and Saskatchewan.

The Kiowa inhabited western Montana, the Crow resided north of Montana's Black Hills, and the Comanche (from the Ute word *Comanche*, meaning "enemies"), and the Ute occupied northern Wyoming. The Apaches spent winters on the eastern borders of the Great Plains in what is now southwestern Kansas, but they traded with the Pueblo tribes in the Rio Grand region and therefore, controlled the southern Great Plains across their entire width and from northern Texas to the Arkansas River.

Native American art suggests that tribes lived in relative harmony until the white man brought horses and guns to the plains. Horses enabled tribes to travel into other tribal lands in search of food and goods and guns turned their minor tussles into major bloodbaths. In

A Bighorn brown (Courtesy of Jeremy Gilbertson of Big Sky Fly Fishers)

the early 1700s, their pictorial art reflects the turbulent changes taking place in their cultures, as rock art images changed from cultural topics to horseback warriors armed with guns.

As European settlers flocked to eastern America, Native Americans were driven from their homelands. They migrated west, some into unoccupied sections of the Great Plains, others into homelands of resident tribes. Both Cheyenne and Sioux moved to the Great Plains from the Great Lakes. The Cheyenne lived just south of Lake Superior, in present day Wisconsin, and the Sioux between Green Bay, Wisconsin, and southern Minnesota. The Chippewa called their longstanding enemy, the Sioux, the name the English used for them - *nadowe-is-iw,* or "snake." The French corrupted the word to *Nadowessioux,* which was then abbreviated to "Sioux" by the English. The Sioux refereed to themselves as the *Otchent iChakowwin,* or "Seven Council Fires," after the seven tribes that formed their nation.

The Sioux, subsequently called the Dakota, were great warriors, hunters, and trendsetters. An English officer, Lieutenant Gorrell, in the mid-1700s, called them "The greatest nation of Indians ever yet found . . . they could shoot (with bow and arrows) the wildest and largest beasts in the woods at 70 or 100 yards distance. They are remarkable for their dancing; the other nations take their fashion from them." Yet, the Chippewa, who acquired arms from the French, forced the once powerful Dakota to migrate west, not as conquerors, but as humble beggars at foot in the vast plains. To survive, they allied themselves with other nations, acquiring horses from Mandan tribes in the south and guns from Cree to their north, a powerful Algonquin tribe also moving west.

The Dakota allied themselves with the immigrant Piegan tribes, temporarily vanquished by the Shoshone, who'd acquired horses and could fight while mounted. The Dakota brought guns to the alliance and the result was the death of many Shoshone warriors, forcing these longstanding plains dwellers to retreat to the plateau region. Similarly, the Comanche, who acquired guns from their French allies, drove the Apache from the southern plains. The Dakota established their strongest bond with the Cree, and together, along with the Blackfoot, dominated the northern plains. The Cree were the principal suppliers of guns, while the Sioux supplied the horses— two essentials for the plain's lifestyle. Paul Kane, the notable artist of the Canadian scene, captured the importance of horses to Native Americans in his famous painting, *Catching Wild Horses.*

White Man's tools of war transformed the pedestrian, bow carrying and relatively peace-loving nomadic Native Americans into equestrian, gun-carrying, aggressive warriors. By the time Lewis and Clark traveled to the region in the early 1800s, tribal warfare was the predominate theme in Native American culture from the Saskatchewan River to the Rio Grand and from the Missouri River to the foothills of the Rockies.

Forced relocation of Native Americans began on a small scale after the

A Bighorn rainbow (Courtesy of Jeremy Gilbertson, Big Sky Fly Fishers)

War of 1812, but when President Andrew Jackson passed the Indian Removal Act of 1830, forcing tribes to relocate west of the Mississippi River, conflicts between native Americans and white settlers increased ten-fold. After the tribes resettled in the West, our own westward migration began. Forced to flee from their original homelands, they now faced the loss of their hard won new homelands on the plains.

Pushed into corners, they actively resisted our rapid westward movement. After almost 40 years of war with our armies, and numerous battles won, treaties were passed granting Native American tribes permanent lands in which to dwell. The 1865 Harney-Sanborn Treaty guaranteed the Dakota, Arapaho, and Cheyenne use of the Powder River region, a vast area lying between Montana's Black Hills, Yellowstone River, and the Rocky Mountains, land that included the best buffalo country of the central plains.

Yet, white Buffalo hunters, as many as 2,000 on the plains at one time, decimated the buffalo, the lifeblood of many tribes. To keep tribes from interfering with the construction of railroads and the settlement of frontier towns, we pressured them to abandon their nomadic life and take up farming. The tribes feared that completion of the Kansas and Pacific railroads would bring even more white hunters to slaughter buffalos for their hides or just for fun. The great Dakota leader, Red Cloud, among others, visited Washington four times to plead the Indian's cause.

The discovery of gold in Montana further contributed to their misfortune. J. M. Bozman, a gold prospector, looking for a short route from the Oregon Trail to the gold fields of Montana, discovered a course that passed directly through the Dakota lands in Powder River Country—Big Horn Country, the richest hunting grounds in tribal territories. Demands to render this trail safe for travelers resulted in the army improving Bozman Trial into Powder Ridge Road. Jim Bridger, famous for his discovery of Utah's Bridger Pass. assisted the army in this task. The military rebuilt the rudimentary trapper forts along the trail into strongholds, establishing four military bases along Powder River Road. Fort Smith, located just upriver from where the trail crossed the Bighorn, was one of the bases.

Red Cloud bitterly opposed construction of the forts, particularly Fort Phil Kearney, built on the banks of Little Piney Creek in the heart of Power River Country. The 1,000 soldiers garrisoned at the fort saw more bloody action than those on any military post in frontier history. In 1868, another treaty was passed at Fort Laramie, the most eastern fort on Powder River Road. Our government agreed to abandon all the forts along Bozeman Trail and Red Cloud signed the treaty only after they were burned to the ground.

The 1868 Laramie Treaty confirmed the earlier Harney-Sanborn Treaty and set aside a large track of land for Native Americans, where the last free bands of Dakota and Cheyenne continued to roam, under the leadership of Red Cloud, Sitting Bull (son of Standing Bull), Gall, Crazy Horse and Spotted Tail, the nephew of Crazy Horse, Long Knife, and others. Nevertheless, in 1871, the Indian Appropriation Act, passed under President Grant, made all Native Americans wards of the United States and nullified all past treaties.

Several events ended, once and for all, tribal sovereignty over their lands. First, railroad surveying parties, together with military escorts, invaded tribal territories in 1872. Second, gold was discovered in the Black Hills in 1874. Eastern newspaper exaggerated both the mineral wealth and the farming and lumbering potential of the Black Hills and miners and settlers flocked to tribal territories. By 1875, more than 800 miners were working streams in the Black Hills, in spite of General Custer's half-hearted attempts to expel intruders. Our government, in an attempt to solve the conflicts, offered to buy the Black Hills from the Dakotas, but Red Cloud and Spotted Tail demanded more than ten times the unfair amount offered and the negotiations stalemated. Sitting Bull summed up the attitude of the free Dakota: "We want no white men here. The Black Hills belong to me. If the whites try to take them, I will fight."

In response, President Grant and his Commissioner of Indian Affairs notified the tribes that they must relinquish their lands and move to reservations. Those that did not would be considered "hostile groups" and, therefore, law-breakers rather than "hunting parties." Tribal lands were opened to settlers and by 1876 15,000 miners were working the Black Hills. Congress declared in 1876, "Until the Sioux relinquish all claim to Powder River Country and the Black Hills no subsistence would be furnished them." Crazy Horse made his position clear when he spoke disparagingly to those who moved from the free lands to the reservations: "Look at me—see if I am poor or my people either. You are fools to make yourselves slaves for a piece of fat bacon, some hard tack, and a little sugar and coffee." Lieutenant Colonel George A. Custer entered the picture and you know the rest.

Both Spotted Tail and Red Cloud, realizing their situation was hopeless, advocated for compromise and kept their followers out of the wars immediately proceeding and following "Custer's Last Stand." Both chiefs persuaded Crazy Horse to surrender in 1877. Unfortunately, their expectations of fair treatment went unfulfilled. Crazy Horse was shot and killed and Spotted Tail assassinated by Crow Dog. Most likely, reservation agents, wanting to diminish the chief's power on the reservation, bribed Crow Dog to do the dirty deed. In 1889, Sitting Bull decreed, "A warrior I have been, now, it is all over, a hard time I have."

The Battle of Bighorn has been the subject of many paintings and poems. Many American poets attempted to capture the experience in prose, but only from Custer's viewpoint. For example, Henry Wadsworth Longfellow wrote:

> In his war paint and his beads,
> Like a bison among the reeds,
> In ambush the Sitting Bull
> Lay with three thousand braves
> Couched in clefts and caves,
> Savage, unmerciful.

In contrast, Silverbird, a Navaho rock group popular in the late 1960s, included in its album, *Broken Treaties* (Capital Records, 1970) a song with the following lyrics:

> Custer's Last Stand,
> Custer's Last Stand,
> Everyone remembers Custer's Last Stand.
> But who remembers the Indian man?
> Who remembers the Indian man?
> Who remembers the Indian man?

Our Second Trip

On my second trip to the Bighorn, with Bob and Scott, we rented a drift boat and floated the river. There's only one spot where you can get into trouble—a whirlpool below some rapids. We watched other boats navigate it and followed their example. When working a drift boat, I suggest that all lines be reeled in when approaching rapids. During my turn to row, I misjudged a rapid and the boat swung around and grounded in the shallows and Bob's line broke when it wedged under the boat.

The Bighorn, more popular on our second than on out first trip, had become too crowded to drift to a long riffle, stop and work it once, and then drift to another riffle. In the mornings, the first three miles of river was a flotilla; there were more boats than riffles to fish! If our August experience was typical, then anglers planning to riffle-hop will find the next riffle reached surrounded by other fishermen. Two boats will be beached at its head, two at its tail, and, perhaps, two more at the first pool below it

We left early in the morning to stake a claim to an island with good runs and riffles above and below it. Bob and Scott worked the riffles for rainbows, but because three anglers on a riffle is a crowd, I quartered nymphs upstream in the slick water runs above them. The fish were actively feeding and took my small Brassie as soon as my line was straight across the river. At this point in the drift, the nymph was deep enough to flow through the troughs between weed beds where the fish held. One of several in the trough would grab my nymph and tear across the river, accompanied by the sound of a singing reel. I caught a dozen 18-inch look-alike browns on the Brassie each morning before eleven o'clock, all of which put up a credible fight.

I hooked one brown that ran across the river's width before I could gather my wits. I hollered to Bob and Scott, "Here's one over 20 inches!" They turned and looked momentarily, but they were both into their own good fish; doubles, and even triples, was not that uncommon! After working the fish back across the river and chasing it along the near bank, I finally beached it, only to discover that, like the rest, it was 18 inches. Some fish, like men, simply fight better than others! This experience was repeated on a number of occasions.

In the hour before noon, with the sun directly overhead, and the water a few degrees warmer, the fish became lethargic. Using polarized sunglasses, I walked along the bank, located pods of fish, and cast directly into them, but I'd catch only several fish during this hour period. The nymph had to pass directly by a brown's mouth before it would take it; it wouldn't move an inch for the fly! Several casts were needed to position the fly correctly, and then, if my casting hadn't spooked them, I might fool one. During gusts of wind, I didn't cast because I couldn't see the fish. Earlier, when the fish were active, the wind made no difference and blind casting was productive. When the gust changed to steady winds, it was time for lunch, a cigar, and a nap on the island or in the boat. It might be 95 degrees out, but the evaporation of 55-degree waters into the dry air enabled naps in direct sunlight.

Both Bob and Scott hooked rainbows in the fast water, but they caught less trout than I did. This was not unexpected because browns outnumbered rainbows six to one near the dam and two to one in lower sections. A strain of rainbows had been found that learned to spawn in the river, but many of the stream-born ones we hooked didn't fight in keeping with the rainbow's reputation. Perhaps their relatively poor fight was due to their residing in riffle water where most fishermen concentrate their efforts. Perhaps they'd been caught many times and curtailed their struggles.

In the hours between three and five o'clock, we each caught several more trout. Unlike others, we didn't fish nymphs while floating through the runs. Instead, we waited to cast a high-floating fly into eddies when drifting through rapids. We don't enjoy nymph drifting or even catching fish from a drift boat. A six-foot angler with a nine-foot rod places the fish at a serious disadvantage. We traveled 2,000 miles to the Bighorn to fight big fish, not just to land them. When drifting rapidly through rapids and hooking fish, they have the advantage because considerable line is striped off the reel and lots of line on the water results in lots of pressure on the tippet!

Around five o'clock we arrived at Bighorn Access (once called Thirteen-

The Bighorn when busy (Courtesy of Hale Harris of Bighorn Trout Shop)

Mile Take-Out). We then rowed back upriver a short distance and fished until dark. Bighorn Access is hard to find after dark. Unlike Three Mile Access, where lights from the campground guided our way, the access was an isolated spot. Anglers can become so focused on casting to rising fish that they fail to allow enough time to reach the takeout when it can still be easily seen.

Just above Bighorn Access, we cast Pale-Evening Duns along the foam, or scum, lines that gathered along the banks. Sparse Gray Hackle, *in Fishless Days, Angling Nights*, described this type of fishing:

> The hawked-eyed angler sees not only the fish themselves, but the faint, fleeting signs of their presence—the tiny dimple in the slow water next to the bank, which indicates a big fish sucking down little flies; the tiny black object momentarily protruded above the surface, which is the neb of a good, quietly feeding fish.

Being somewhat irreverent, I used interchangeably Pale Evening and Pale Morning Duns. The effort to distinguish cream-colored flies hatching in the morning from those hatching in the evening seems pedantic. Charlie Fox, famed Pennsylvania angler, first tied the Pale Evening Dun, but I have no idea what "innovative" angler first tied the morning version! A huge hatch of Black Caddis occurred in the late afternoons, but no fish took them. Fly shop staff told us that fish continue to feed on Pale Morning Duns until the hatch is exhausted; then, and only then, do they turn to the caddis

When I wasn't using my Brassie, I hooked lots of fish on a shrimp imitation I purchased, for fifty cents a fly, from a local Fly Shop's bargain box. I bought two dozen. Other anglers bought the higher priced scuds recommended by shopkeepers, with some actually mocking me for my purchase. "What good is cheap if the fly doesn't catch fish," they laughed. "Trust me," I replied, "The fish will love it! You really think trout can distinguish my fly from yours as it drifts by them in the current?" Trout suck-in and spit-out lots of floating debris that isn't food and when a fly floats by them in a swift current, they won't spend the energy it takes to examine it closely.

The Bighorn is a wonderful river to fish. Wading is easy, the fish are plentiful, and beginners can catch them from drift boats. All the fish we hooked were about the same size. Most were 18 inches and several approached 19. On our two trips, we caught only one fish over 20 inches. Bob hooked it casting to the scum line just above Bighorn Access. There are a number of short riffles above pools where a beginner can flip the fly downstream and catch fish. I've caught bigger trout in Calgary's Bow River, more trout per hour in Utah's Green, and better fighting rainbows in the Delaware, but nowhere have I caught as many hard fighting 18-inch browns per day as I have on the Bighorn.

The average air temperature in July and August is 74 degrees, although it can get into the 90s. The average temperature drops to about 63 degrees in September, 52 degrees in October, and 39 degrees in November. And you won't be caught in a heavy rains in any of these months because the average monthly rainfall in each is about half an inch. Friends who've fished the river in October report pleasant breezes shacking the limbs of yellowed cottonwoods, pheasants screeching in adjacent fields, fish more explosive then in the summer, and considerably more solitude.

Accommodations

There were only three motels at Fort Smith when we first fished the river, but now they're many and their cost is no more than those in Hardin, over 40 miles away, so book early and stay right at the river. We stayed in Hardin on our first trip and the restaurants were closed by the time we returned from the river. As a result, we ate pizza every evening!

All the Fort Smith motels are attached to fly shops and each has food service. They are: Bighorn Anglers (406-666-2333), Bighorn Fly and Tackle Shop (888-665-1321), Bighorn Trout Shop (406-666-2375), Fort Smith Fly Shop and Cabins (406-666-2500), and Polly's Place (866-6-POLLYS), associated with Bighorn River Fly Fishers (406-686-2255) which also is associated with Bluff's Bighorn River Lodge (866-9-BLUFF), located a mile above Three Mile Access.

The Bighorn River Resort (800-665-3799), an Orvis endorsed lodge, sits on a bluff on the old Bozeman Trail overlooking the river, about one-half mile downstream from After Bay Dam. Bighorn River Country Lodge (866-582-8767) is located at Three Mile Access and Bighorn River Lodge (formerly Bighorn River Fishing Lodge) (800-235-5450), a high-end resort, is located on the river just above Bighorn Landing. Others are: Riverbend Angler Resort (877-55-Trout), Angler's Edge Outfitters (406-666-2417), located one mile north of Fort Smith, and Eagle's Nest Lodge, located just outside of Hardin (866-258-3734), another Orivs endorsed high-end lodge popular with those who both hunt and fish. In contrast, there're only two motels on Utah's Green River, discussed in the next chapter, a river with equal fish numbers, but a longer drive from a major airport.

Camping is popular in Bighorn Canyon and sites are available in a variety of environments. The National Park Service (406-666-2412) provides information about their sites. One free 30-site campground is at After Bay Dam. Cottonwood Camp (406-666-2391) also rents boats and offers a shuttle service.

Other Activities

Evening campfire programs are offered at After Bay Campground every Friday and Saturday evening from Memorial Day through Labor Day weekend. Fishing, recreation, history, and wildlife are topics at these gatherings. Ranger-led activities are offered at the Fort Smith/Yellowtail Dam area. Arrangements can be made for self-guided tours of two to three hours, a half day, a full day, or more than a day. Bighorn Lake was once noted for large walleye, but other species, including trout, occupy its waters. Boats can be rented at Ok-A-Beh-Marina (406-666-2349).

Indians led by Crazy Horse and Gall, Sitting Bull's adopted son, with Sitting Bull watching from the hilltops, defeated General Custer's soldiers near Little Bighorn River, a tributary to the Bighorn just below Hardin. The site of the battle is a short drive from the Bighorn. The Custer Battlefield National Monument was created in 1879 to honor Custer and the U. S. Soldiers killed there on June 25, 1868. Later its name was changed to Little Bighorn Battlefield National Monument to also memorialize Native Americans for their last major victory over European invaders. Both the Museum/Visitor Center and the National Cemetery are open every day.

Every June the Crows put on a "Custer's Last Stand Re-Enactment," part of a four-day festival that features a rodeo, casino night, parade, street dance, arts and crafts demonstrations, gospel services, and other activities. Perhaps more interesting is the Crow Fair, held on the third weekend in August along the banks of Little Bighorn River. It's the premier pow-wow of North America's native peoples and helps to keep the Crow culture alive and strong. Wet wading the Little Bighorn, a scenic river, is a pleasant diversion from fishing its bigger neighbor.

The Cheyenne reservation can also be visited. Their lands include 400,000 plus acres that extend from the Crow reservation east to the Tongue River, an excellent wild trout stream above the Tongue River Reservoir in Wyoming, but a warm water fishery below it in Montana. The Cheyenne helped the Dakota to defeat Custer. After their pursuit and capture following this victory, they were placed, along with the leaderless Dakotas, in Oklahoma Indian Territory. Sick and hungry, but determined to return to their homelands, Dull Knife (also called Morning Star after the official emblem of the Northern Cheyenne) and Little Wolf led an escape. Pursued by the military, they fought, froze, and starved to death in efforts to reach their homeland. An executive order in 1884 finally set aside the track of country the Dakota now occupy next to the Crow Reservation.

The Cheyenne Indian Museum, at Ashland, has an extensive collection of Native American artifacts. Their annual pow-wow is held in Lame Deer from July 1-4, with competitive Native American dancing contests, parades, and other activities. The Northern Cheyenne Arts and Crafts Center features Cheyenne-made moccasins, belts, jewelry, and other beaded gifts. They also hold pow-wows over Memorial Day, Labor Day, Veteran's Day, Christmas, and New Years. Campers can stay at the Holiday Campground (406-784-2244) in Custer National Forest

The Crow, rather than the Dakota, were given the land surrounding the Bighorn River, perhaps because they scouted for the U. S. Army. In fact, a story circulates that the Crow scouts, having discovered the Dakota and Cheyenne camped in preparation for Custer's troops, warned Custer that there were too many Indians for him to whip, but that Custer merely responded that more Indians just meant more time would be needed to kill them. The head Crow scout, Curley, reported that only he escaped the battle, urging Custer to accompany him when all seemed lost, but Custer refused. Others believe that all six crow scouts, including Curley, quietly slipped away before the actual battle, realizing that Custer's army had no chance.

The Crow inhabited the Big Horn Mountains long before the Dakota migrated west, participants in a complex trade pattern across the plains. The River Crow, along the upper Missouri, traveled east, and the Mountain Crow traveled west, both meeting at the central rendezvous point at the headwaters of the Bighorn. It is fitting that some of this land is now theirs.

The Bighorn can be fished in the winter because the water temperature remains constant throughout the year. Skiers can fish the river and then drive north to Red Lodge, a western town with all the expected amenities. Red Lodge Mountain Ski Resort, where the sun shines more than 300 days per year, has runs for skiers at all ability levels and the lift prices, especially on Mondays and Tuesdays, are relatively cheap.

Southern Alberta's Castle River (Tom Royster Photo)

Yellowstone Park's Slough Creek in a meadow stretch (Mike Zelie Photo)

Southern Idaho's East Fork Big Lost River

Montana's Big Horn River (Courtesy of Hale Harris of Big Horn Trout Shop)

Fighting a 20-inch brown in Alberta's Bow River

Netting a big one from Montana's Big Horn (Courtesy of Big Horn Trout Shop)

Alberta's Crowsnest River

Wyoming's Madison River in Yellowstone Park (Harold McMillan, Jr. Photo)

Alberta's upper Oldman River

Utah's Green River below Little Hole (Scott Daniels Photo)

New Mexico's San Juan River below Navajo Dam

Alberta's Crowsnest River (Tom Royster Photo)

New Mexico's San Juan River at Baetis Bend

Yellowstone River at Buffalo Ford in Yellowstone Park

New Mexico's San Juan River at Jack's Hole

Idaho's Salmon River near Stanley and the Sawtooth Range

Montana's South Fork Flathead River (Mike Zelie Photo)

Southern Alberta's Oldman River

Colorado's Roaring Fork River above Aspen

Idaho's Silver Creek (Courtesy of Terry Ring of Silver Creek Outfitters)

Colorado's Frying Pan River at Seven Castles

Colorado's Frying Pan River at the "spring creek" section

Many anglers dream of casting a fly in the Green River below Flaming Gorge Dam, a popular western destination for fly fishing enthusiasts. The dam, 502 feet high and 1,189 feet long, created the famous reservoir in the Flaming Gorge, named by Major John Wesley Powell and his company of men who were impressed by the sun reflecting off the canyon's red rocks as they explored the Green River in 1867. Construction of the reservoir was completed in 1962, but the 39-degree water surging through its bottom portals was too cold for both mayflies and fish.

In 1978, ladders were installed in the dam to let surface waters mingle with deeper waters, producing water temperatures of about 55 degrees, the perfect temperature for optimum trout growth. Weed beds began to flourish and a wide variety of aquatic life evolved, but liberal bag limits and high mortality of released trout by bait fisherman kept the fishing poor. In 1985, a slot limit was created (two fish less than 13 inches and one fish more than 20 inches) and bait fishing was disallowed.

The fishing improved dramatically after these new regulations. In October of 1986, state biologists estimated 21,000 trout in the first mile below the dam, more trout than in any mile of river in America, and 8,000 trout per mile at Little Hole, about seven and a half miles downstream. Because of high water releases, needed to generate electricity for homes, more than 50 percent of the fish in this stretch died over the winter or were flushed downstream by dam overflows in the spring.

Green River in Red Canyon

In an effort to combat this problem, the Utah Division of Wildlife Resources developed a computer model that determined the optimal trout carrying capacity of the river. Working with the Bureau of Reclamation, whose staff operates the dam, water releases were modified and stocking plans altered. When large amounts of water were released, the ramp rate was lowered from 1,200-cfs to 800-cfs, which made for milder level changes and trout were neither flushed downstream nor stranded in shallow backwaters. As a result, fish prospered and fewer were stocked, the number per mile leveled off, and winterkills decreased. River guides now estimate about 9,000 trout per mile from Flaming Gorge Dam to Little Hole and 7,000 per mile from Little Hole to Indian Crossing, about 17 miles below the dam.

Because the river was subject to highly fluctuating water flows over the years, particularly high spring flows when rainbows spawn, its carrying capacity was, and still is, poor for juvenile rainbows that find few shallows in which to seek refuge. Consequently about 20,000 catchable-size rainbows, and 880 cutthroats, were, and still are, stocked annually, toward the end of spring flows, along the seven-mile stretch below the dam and 5,000 rainbows stocked downstream at Brown's Park. Brook trout were stocked at one time, but didn't survive. Because water releases were much lower in the fall, stocked brown trout fry did well, the adult fish reproduced, and they're no longer stocked in the river. Green River trout grow 13 inches in their fist year and approach 20 inches by year two, with a 30-lb. brown landed in 1996, although the average brown caught is around 16 inches.

In February of 2006, in keeping with the Endangered Species Act, the Bureau of Reclamation agreed to release waters in ways that better mimic natural flow patterns and water temperatures to help the recovery of endangered native fish, such as bobtail chubs, Colorado pike-minnows, humpback chubs, and razorback suckers, that need both warmer waters and flooded lowlands for nursery habitat. These releases not only will increase riparian zone habitat in lower stretches of the river, but also create small habitat increases in trout waters. Part of the plan calls for an increase, starting in early May, from the normal pre-runoff release of around 800-cfs, to the maximum release of 4,600-cfs of warmer water from the power plant. These high releases, combined with the spring flush from Yampa River, which flows from the southeast into the Green at the Town of Jenson, will not only flood the lowlands, but also ensure that silt is washed further downstream and away from native fish spawning sites.

Releases from the dam are planned in keeping with estimated spring flows from the Yampa River. Flows of at least 15,000-cfs for 5 days are needed at Jenson to facilitate recovery of endangered native fish, but much more than that causes Jenson residents to complain about high waters. If the Yampa River Basin has an especially wet year, as it did in 2008, then releases from the dam are lowered accordingly. How this new flow plan will affect the river's trout is yet to be determined, but even though the number of browns has changed from year to year during the river's long history of highly fluctuating flows, they've survived and prospered. In fact, in sharp contrast to Bighorn browns, their numbers have increased dramatically during the recent long dry spell.

The upper stretch of the river, paralleled by 1,000 to 2,000 foot canyon walls in the Red Canyon Stretch, runs for about seven miles. The first half of the stretch is flat and deep, with several Class I and Class II rapids. The second half flows more rapidly and contains nice pocket water, with shallow areas well suited for wading. There's a boat launch about a mile and a half below the dam and a take-out spot at Little Hole, seven and a half miles downstream.

The Green in Red Canyon

The middle section of the trout water runs from Little Hole eight miles downstream to Indian Crossing, in Brown's park, but three miles below Little Hole, Red Creek can turn the river's waters mucky after heavy rains. In addition, the foot trail along the river, which begins below the dam on the river's north side, ends about three miles below Little Hole. The 17 miles of river between Indian Crossing and the Utah-Colorado border, where the river and the surrounding terrain are flatter and subject to strong winds, is marginal trout water, referred to as "transitional waters" in my book, *Capturing Rogue Trout,* and it holds the river's largest browns. Below the border, the river continues south and, after joining White River, discussed in Chapter Three, it joins the Colorado River before it flows into Lake Powell.

I first fished the river with Scott in August of 1995. I rented a car at the Logan International Airport in Salt Lake City and took Interstate 80 west to Rt. 40 and then Rt. 40 southwest for 125 miles to Vernal, where I picked up Scott who'd been rafting with his son on the Colorado River near Moab, Utah. We then took Rt. 191 north for about 40 miles to Dutch John. The complete trip from Salt Lake City took about three and one half hours, with the imposing Uintah Mountains visible along the entire route. Eleven of the Uintah's s peeks exceed 12,000 feet, with Gilbert Peak the highest at 13,434 feet. We stayed at the Flaming Gorge Lodge, four miles south of the dam, the only motel in the area at the time, but one with reasonable prices.

Rafting Below the Dam

Magazine articles about the river recommended hiring a guide, but friends familiar with the river claimed that access was easy and guides were necessary only for beginners. Fish were plentiful, easy to locate, and fooled with typical techniques. We rented a raft from Flaming Gorge Recreation Services, situated next to the lodge, and put in at the base of the dam. The water was extremely clear and fish were easily spotted. After marveling at the canyon's beauty, we beached the raft at the first good looking spot and cast nymphs and dry flies to trout holding in eddies.

After each of us caught half-a-dozen trout on nymphs, we ate our lunch on the raft. Scott inadvertently dropped a scrap of bread into the river. Instantly, several rainbows appeared and one grabbed it. We deliberately threw in several more pieces and it wasn't long before two-dozen rainbows circled the raft. Evidently, many trout in the Green, especially the stocked rainbows, are used to being fed by recreational rafters and eagerly await their offerings. The knowledge that the river's fish were this tame distracted somewhat from our initial enthusiasm.

We left our lunch spot and resumed our float downstream. Although we didn't catch anywhere near the number of trout that fed on our bread, we both caught another half-a-dozen good sized ones by the time we reached the take out at Little Hole. The shuttle service picked us up at around five o'clock. The return drive from Little Hole to our car at the dam took only 20 minutes, giving us some time to fish near the base of the dam until dark. We both took several more fish during this period. All the anglers we talked to at the lodge had similar, if not better, success, particularly those who concentrated on mending line to create drag free floats of their offerings.

Fleets of rafts drifted between the dam and Little Hole, but, unlike the Bighorn and San Juan, most floaters were recreational rafters, including many young people splashing each other with their paddles, jumping in and out of

Scott, trying to keep a nice fish from using the faster waters to escape

the rafts trying to swamp each other, and otherwise having a good time. Enamored with themselves as playmates, I don't think they even noticed the spectacular and unique canyon views. As many as 10, 8-person rafts in one teenage group floated along with us during our journey down the river! Although fun to watch for a while, reminding us of our own youth, eventually we stopped to let them by, but more came from above, always heard before they were seen. Where all these "screaming-memmies" came from was a mystery to me because the Green sits in the middle of nowhere. Either the kids were staying at a nearby campground or were bused from Salt Lake City to either Dan Hatch River Expeditions in Vernal, where guided raft floats are arranged and transportation provided to the river, or directly to Dutch John, where rafts can be rented.

Scott and I figured the weekend would bring even more floaters so we decided to fish Saturday and Sunday in a more secluded area. We thought about fishing Indian Crossing at Brown's Park, but it required an 80-mile round trip drive, with 50 of those miles on gravel roads. We would have to drive north into Wyoming, then southeast, back into Utah, and then south to get to this spot. We felt this distance was too far to travel.

I'm sorry we didn't go to Brown's Park, named after Baptiste Brown, an early fur trader. I wish I'd walked where Ann Bassett, the Queen of Rustlers, and Butch Cassidy and the Sundance Kid and their Wild Bunch, the last of the famous outlaws of the Old West, hid out between their notorious activities. Brown's Park was, and still is, a secluded area, visited for many years only by rugged mountain men. Nevertheless, it provided quick access to three states, making it an excellent retreat after the Wild Bunch had robbed a bank or a train, or had stolen horses. A flood in the early 1900s washed away the original buildings they occupied, except for a stone house, although a cabin built in the late 1800s was relocated to the park. The area is now a national wildlife refuge, a major stopover spot and nesting area for migratory waterfowl.

Butch Cassidy and the Sundance Kid

Butch Cassidy acquired his last name from an early mentor. One of 10 neglected children, Robert Leroy Parker, born in 1866 in Circleville, Utah, became a cowboy in his teens. He met outlaw Mike Cassidy, who took an interest in him and taught him to shoot. Parker mastered the skill quickly and could hit a playing card dead center at 50 paces. Because Cassidy was the first father figure to show any interest in him, he adopted "Cassidy" as his last name. "Butch" was later substituted for Le Roy after he tried "going straight," working as a butcher for several years in Rock Springs, Wyoming.

Cassidy was a fun-loving and easy-going outlaw who preferred using his brains to his six guns. He could afford this attitude, not just because he could shoot accurately when he needed to, but also because he was backed-up by the lightening-fast draw of Harvey Longabaugh, more popularly known as the "Sundance Kid." Because Longabaugh was so fast on the draw, other outlaws had to tolerate his infamous lectures about the healthy properties of Ralston Cereal, his favorite breakfast food. Longabaugh, born in 1863 in Mint Clare, Pennsylvania, acquired his outlaw name after moving west and serving time in jail in Sundance, Arizona.

Butch Cassidy, the Sundance Kid, and Kid Curry, perhaps the gang's most ruthless member, were the most famous members of the Wild Bunch, a gang with many different members during the years it operated; a loose federation of more than 100 cowboys, most of whom turned outlaw following the disastrous blizzards of 1888 that drastically reduced cattle herds and caused the collapse of thousands of small ranches and the unemployment of many cowhands.

After their escapades, members of the Wild Bunch went to one of three major hideouts: "Robber's Roost," in the southwest corner of Utah, the "Hole in the Wall," in the southeast corner of the Big Horn Mountains in North Central Wyoming, and "Brown's Park," bordering the states of Utah, Colorado, and Wyoming. Because access into each of these hideouts was difficult, neither lawmen nor sheriff's posses dared to enter. Many outlaws could be hidden along their rocky accesses, making entering lawmen easy targets. In fact, the Hole in the Wall hideout acquired its name because it was accessed by traversing a steep v-shaped notch, or pass, in a section of a vertical wall that paralleled the mountains for many miles.

The outlaws preferred Brown's Park to the other two hideouts because it offered amenities the others lacked. Ranch owner John Tarvie, whose holdings included a store, post office, river ferry, and cemetery, provided these amenities. Tarvie, a Scotsman, came to the area in the late 1800s. He ran the ferry and entertained visitors by playing the organ and the concertina. His first home, called "The Dugout," was where the Wild Bunch met. But it you mix with outlaws, you're asking for trouble. Tarvie was murdered in 1909 by two transients that didn't play by the unspoken rules.

In addition to robbing trains and banks, Butch and Sundance ran a protection racket. Those ranchers who didn't pay for their protection from cattle rustlers often found their cattle missing, stolen by Butch and Sundance themselves. After telegraph and telephone systems eroded their escape routes, Cassidy fled to Argentina, where Sundance and his girlfriend, Etta Place, later joined him. They became partners in a cattle ranch they later sold when they migrated to Bolivia. Their efforts to go straight in a foreign land might have worked if Sundance hadn't had a wondering eye; he bedded a rancher wife and then shot the rancher when caught in the act.

After arriving in Bolivia, they both worked for a mining company, but supplemented their income with an occasional bank robbery. In 1911, they robbed a mule train carrying ore from the mine near the town of San Vicente. Recognized in the town several days later, they were surrounded by a posse and reportedly shot and killed.

Stories about their exact death vary. In fact, Cassidy's sister claims he wasn't killed at all—that he escaped from Bolivia and lived in California until he died in 1943. He was also reportedly seen attending a wild-west show in 1915 that featured Jess Willard, the Great White Hope, who knocked out Jack Johnson, the first black American to hold the heavy weight title. Willard was somebody Cassidy would pay to see, especially because Willard starred as a western gunslinger in the show.

Legend has it that Longabaugh also returned to America where he sought out Etta, married her, and lived under an assumed name until his death in 1954. Both these stories might be true because, in 1992, human bones were removed from the graves in the Bolivia village where the two were reportedly buried in 1911. The bones were sent to the United States for

Scott and another angler well downstream

forensic study. The study's findings, reported in 1993, suggested that the bones were not those of either Parker or Longabaugh.

Below Little Hole

Saturday morning we went to the fly shop associated with the lodge to replenish our stock of flies. Two other fly shops now exist in Dutch John, Green River Outfitters and Trout Creek Flies, but at that time only the lodge sold flies. The shop sales person recommended a fly we'd never heard of—the "Royal Trude, claiming it was a "killer" on rainbows when nothing else worked. We both bought some, although I believe fly shop staff everywhere promote flies that visiting anglers don't typically bring with them. I didn't find Green River trout to be particularly selective and caught most of my fish on attractors, the Royal Trude being in that category. Nevertheless, local fly shops provide a needed service and I always buy some flies from them to help them to prosper.

Armed with ample flies, we decided to fish the river directly below Little Hole. After working our way downstream to a sharp bend in the river, we were faced with a deep run along the side of a steep cliff. With the water approaching the top of my waders and still deeper water ahead, I realized we could go no further downriver.

We returned to our car, took out the cooler containing our lunch and drinks, and hiked a trail up and along the cliff, taking turns carrying the cooler and taking short rests. We spotted, from the cliff, some large rainbows feeding in quite backwaters below. We came back down to the river just above Joe's Hole and Stonefly River Camp. We had this section to ourselves, except for the occasional John Boat drifting from Little Hole to Brown's Park. Drift boat anglers always hooked at least one trout from productive waters we'd just fished, evidence for the large numbers of fish in the river.

About five o'clock, we hiked back to Little Hole, returned the cooler to the car, and fished the 300-yard section from Little Hole to the beginning of the bluff we'd hiked over. I witnessed two trout several feet long chasing each other downstream in the slow moving water along the shore. One must have had a minnow that the other wanted. They both disappeared into a backwater below a bend in the river. I repeatedly cast into the backwater, but had no hits. About an hour later, I cast a streamer into this quite water on my way back upstream and landed two 18-inch browns, but they were definitely not the two I'd seen earlier

On Sunday, once again, we carted our cooler up and over the bluff. Once more, we spotted the big fish feeding below the cliff, but we'd learned earlier that we couldn't place a drag free float over them, so we ignored them and went directly to the long run we now called our own; it had become a familiar friend and we now knew where most of its fish hung out.

Above Little Hole

On Monday we decided to take the trail that runs the entire length of the river between Little Hole and Flaming Gorge Dam. We hiked up the river from Little Hole until we reached Dripping Springs Rapids. I worked my way up the rapids using an Adams. Within a few minutes, I hooked an 18-inch cutthroat that fought like no other cutthroat I'd ever hooked. Fighting and landing this fish was the highlight of my trip. It was a strong fish that ran and dogged, ran and dogged, until it finally tired. Scott came down from his upriver location, waded into the river, and netted it; otherwise I doubt I'd have landed it.

Unlike the darker Yellowstone cutthroat, this fish was cream-colored with black spots. Its iridescent sides and its brilliant orange-red patches, below and to the side of each gill, the patches that give it its name, were magnificent to behold. With wet hands, I carefully lifted it from the water, while Scott took its picture, and then watched it dart back into the rapids. Scott had been upstream observing an 18-inch brown feeding in a little backwater alcove. After photographing my fish, he returned upstream, cast to the brown, and landed it, but it didn't fight nearly as well as the cutthroat, probably because it didn't have the girth the cutthroat had—my cutthroat was a strong, fat fish.

The fight my cutthroat displayed was not typical of other Green River trout. To the contrary, the average trout fought poorly relative to its size. This was not just our observation, but also that of other anglers who fished the river that summer. I talked to a Utah resident who'd fished the river for years and the poor fight of the average fish also puzzled him. In other heavily fished rivers, the fish fight poorly because they've been caught repeatedly, but this didn't seem to be the case in the Green. We did catch some trout above Little Hole that we thought were caught before, but many of those fooled below Little Hole had probably never felt a hook. In addition, the stream-born browns fought no better than the stocked rainbows. Perhaps the river was warmer than usual, as trout fight less rigorously in warmer water, but we never took its temperature so we don't know if temperature was a contributing factor.

Nevertheless, our venture on the Green was a meaningful one and the river well worth more than one

Author with an 18-inch cutthroat

visit. In defense of the river, I recently talked to an angler who fished the Green in the fall and he was well satisfied with the fight of the many 20-inch fish he caught. Since we didn't hook any fish that size, our experiences aren't really comparable!

The Green's Troubles

Like the Bighorn, the Green is not without it's struggles. Unlike Bighorn Lake, Flaming Gorge Reservoir is a renowned trout fishery, especially for lake trout, many of which weigh in the 30-pound range. They drifted into the reservoir from the upper Green River drainage and established themselves as a wild population. The state record fish, a 51.5-pound fish, was fooled in the reservoir. The reservoir's relatively high elevation, 6,040 feet, keeps air temperatures moderate throughout the summer and fish can be caught without having to troll exceptionally deep. Huge browns, those up to 30 pounds, were caught in the 1970s, mostly by anglers trolling large lures in the reservoir, but also by some anglers fishing the Green River above the reservoir in the fall. Rainbows up to 25 pounds, the first fish stocked to help curb the burgeoning Utah chub population, that along with catfish, were the only fish in the reservoir when it was first created

Unfortunately, the reservoir's wild brown trout population has dwindled since their initial introduction in 1967 and browns pushing 30 inches are now difficult to find. Not only because the browns consumed almost all the Utah chubs, but also because young browns are eaten by smallmouth bass introduced in the 1960s in the reservoir's northern end, near the mouth of the Green, and by the reservoir's large lake trout, as were the stocked rainbows, whose stocking has now been delayed until the lake trout stop cruising shorelines and head for deeper water. Nevertheless, because the lake trout were forced to switch from eating chubs to eating kokanee salmon, 80,000 of which are stocked each year, the chub population is on the rebound. As a result, rumor has it that browns may be stocked in greater numbers in the hope that they'll grow big once again. Currently, about 63,000 tiger trout, a brown/brook hybrid, are stocked in the reservoir, but they don't grow as big as browns and, being sterile, don't run up tributaries to spawn.

In the late 1970s, I read an article about Robert Bringhurst, who holds the state record for brown trout, a 33-lb., 10 oz. fish. This catch was not the result of luck, but of hard work. His avocation was catching big trout in Flaming Gorge, using hand painted, deep diving lures to imitate rainbow trout, and each year he caught browns weighing more than 10 pounds

The problem, however, lies not with the disappearance of big trout, but with the reservoir's kokanee salmon, the main forage fish of the lake trout and, behind rainbows, they're second in harvest and popularity. Unfortunately, kokanee are not fussy about water depth when they spawn, with many choosing waters less than a foot deep. If the reservoir is lowered in

November, after they spawn in the early fall, their eggs will either be left high and dry or in waters that freeze along the shoreline.

Although new, more efficient, turbines were recently installed in the power plant to reduce the flows needed to achieve power capacity, with increasing population growth, increased releases are constantly being requested by the Power Authority, as well as requests for "double peaking," or the release of high volumes of water twice a day to make better use of the power plant's 150 megawatt capacity. These request are made in the late fall when angler visits are low, placing few in danger, although efforts are underway to promote the river as a winter fishery. Currently, power is generated in the fall during a single peak, with an average daily release of about 1,000-cfs, a level excellent for wading anglers.

Double peaking not only lowers reservoir waters, but also wreaks havoc with the river's trout. Although many browns survive, the stocked rainbows suffer and their numbers dwindle. During the drought years, when the reservoir was at historical lows, double peaking didn't occur, but with higher levels in future years, that situation could change. Nevertheless, higher levels, like those in 2008, may become the exception. Global warming experts predict that water shortages in the West are going to get worse, with two scientists publishing an article in 2007, in *Southwest Hydrology*, in which they predict that the recent drought conditions will become average conditions throughout the West and severe drought will occur by 2035 in Arizona, Colorado, New Mexico, Utah, and Wyoming, homes to many of the country's best trout streams.

Scott into a good fish at Joe's Hole

A unique problem occurred following the fires in 2002 when tons of silt was deposited in the river, silt that has now hardened on the bottom, and river flows have not been high enough to flush it out. Guides and outfitters have called for a flush-release for 24 hours to clean the river, but until this year, not enough water was available to do so. Nevertheless, considering the warnings of Global Warming Experts, I doubt their request will be granted, considering the fear of future droughts.

There are currently two books about the Green River. In 1993 Larry Tullis published *Green River* (Journal Series, No 3) and in 1998 Dennis Breer published *Utah's*

Green River: A Fly Fisher's Guide to the Flaming Gorge Tailwater, but I haven't read either.

Accommodations

There are only two motels near Flaming Gorge. The Flaming Gorge (Lodge) Resort (435-889-3773) at Grendale, which includes a restaurant, full-service fly shop, and raft and mountain bike rentals, and the Red Canyon Lodge (435-889-3759) in Dutch John, which also includes a restaurant, a stocked lake, and a stock pond that only children can fish. Anglers can camp on National Forest Campgrounds (800-283-CAMP) on the river below Little Hole or on the reservoir. One of the nicest campsites is the Dripping Springs Campgrounds on 18 wooded acres on the river. Campers with family members who like to swim can camp on the reservoir at either Mustang Ridge or Antelope Flats, both of which have sandy beaches.

Other Activities

The Flaming Gorge Visitors Center, on Federal. Hwy. 198 at the top of the dam, offers free daily tours of the dam and shows the film, *Flaming Gorge: A Study Written in Water*, which presents the natural and human history of the Gorge. The Red Canyon Visitors Center, west of Dutch John, on State Rt. 44, provides a stunning view of the reservoir situated 1,300 feet below its plate-glass viewing window.

For those enjoying still water activities or wanting to explore the reservoir, the Cedar Springs Marina (435-889-3795), located about three miles before the dam, rents pontoon and ski boats by the hour. The Lucerne Valley Marina (435-784-3483), located seven miles northeast of Manila, off Rt. 43, rents small fishing boats for about $75 dollars per day. The history of Butch Cassidy and the Sundance Kid can be relived in Vernal, where The Outlaw Trail Theater (888-240-2080) puts on a musical entitled, "The Mostly True Story of Butch Cassidy and the Wild Bunch."

For $10 dollars a car, Dinosaur National Monument, about 30 miles west of Vernal in Dinosaur, Colorado, can be visited, although the Dinosaur Pits can be accessed seven miles south of Vernal at Jensen, Utah, at the end of Rt. 149. The Park has complete skeletons of dinosaurs encased in rock. Ancient petroglyphs are visible along the road to the campsites in the park's western section. The Desert Voices Trail is a two-mile loop offering sweeping views of the surrounding mountains. The temperature is said to vary as much as 150 fifty degrees between winter and summer.

Before or after you fish the Green, you can fish the Provo or Webber rivers, neither of which is more than an hour from Salt Lake City. The Provo River is in Provo Canyon, above the town of Provo, the location of Brigham Young University. Scott has fished the Provo in two sections, but did his best

The mixed landscape at Little Hole

in Heber Valley, located between Jordanelle and Deer Creek reservoirs. This middle section of the Provo is a tail-water river, with dense aquatic insect hatches and a fish population of 3,000 brown trout per mile.

On one trip, Scott's son, Mathew, accompanied him. At the time, Mathew worked for a stream restoration company in Hamilton, Montana, through which the Bitterroot flows. When Matthew was interviewed for the job, he was asked two questions. First, "Do you fish?" When he responded with "Not really," the interviewer exclaimed, "Good, you can row the drift boat." Second, he was asked, "Do you hunt?" When he again replied in the negative, the interviewer exclaimed, "Good, you can cook." Today. Mathew owns his own stream restoration company in Whitefish, Montana. Unlike the preacher's sons in Norman Maclean's, *A River Runs Thru It*. Matthew showed no interest in fly fishing until he and Scott camped in the Wind River Wilderness, where he taught Scott wilderness camping and, afterwards, let Scott teach him to fly fish. A lesson other fathers should pay heed to!

Chapter Seven

Glacial Rivers of Northwest Montana
Emerald Green in August

The world has definitely gotten smaller during my lifetime. Who would have thought that my fishing companion of 40 years, Scott Daniels, the first friend I made after moving to New York, would retire in Whitefish, Montana, where he fishes with both his daughter, Durae, and his son, Mathew, both Whitefish residents for about a decade? I first fished the area in August of 1992, when Scott's children were too young to think about moving from New York State.

Durae moved to Montana after college graduation and took a position in Montana with the United States Forest Service. When she and her co-workers traveled to clear-cut a forest area, Scott would fly to Montana, rent a car, and meet her. While she worked during the day, he would fish nearby rivers and visit with her in the evenings.

To date, Scott's favorite Montana rivers are the Beaverhead and Ruby in Montana's Gold West Country, although he enjoys the Missouri River in the fall, when cookie cutter rainbows, all about 19 inches, feed on Tiny Blue Olives. He also likes picturesque Rock Creek, a tributary to the upper Clarks Fork of the Columbia River east of Missoula. He fished the Beaverhead between Clark Canyon Reservoir and Dillon for three days, but said bush-lined banks limited his access. Lots of anglers passed him by floating the river, but few waders were encountered. Nearby Big Hole River, an excellent trout stream, can get low in July and August and the variable nature of spring runoffs rule out advanced planning of earlier visits to it.

In 1999, Durae left the Forest Service to take a job with Montana Department of Fish, Wildlife and Parks. Her first task was to help monitor the spawning runs of endangered bull trout in the North Fork of the Flathead. Bull trout, which don't usually spawn until their seven years old and at least 17 inches long, do so in the fall in the headwaters of small tributaries where water temperatures are 45 degrees. In such waters, anchor ice can form on their redds and starve their eggs of oxygen and spring runoff can scour their eggs from the bottom. In addition, the harsh and sterile conditions at the headwaters stress the fish and many don't repeat spawn. Although man can do nothing to prevent these acts of Nature, actions can be taken to prevent other hazards, such as silting of spawning beds.

Because the two million acre Flathead National Forest is subject to clear-cut logging and road building, practices that increase the sediment levels in many Flathead tributaries, it's important to discover where the endangered bull trout, or Dolly Varden, actually spawn. Less than a one-third increase in silt results in more than a two-thirds increase in trout mortality. In addition, clear-cutting removes the protective tree canopy and results in more rapid snowmelts and runoffs that cause bank erosion, scoring, and stream braiding.

At the Flathead River's inlet into Lake Flathead, her colleagues would electroshock the water and she would plunge into it to net the big bull trout before they recovered. Radio transmitters were then surgically implanted in the fish and Durae would don a wet suit and scuba gear and follow the fish in the cold glacial waters on their journey upriver to their spawning grounds in tributaries near the Canadian Border, grounds currently threatened by a huge mining project in Canada. Future plans called for state employees to clear the barriers to these sites, improve important habitat elements, place spawning sites off-limits to river fishermen, and help the rearing habitat to maintain the needed detritus and woody debris

Durae reports that efforts to save bull trout are not without complications. Although electroshocks can permanently injure fish if not administered properly, the surgically implanted transmitters cause the most fatalities. About half the bull trout implanted never make it to the spawning grounds. In most cases, the transmitters catch in bottom structure, rip free of their bodies, and leave them with wounds too large to heal.

Priest River

I first fished the rivers near Glacier National Park in the summer of 1992. Melody and I flew into Spokane, rented a car, and headed for Sand Point, Idaho, where we planned to fish the stunning Priest River. Unfortunately, I couldn't find a trout in the two different sections I explored. I poked into undercover banks, walked through riffles, and stared into holes, but I neither saw nor scared up a single trout. Later inquiry revealed that the Priest is a good cutthroat river earlier in the year, but by July, the fish have moved into cool feeder creeks because water is held in Priest Lake, a man-made reservoir on the river, and the river below it runs low and warms up. The average depth of the river in the summer is less than three feet, slow lazy stretches predominate, and canoes and rafts often scrape the bottom.

The drive north to see Priest Lake took us through tall pines that reached far up into the sky and then arched over so that the road was without sunlight. I believe the trees were Ponderosa Pines because the forest floor was devoid of other trees and even of small bushes. The 30-foot root systems on Ponderosa Pines consume all the nutrients at their base.

In spite of the lifeless river, I was impressed with Sand Point's public park on Lake Pend Oreille and with the lake itself, a glacial-made lake deeper than any of the Great Lakes, at 1,500 feet, and with more than 100 miles of shoreline. It's home to Kamloops rainbow trout up to 20 pounds. The quaint tourist town of Sand Point, a town soothed by a Pacific Northwest climate, where one can sail and fish in the lake and ski Schweitzer Mountain, Idaho's second largest ski area, is a good spot to vacation or even to retire.

Kootenai River

After leaving Sand Point, and heading toward Glacier National Park, we stopped at a market in Libby, Montana, where I engaged in a brief conservation with a resident while pumping gas. He spoke enthusiastically about Kootenai River, flowing just north of the town, claiming, "It's the best river in Montana; had been for many years, but because it's 'a piece' from major cities, it's unsung." He promised I would catch "fierce fighting rainbows between 15 and 18 inches during the day and bigger ones at dusk."

We arrived at the Kootenai at noon and I fished a section within sight of the dam. It was hot and sunny, but I caught a number of 10-inch bull trout along a narrow section of shoreline where I could comfortably wade. I quit about one o'clock, and after a quick lunch, visited the visitor's center at the dam, where huge trout caught below the dam were mounted for display, with the biggest weighing 28 pounds.

At the base of the dam, trout feed on Kokanee salmon fry that become entrapped in the outlet flow from Koocanusa Reservoir and pass through the turbines. Bait fisherman catch these big ones by dropping special weighted rigs down into the turbulent water. About 50 feet downstream from the dam, the trout are of normal size.

At the visitor's center, a ranger informed me that, in August, the Kootenaii is an evening river. Unfortunately, we planned to be in Kalispell that evening, keeping me from catching any of the rainbows he said, "fight exceptionally well for their size." Long experience has taught me that blind fishing for native rainbows in the heat of the day is wasted effort. I went after the small bull trout because they were rising along the shoreline in a clear, deep grassy section about 100 yards below the dam.

The ranger said I should stay at least until late afternoon because around four o'clock rainbows would start feeding on emerging Pale Morning Duns. I should look for silver flashes near the tails of seams. With Melody's permission, we put off our drive to Kalispell and I followed the ranger's advice. Unfortunately, no hatch came and we left at five o'clock.

An angler in Whitefish told me I should've waited a bit longer, put on a Pale Morning Dun, with a #18 Pheasant Tail Nymph dropper, as he had done, and cast into the weedy channels in the deep waters several hundred yards below the dam. He said the rainbows feed deep among the reeds, where they feel safe, but move out of the troughs when the hatch begins and, as it progresses, confine themselves to narrow feeding lanes, referring to the river's rainbows as "narrow minded." Still later, he moved downstream and fished the shallow riffles, where more flies were emerging.

My informant told me he always does better when he matches the exact color of flies, so he netted a few duns to determine the underbody color, as it can vary from creamy-yellow to burnt-orange. The Pale Morning Dun hatch reaches its crescendo around 7:30 in the evening (why locals don't call it a Pale Evening Dun hatch escapes me). Right at dark, the caddis hatch begins, and anglers do well who fish into the night. Below the falls at Libby, the rainbows reside in the long step-pools that characterize this section.

Kootenai River below the dam

North and South Forks of Flathead River

During our stay in Kalispell, Melody and I planned to fish each of the three forks of Flathead River, the nation's longest wild and scenic river system. Both the river and the lake into which it flows were named after the Salish and Kootenai Indians, referred to as "Flatheads," although neither tribe swaddled their infants on boards, a practice that flattens infants' heads. We skipped the Middle Fork because rafting tourists were everywhere. In addition, we were told that it didn't fish well in its lower, more easily accessible, sections. Lower stretches of the North Fork were said to fish better and it was readily accessible in many spots off a gravel road that ran parallel to it. We caught a number of 11-inch cutthroats, as well as whitefish, immediately below riffled waters.

North Fork Flathead River

To fish the South Fork, we had to drive 50 miles on a gravel road on the southern shore of Hungry Horse Reservoir, at 25 miles per hour, to reach the river above the reservoir. The riverbed is wider in its lower reaches than sections of the Hudson River near my home, although in August the river is not as wide as the Delaware. The Dinka peoples of South Africa, who live along the White Nile, speak of the Nile as "breathing in" when it recedes in the summer. The Flatheads definitely "breath in," if not inhale in the summer. I can't imagine what the river looks like when it "breaths out" during runoff!

We checked in at the Spotted Bear Ranger Station and walked upstream to find a spot where Melody could read and sun herself while I fished. The primitive area above the ranger station illustrates the saying that "nature thrives where humans give up." I left Melody on the wide rocky riverbed and went further upstream. I didn't go too far, however, as I worried about her being all alone and out of my sight in Grizzly Country.

All three forks, being glacial streams, were relatively barren of insect life. When I picked up rocks from the emerald green waters of the South Fork, I found only small nymphs clinging to them. Yet small cutthroats eagerly took my Adams almost anywhere I threw it. They were either river residents or young fish yet to migrate downstream to the reservoir, the offspring of migratory cutthroats that entered the river two summers ago.

When Scott first fished these waters, some eight years later, he went about a mile further upstream, but then became troubled by crackling noises in the woods, wondering if a grizzly made them! He knew such thoughts were foolish, but being alone in the wilderness can be spooky. Nevertheless, a deputy sheriff in Libby told me that I would be safer on the Flatheads than on the Yaak, a tributary to the Kootenai that I thought I might fish. He said there was a greater chance of being shot by militia group members, whose

South Fork Flathead River at mouth of First Twin Creek (Mike Zelie Photo)

organizations headquarter along the Yaak, than being attacked by a grizzly on the Flathead's South Fork.

One angling writer states that the South Fork is alive with cutthroat that often top three pounds. As just mentioned, eight years apart, both Scott and I fished upstream from Spotted Bear Ranger Station in wilderness country and neither of us caught any close to that weight. Scott walked further upstream than I did and was rewarded for his efforts with several decent fish, but none approached two pounds. Scott has also fished this stretch more recently with Mike Zelie and their biggest fish approached 15 inches. Perhaps the author fished before the spring flush, when trout from Flathead Lake, which had run the river to spawn, remained in it to feed before their return.

I'd heard that the cutthroat fishing was superb on Spotted Bear River, a feeder stream to the South Fork just above the reservoir, but it required a steep hike down to access it from the road that paralleled it. In addition, the river was low and crisscrossed by uprooted trees. When Mike Zelie visited Scott in 2006, they made the strenuous climb down, but neither caught any fish.

Scott and his children drive to the end of the road paralleling Spotted Bear River and hike 15 miles into the Bob Marshall Wilderness Area, where they fish the Flathead's upper South Fork. Because waters flowing through limestone deposits feed the upper river, it contains considerable aquatic life and big cutthroats, with both Durae and Scott landing some approaching 20 inches. Adding to the experience is the occasional bull trout exceeding 28 inches that grabs a hooked cutthroat and the hook dislodges and imbeds in it, enabling these monsters to be landed after long, drawn-out battles.

Our return trip from the South Fork took three hours instead of two. Melody was into flower pressing and I stopped numerous times so she could pick samples of the different wild flowers that adorned the roadside. The end result was that I spent five hours driving and about 90 minutes fishing, although such a ratio of travel to fishing time is not unique to rivers in Glacier National Park.

In the past, outdoor writers featured the capture of big bull trout in the North Fork of the Flathead during their August migration up river from Flathead Lake, but few visitors caught these big fish. In fact, even locals had difficulty catching them. Their primary diet is whitefish and although they'll feed during their late summer and fall trips up the river, it's difficult to throw the large streamers needed to interest them. It's no longer legal to fish for bull trout in Montana, even under catch-and-release conditions.

Other Waters

Driving on the "Going to the Sun Road," that parallels the eastern shore of Lake McDonald, a finger of blue pointing the way to the mountains, said to contain bull trout, cutthroat, kokanee salmon, lake trout, and rainbow, I stopped to cast to some cutthroats rising close to the shoreline. After catching a few, and realizing that all the risers were less than 10 inches, I quit and concentrated on sightseeing. The Going to the Sun Road, or "Transmountain Highway," as it was first named, was completed in 1933, after three decades of work. The road, 52 miles long, penetrates the park's interior, climbing nearly 3,000 feet from the valley floor and then descending on the Canadian side of the park. Driving it is not for the squeamish.

Architects with the National Park Service landscape insisted that the bridges, retaining walls, and guardrails be made of native materials and required contractors to use numerous small blasts of explosives because large ones destroy more landscape. Locals opposed the road, favoring construction of a less expensive one along the park's southern boundary, next to the Great Northern Railroad tracks, but eventually supported it after realizing that more tourist dollars would flow to the community. The railroad called the area the "Switzerland of America" and built hotels and chalets in keeping with the image of this slogan.

The Going to the Sun Road hugs the wooded shores of Lake McDonald for about 10 miles. After leaving the lake, the road goes through forests of hemlock and red cedar, as it climbs the mountains alongside McDonald Creek, which cascades downward toward the lake. The road passes McDonald Falls, where moose are sometimes seen feeding in the marshes below. Travelers can stop and walk the Trail of Cedars, which starts across Avalanche Creek. Hemlocks, draped in lichen, and cedars, fresh with sent, shade the half-mile of the trail's elevated boardwalk in the ancient forest.

Majestic Avalanche Gorge is located along the trail near Avalanche Campground. Its sculptured rock banks demonstrate stream erosion ongoing since the ice age. At the end of the Trail of Cedars, a narrow two-mile-trail gently climbs to Avalanche Lake, located in a magnificent cirque. Five waterfalls, fed by melting snow and ice, plunge over a 1,000 feet from the cliffs surrounding the lake. Park rangers report good fishing for cutthroats in the lake's turquoise waters.

As the road climes higher, scattered strands of spruces replace the sturdy hemlocks, and a sheer ridge, cresting thousands of feet above the valley, comes into view. The ridge is called "The Garden Wall." Beneath the shadow of the wall, the road takes a lengthy zigzag, known as "The Loop," climbing higher and higher. Waterfalls, peaks, and plummeting valleys make up the view, with the highest falls called "Birdwoman Falls" The road reaches it zenith at Logan Pass, where a stunted forest of contorted firs line its edge.

Few areas in the world accessible by car provide the grandeur of Logan Pass. From the Visitor's Center, a seven and one-half mile trail leads across the Garden Wall to Granite Park Chalet, where overnight lodging and meals can be arranged. Less adventurous visitors can hike a self-guided nature trail that winds among the flowers of Hanging Garden, along snow banks, and over Hidden Lake Pass, where Hidden Lake comes into view, situated in a half-moon shaped cirque surrounded by the step cliffs of the Bearhat and Reynolds Mountains.

One writer asserts that Hidden Lake harbors large cutthroats that cruise the shallows and drop-offs along the shores. He also writes that the park's interior lakes offer exceptional fishing for cutthroats and huge brook trout, but the best lakes require a two-day hike to reach and are in prime grizzly country. Approximately 45 lakes in the park contain trout, with seven accessible by car. Nevertheless, because of their glacial origin, many of the

South Fork Flathead River

lakes are cold and deep and, as a result, have little plant life and low oxygen levels, both necessary to support abundant fish populations. Most of the deeper lakes never get much warmer than 50 degrees, resulting in small trout because their only source of food is an occasional midge hatch.

The best lakes to fish are east of the Park in Blackfoot Indian Reservation. Trout stocked by the tribe become monsters quickly in their fertile waters, growing as much as 12 inches a year. The lakes lie in the wide-open vastness of upland plains, where strong winds can make fly-casting impossible. The fishing is tough and frustrating, but a back up spin rod may save the day. The lakes are hard to find and accessed by poor roads. In addition, there are no facilities, like running water or toilets. For this reason, I didn't fish them because my wife wouldn't enjoy fishing under such circumstances. Articles on Duck Lake have appeared in many outdoor publications, including one by Greg Thomas in the February 2000 issue of *Fly Fisherman*, with pictures illustrating the bleakness of its surroundings.

After leaving Glacier Park, we drove along Rt. 83, a road that parallels Swan River in the Seeley-Swan Valley above Swan Lake. We stopped at several spots on the 25-mile section of the road between Swan Lake and Lindbergh Lake so I could wet a line. The Swan and Clearwater rivers link a chain of lakes that mirror the snowcapped peaks in the Bob Marshall Wilderness. The water corridors around Seeley Lake shelter the largest population of nesting common loons in the Western lower 48 states

Swan River was very low and warm, no fish were rising, and after working a nymph below some riffles and through some deep pools, I decided that the fish had either moved into one of the river's 17 major feeder streams, such as Beaver, Buck, Holland, Lion, or Woodward creeks, or migrated downstream into Swan Lake. Perhaps I was wrong, but an hour and a half of fishing under overcast conditions revealed no fish. Stories are told of five pound rainbows caught in the Swan on spoons and live bait. If the stories are true, perhaps some large rainbows migrate up from Swan Lake during spawning season, but I wouldn't bet on the truth of such stories, but I would bet that the Swan is better for resident trout in early summer.

After a day in Swan River Valley, we returned to Flathead Lake, the West's largest natural freshwater lake, occupying 200 square miles. East Shore Highway, bordered by Mission Mountains, offers 35 miles of majestic beauty. We stayed in a motel in Polson, a small town on the south end of the lake. A storm had been brewing all day and when it finally hit, four-foot waves broke over the concrete abutment across the street from the motel!

Wildhorse Island can be reached by boat from the southern arm of the lake. It currently shelters a small herd of bighorn sheep. The Salish and Kootenai Indians hid their horses on the island to avoid their capture by Blackfoot raiding parties. The horses, never reclaimed by the tribes, roamed free for a time and gave the island its current name. Just south of the island is a spot called "Mac Alley," where large lake trout (mackinaw) are caught each season. Both the state record lake and bull trout were caught in the lake, 42 and 26 pounds respectively.

On our return trip to Spokane from the Bitterroot River, I also fished the Clark Fork below Missoula for about an hour. I floated a large Humpy through riffle water after I heard, but didn't see, large fish splashing in the fast current. Nevertheless, I couldn't entice them up to my fly and since my fishing license had expired, I quit before I regretted my actions. I learned later

South Fork Flathead River

that the fish might have been big squawfish, a fish that eats fish up to its own size. The Clark Fork is a big river. Its peak flow entering Idaho is more than the combined flows of the Missouri and Yellowstone rivers at their confluence.

Years ago, large numbers of bull and cutthroat trout migrated upstream from Lake Pend Oreille to spawn in the Clark Fork and its tributaries. Dams and environmental destruction changed all that. Now Biologists are not even sure that bull trout still have the "migratory gene" to travel from the lake to Clark Fork, even if good spawning habitats were attainable.

I also liked the looks of Thompson River, a tributary at to the Clarks Fork near Thompson Falls, close to the Idaho border. I'd also heard good things about nearby St. Joe River, a rugged, swift flowing cutthroat stream in Idaho, but we didn't have the time to take the gravel road over the Bitterroot Range to examine it.

Accommodations

Most of the major motel chains are represented in either Kalispell or Whitefish. Glacier National Park has three lodges, with reservations made through one central number (866-875-8456). Glacier Park Lodge, located at the park's southwest corner, has 162 rooms, a main dining room, snack shop, and a lounge serving sandwiches. Rooms are priced according to size rather than location. Many Glacier Hotel, on the shores of Swiftcurrent Lake, in the park's northeast corner, contains 211 rooms and a restaurant, lounge, and store selling snacks. Lake McDonald Lodge, right on the lake, is the least expensive of the three, priced similarly to local motels. Guests can stay in the main lodge, small cabins, or units in a two-story motel. Located in a lovely wooded setting, it includes a restaurant and the Stockade Lounge, which serves light meals. John Lewis operated a fishing and tourist camp on the lake until he built the cabins in 1910 and added the lodge in 1913.

In addition to seven major and eight minor campgrounds in the park, operated on a first come, first served basis, 15 campgrounds in Flat head National Forest are on lands adjacent to Hungry Horse Reservoir, all mixed in among the trees, which includes lodge pole pine, Douglas fir, spruce, and some larch, the later providing soft tent sites because it sheds its needles. The campgrounds have engaging names, such as Devils Corkscrew, Fire Island, and Lost Johnny Point. Most are small, with only 6 to 10 sites, but most are free. Beaver Creek Campground, located among mixed conifers, provides views of Spotted Bear River and Spotted Bear Campground, which charges a small fee, is near the ranger station.

Other Activities

Glacier country offers a variety of activities, but, typical of the West, considerable distance exists between them. Those who've never visited the large estates along New York's Hudson River should visit the Conrad Mansion, located in Kalispell. C. E. Conrad, Kalispell's founder, built the estate in 1895 and later restored it to Victorian Elegance. The Ross Creek Cedar Grove Scenic Area, south of Bull River, offers strolls among cedars more than 500 years old and 250 feet tall. The Museum of Plains Indians, located west of Browning, includes a collection of Blackfoot tribal artifacts and the history of Northern Great Plains tribes. The National Bison Range, on the Flathead Indian Reservation, near Moiese, allows for self-driving tours through parts of the grasslands inhabited by 400 to 500 buffalo.

St. Ignatius, near Moiese, is the home to St. Ignatius Mission. This unique Catholic Church has 58 original murals on its walls and ceilings, but the history of its founder is what makes it interesting. Pierre Jean De Smet, a Jesuit missionary from Belgium, established it in 1854 to serve the Kalispell tribes. The Indians trusted De Smet and his influence extended to many tribes, most notably the Blackfoot and Sioux. Fearless, tireless, and straightforward, "Blackrobe," as the Indians called him, mediated differences between tribes and between tribes and white settlers. He pushed for the treaty at Fort Laramie, mentioned in Chapter Five, where lands were set aside for the Plains tribes. He helped to end the "Morman" and "Yakima" wars, two wars preceding the Battle of Big Horn. De Smet later negotiated a temporary peace with Sitting Bull, after boldly entering the Sioux encampment in Big Horn Valley in 1868.

Chapter Eight
Snake River
Native Cutthroat in Big Waters

I've been to the Snake River in Jackson Hole twice—once with Bob and Tom, and once with members of my family. Bob returned to Jackson Hole several times with his family and reported good fishing in both the Snake and nearby rivers, as did Mike Zelie on his visit with his family. Jackson hole is a good jumping off spot for several excellent rivers, particularly Flat Creek, the upper Green, the South Fork of the Snake, and the Snake River itself. When the "One Fly Contest" was first held on the Snake in 1986, the largest cutthroat landed approached two feet. In 1989 and 1993 the largest were 25 inches and in recent contests the largest typically exceed 20 inches, larger by three inches than any Bob or I landed on our trips, including my two sons, who caught several 17-inch fish, using worms on a float trip. I did work for larger fish in the Snake that were visible from the banks, landed a 19-inch cutthroat in Flat Creek, and lost several cutthroat exceeding 20 inches in the South Fork of the Snake.

The Snake River Valley is called Jackson Hole because it was the favorite valley of noted fur trapper "Davy" Jackson. His partner, Bill Sublette, first called the valley Jackson's Hole and other trappers dropped the possessive. Jackson Hole is the corridor to Teton National Park. Not all Americans wanted the strikingly beautiful Tetons, and the lands surrounding them, set aside as a national park in order to preserve their natural state. Several influential groups opposed the effort. Early settlers, who turned the harsh land into farms, and cattle ranchers, who flourished in the valley, were two such groups. In addition, large numbers of wealthy hunters traveled to Jackson Hole in the late 1800s. A special brand of hunter, called a "Tusker," shot bull elk simply for their teeth, as Elk Club members prized elk teeth as their lodge symbol. The elk herd rapidly deteriorated because Tuskers killed the largest, most virile bulls that provided the most profitable tusks. Eventually, Elk Clubs outlawed elk teeth as a symbol and the trade died, but other hunters, as well as ranchers and farmers, wanted things kept the same.

Congress first established the National Elk Refuge in the valley in 1913. Those fearing that Moose, Big Horn Sheep, Mule Deer and Bear would also be decimated lobbied Congress to preserve the entire region. One proposal put before Congress was to extend Yellowstone Park southward. Opposing groups kept the measure from passing in the Congress, but the idea for another national park was born.

John Rockefeller Jr., enchanted by the valley when he visited it in 1926, wanted it preserved as a national park. He established the Snake River Land Company, whose sole purpose was to purchase as much of the area's land as possible. Ranchers who considered selling land to his company were vilified by many of their neighbors. In 1929, Congress established Grand Teton National Park from national forest land, but to appease the park's opponents, it included only the western drainage area of the Tetons and the little lakes at their feet. Rockefeller tried to denote his company's holdings to enlarge the park, but Congress delayed taking action. In response, the Rockefeller family considered selling the properties; if they weren't going to become part of a park, they weren't going to continue paying taxes on them, having already paid an amount equal to half their original cost.

To prevent loss of these lands from the public domain, President Franklin D. Roosevelt decreed a national monument that included the Rockefeller holdings, plus some additional national forest land. Although presidents can create national monuments, only acts of Congress can create national parks. Valley residents complained that Roosevelt had undermined the democratic process and pressured Congress to pass a bill abolishing the monument. President Roosevelt vetoed the bill. After more clashes, Congress finally incorporated the monument into the Park in 1950.

Snake River

There are approximately 80 miles of water between the outlet at Jackson Lake Dam, and the Palisades Reservoir at Alpine, with about 50 of the miles below Wilson Bridge (Rt. 22 Bridge), although long stretches below Hoback Junction flow through Snake River Canyon and others through the Class III/IV rapids just above Alpine, where white water rafting is popular. Year-round fishing is allowed, with catch-and-release regulations between November 1 and March 31. Several access sites are situated along the 30 miles of river between Oxbow Bend, where the river flows out of Jackson

Lake, and Wilson Bridge, just south of Teton Village. Federal Hwy. 191 parallels the river for part of this stretch, enabling anglers to park, hike into the river, and walk along its steep banks, but it's more easily assessed at two raft launch cites, one just above the famous Snake River Overlook and the other just south of Teton Point Turnout. The dirt roads to these two sites are fairly dry in August, but earlier in the season four-wheel drive vehicles may be required, although with 400 inches of snowfall in the Tetons each winter, the river isn't really fishable until August.

More specifically, the first five miles of water below Jackson Lake Dam is relatively slow moving and usually too deep to wade in August. From Moran Junction, where the river is joined by its Buffalo Fork, it turns south to Deadmans Bar, moves faster, and braids up some, with riffles in spots. From the boat launch at Deadmans Bar to Moose (formerly Moose Landing), side channels with riffles develop that can be waded if they can be accessed. In the stretch from Moose to Wilson Bridge, the river drops in elevation and the Army Corps of Engineers has built rock levies for flood protection, making the fast flowing water usually too deep to wade.

The best spot for wading anglers is the 12-mile stretch from Wilson Bridge to South Park, a housing development adjacent to the Rafter J Ranch resort community, south of Jackson, but the only access site is at the bridge. This stretch widens out from levy to levy, resulting in side channels, riffles, and pocket waters. The waters below the bridge are heavily fished in the first several miles, more fish can be kept than allowed in the park, and many of the remaining trout are small. On a float trip I took in this section when I visited the Park with my family, the guide stopped at several spots so I could fish the riffles and along the shorelines of islands.

Section of the Snake where we fished from the banks

In summary, from Moran Junction to Wilson Bridge, other than the turn visible from Snake River Overlook, the river flows rapidly along a relatively straight path, making it a drift-boat-angler's river.

On my first visit to the river, with Bob and Tom, the river was unusually high, probably flowing more than 2,000-cfs, so we fished it for only a short time and then headed to Yellowstone Park. We worked the stretch pictured on the previous page, one that can be waded in August only in low water years and, even then, it's best fished from drift boats, as do contestants in the annual One Fly Contest, held during the first week in September.

When river flows are around 1,400-cfs, it can be waded in some spots, but the gravel/cobble bottom can be unstable and wading should be restricted to knee-deep levels. About the middle of November, when skiing begins, the release from Lake Jackson is lowered in wet years to around 450-cfs, making for easy wading, with large terrestrial patterns fooling some of its fish at this time, but levels less than 450-cfs stress the fish and large winter kills of young fish usually occur.

The river's biggest cutthroat, more solitary than their smaller peers, hold in small sanctuaries adjacent to the power water, as well as in narrow chutes where the river gradient drops. They do so not only because more foods drift through these spots, but also because they seek cover from the many birds of pray that inhabit the Park.

Snake River cutthroats, a unique species called, "Fine Spotted Snake River Cutthroats," a fish accustomed to a short growing season, feed opportunistically and aggressively, preferring large to small foodstuffs, and, therefore, large attractors can bring them to the surface, the major reason dry fly enthusiasts should visit the Snake between late August and early November. It's one of only a few rivers in America where two-foot trout can be caught on dry flies. And the best fishing is midday because its cold waters need warming before the cutthroat actively feed.

We walked along the high banks looking for spots where we could climb down and wade, but the banks were either too steep or the power water ran adjacent to them and undercut the banks. Nevertheless, we could see large fish holding behind shoreline boulders and took turns casting to them from the high banks. Evidently, we didn't get good drifts casting from above because each fish rose about half way up to the fly and then dropped down to its holding position, all while drift boats and large touring rafts passed us by.

We also checked, but didn't fish, the river at Deadman's Bar, the scene of a triple murder in the gold rush days. Four men camped on the island, set up a sluice near the bar, and panned for gold. Several months later, one of the men showed up at a local ranch looking for work. When asked about his three companions, he replied that they'd gone hunting. The ranch owner became suspicious when the hunt lasted longer than usual trips. Eventually, a posse arrived because three bodies had been discovered weighted down with rocks at the edge of the river. The prospector claimed that he'd killed his companions in self-defense when they attacked him following an argument over finances. He had grubstaked the entire operation, but when their efforts turned sour, his partners turned on him to avoid paying their debts.

As discussed in Chapter Two, the trick to finding cutthroat is to locate them, as they don't hold in specific spots, but, instead, move about in search of food. In addition, in the section below Wilson Bridge, they school-up in slower waters next to long riffles. Once located, they usually strike attractors in large sizes, even when not rising. When one is caught in a spot, several others will usually be caught as well. Unfortunately, they can't always be located! On my family trip, also in late August, my boys had better luck than I by casting worms at the junctions of side channels and into deep holes off island points. No trout were interested in either my attractor pattern or my streamer. In fact, my boys wondered if there was a purpose to my fishing since I wasn't catching any fish. On numerous occasions, they offered me their poles out of sympathy for my situation.

During several afternoons on my trip with my family, I didn't catch a cutthroat over 12 inches below Wilson Bridge. My sons continued to catch larger ones on worms, but eventually became bored and found a spot in a side channel where they could jump into the water and float downstream to a shallow sand bar. Nevertheless, I enjoyed my efforts and believe that had I fished more of this stretch on my own, instead of helping to supervise the activities of our sons, I'd have caught some of the river's bigger fish.

The famous view from Snake River Overlook (Mike Zelie Photo)

Flat Creek

Jackson Hole provides a relatively unique fishing opportunity. Flowing from Gros Ventre Mountains, east of Jackson, and through the National Elk

Refuge in the South Park Feeding Ground, is a small creek called Flat Creek. Fly fishermen can fish the creek during the summer months after the elk have sought cooler, higher ground. Before an early settler dredged the creek and drained the marshland into which it flowed, the creek spread over the flat lands, but once marshlands no longer swallowed it up, it flowed into the Snake and cutthroats ascended its gentle gradient to spawn.

Following habitation degradation resulting from water diversion, the Jackson Hole Chapter of Trout Unlimited placed numerous boulders in the creek in the mid-1980s to create better spawning grounds for cutthroats, but, to everyone's surprise, some very large fish became permanent residents.

Several wooden bridges have been built over the creek, enabling access to different sections without climbing up and down the banks and contributing to soil erosion. The creek twists and turns on the flats near Jackson National Fish Hatchery, which can be visited daily and where, in addition to tanks teeming with fry, several aquariums display adult trout.

Unless there's a major rainstorm, Flat Creek is always clear and holding trout are easily seen from the banks. A careful approach is demanded; otherwise fish dart rapidly away and disappear into deep holes occupied by numerous whitefish. Morning fishing is required for dry flies because the hatches cease immediately with the arrival of prairie winds, usually around 10:30 in August. Because of its many dramatic twists and turns, anglers can find sections to fish where they can cast with the wind, but the winds usually push the fly away from holding trout.

Fish exceeding 20-inches inhabit the small creek, but they're not easily caught. In fact the 19-inch fish I spotted nymphing in shallow water next to the bank took my nymph imitation just as the creek's water began to cloud up after an hour of rain. Daniel Lamoreux wrote, in the Summer 2001 issue of

Buffalo Fork at Moran Junction

Northwest Fly Fishing, that fish over seven pounds are caught in the creek. I though they might be brood fish that escaped from the federal hatchery, but Howard Cole, of High Country Flies, assured me that they were wild fish.

One perk to fishing Flat Creek is that after the wind comes up, you can walk to the craft booths that open, on scheduled summer weekends, near the information center. Here the creek is damned and a small lake has formed. Along with other waterfowl, several pairs of trumpeter swans, less than 2,000 of which are left in the world, gracefully swim and feed along the pond's shoreline. These once endangered birds have wingspans up to seven feet.

One afternoon, I drove along Gros Ventre River up to Lower Slide Lake. The road was once part of an old entrance route to the valley used by mountain men and early explorers to cross, from the east, the Gros Ventre Mountains and the Wind River Range, first using Union Pass, located at the Continental Divide, just above the headwaters of the river. Jim Bridger, the famous mountain guide, used the trail to guide an Army Engineer exploration party from the east to the valley in 1860. Along the way, I was struck by the large boulders that doted the surrounding farmland.

Cutthroats inhabit Gros Ventre River, but because it was so shallow that August, it wasn't worth a try. To avoid high spring flows and to successfully spawn, most Snake River cutthroat migrate up tributaries, like the Gros Ventre, and don't return to the Snake until the water drops in early August, but even in the tributaries, young trout have a hard time, with over 50 percent of juveniles dying each year. If you want to catch large cutthroats in tributaries, a July visit is recommended, but fishing the Snake will be difficult.

Lower Slide Lake, a 1,300-acre lake, was created in 1925, when fifty million tons of stone and soil slid down the mountain and across the river at Gros Ventre Canyon, forming a natural dam. From the road, you can see the scar on the mountain's side, called Gros Ventre Slide. Unfortunately, a boat was needed to fish the lake, as the fish were deep and unlikely to rise along the shoreline. After enjoying a brief walk, I returned to Jackson. Later, I learned that Slide Lake was bigger when first created. After a period of stabilization, water began to seep from the dam at the same rate as it flowed in. A huge winter runoff in May resulted in water cresting at the dam and washing out part of its south end, causing a flood that wiped out the town of Kelly in the valley below. Six lives were lost and 30 families left homeless. The flood's waters deposited the large boulders I saw in the fields.

The Upper Green

Gannet Peak, the highest point in Wyoming, at 13,804 feet, is located at the north end of the Wind River Range, just west of the Continental Divide. Weaving its way down from this peak, the upper waters of Green River, discussed in Chapter Six, runs south through national forest lands from lower Green Lake to privately owned ranch lands, and then through public water to the Hamlet of Daniel. From Daniel, the river flows through private lands and is largely inaccessible to wading anglers. To access public water upstream from Daniel, I took Federal Hwy. 189/191 from Jackson and when I crossed the river, just east of Daniel, I took a dirt road north along the river. This section of the Green is called the Warren Bridge Easement and the U. S. Bureau of Land Management oversees it.

Approximately 10 miles of water upstream from Hwy. 189 are open to the public, with dozens of access points and a number of campsites along it. The trip from Jackson should take about an hour, unless you stop, like I did, and fish the riffles and deep pools of Hoback River, which parallels the highway. I'd recommend going straight to the Green in August, as my hour sojourn on the inviting Hoback resulted in one 10-inch cutthroat.

Anglers also can find spots to wade the Green in the section between Warren Bridge and Daniel. The Forty Road access has several sites that can be reached by turning off Hwy. 191, just north of Daniel, and following a dirt road to the access-sites just north of the hatchery. The dirt road then loops

back to the highway north of the Forty Road access. The river in this section offers excellent fishing for stocked rainbows, wild browns, and native cutthroats, but it receives heavy fishing pressure from guide boats. Anglers at our motel didn't catch any big fish near Warren Bridge, but the many fish they did catch readily took a dry fly, while floating anglers passed them by.

The angler wanting to avoid crowds can travel north and fish in the Bridger Teton National Forest, where 30 miles of the Green is open to the public. To reach this section, about five miles north of Daniel, turn east on the road to Cora and then north on Ct. Rd. 352 and drive 25 miles to the National Forest boundary.

Cutthroat from a Teton Park mountain stream

Good forest roads go to the lower end of the Green River Lakes and past campgrounds at Whisky Grove, located just below Kendall Warm Springs. The trout in this section are not large, but an angler I talked to enjoyed fooling 25 fish on the day he fished this water.

During the summer of 2000, Scott Daniels and his son, Matthew, fished the upper Green before they hiked into Wind River Wilderness to fish some mountain lakes. In addition to good fishing, they also felt the spirit of Sacagawea, the Shoshone wife of French Canadian trapper, Toussaint Charbonneau, who, along with Sacagawea, guided Lewis and Clark on their journey to the Pacific Coast. The explorers specifically wanted Sacagawea to accompany them to facilitate their contacts with Shoshone in Montana. Although Sacagawea reportedly died in 1812, in Omaha, a woman claiming to be she was found living with the Wind River Shoshone. This woman died in 1884, and if she were Sacagawea, she would have been nearly 100 years old!

South Fork Snake River

In August, the South Fork of the Snake, the name given the Snake between Paradise Reservoir and its junction with the Henry's Fork below Rexburg, Idaho, flows out of Paradise Reservoir to irrigate downstream farmland. I drove along its northeast side for several miles, looking for a place where I could wade it, but it was too deep. I returned to the dam, crossed over it, and fished flooded backwaters on the southwest bank just below the dam, where I fooled several fat cutthroat short-sticking weighted nymphs. I returned the next evening with my son, Marten, and we both lost fish exceeding 20 inches that raced into the fast water flowing from the dam. Marten was so shook up by one fish that he handed me his rod and was surprised when I simply watch the fish strip the backing until it broke off.

On our departure from Jackson Hole Airport, I talked to a young angler who'd spent three days with his dad fishing the South Fork and staying at Swan Valley Lodge. He and his dad caught trout up to two feet, but he didn't enjoy it much. They floated to a hole, anchored, and cast large, weighted Woolly Buggers on 0X tippets into the hole's depths. When a big fish was hooked, the guide admonished them if it wasn't rapidly brought to the net, concerned that once it got into the current, the long fight to retrieve it would kill it. The young angler said that horsing in fish wasn't his cup of tea. He would like to come back during a month when the water level was low and he could cast dry flies to these big fish.

Unfortunately, times when the river is low are few and far between! In early summer, the reservoir is still full from winter runoff and water releases create high water conditions. When the runoff is over, large volumes of water are released for irrigation. I would imagine that early spring and late fall would be the best times to fish it. The river averages about 7,000 trout per mile, but if the water is high when you arrive, you can fish the Gray's and Salt rivers, rivers that empty into the reservoir from Wyoming. Both rivers have good populations of resident fish and big wild browns move up these rivers from the reservoir to spawn.

Accommodations and Other Activities

It goes without saying that there's a lot to do in Jackson Hole. My family took horseback rides, mountain bike tours, and shopped in local craft stores. We went white water rafting on the lower Snake and hiked some of the 200 miles of the well-marked trails in Grand Teton National Park. I'll never forget our hike up the Cascade Canyon Trail west of Jenny Lake. The views of Teewinot Mountain and Mount Owens in this glacially sculpted backcountry were spectacular.

Both Leigh and Jenny lakes were named after a local trapper, Richard Leigh, better known as "Beaver Dick," and his wife, Jenny. Leigh had guided a group of governmental surveyors through the area in 1876 and, in appreciation for his effort, they named one lake after him and another after his wife. Later, Jenny, and all of their five children, died from smallpox.

One plus was that I found a river guide who took four of us on a float trip for a reasonable price and I had plenty of time to fish alone in majestic surroundings without alienating Melody, perhaps making up for trip's cost.

My son, Mason, floating a mild rapid while I cast into the slack water

Chapter Nine
San Juan River
Rainbows on the Flats

Anglers return to the San Juan year after year. For many, it's the only river they fish. They make an annual trip to this red and rugged country, first populated by the Ancient Pueblos, and rarely fish anywhere else. When checking in at Abe's Fly Shop and Motel, I talked with a Californian who proudly informed me that, for the last five years, his only serious fishing was during his week's vacation at Abe's. I asked him why he repeatedly came to the San Juan, a stocked trout stream, when excellent wild rainbow rivers, like the McCloud, were in his home state. He replied, "Yes, there are good rivers in the High Sierra, but none like the San Juan!" Not only had he never fished the McCloud, but he also didn't know where it was located! I subsequently asked him about the Fall and Hat rivers, rivers fished regularly by my Uncle, but he only shook his head in puzzlement! I learned that many San Juan enthusiasts are similarly uninformed. Their attitude seems to be, "Why learn about other places when the San Juan is so good?"

Many anglers fish the San Juan because they first learned to handle a fly rod in its waters. But few are locals. The opportunity to catch big rainbows, like the one depicted in the movie, *A River Runs Through It*, attracted them to it and they hired a guide who taught them to fish it with nymphs. Abe, who operated a gas station and the areas only post office before the dam was built, had 19 guides in his employ during our stay and we saw three other fly shops in the area. Michael Shook, author of, *San Juan River Fly Fishing Guide*, states that 20 licensed outfitters operate on the river, with some employing a dozen guides, quite a lot for a seven-mile stretch of water.

The San Juan River in the first few miles below the 400 foot high Navajo Dam is too cold for mayflies, but it's full of midges. Trout feed all day long on midge larvae and pupae in the 40 to 44 degree water below the dam, rarely coming to the surface to take an adult fly. For this reason, nymph fishing with midge imitations in the first few miles is the preferred angling method. In fact, I never met so many fishermen on a river who admitted they fished only nymphs and didn't know how to fish a dry fly!

I could understand this phenomenon if anglers came only from Southern Colorado, Arizona, New Mexico, Southern Utah or the nearby states of Texas, Oklahoma, or Kansas. A number of fair trout streams meander through the mountains above this dry and arid desert country, such as the Dolores and Rio Grande in Colorado and the Upper Pecos in New Mexico, but there are no "blue ribbon" trout streams and, therefore, the San Juan would be the best place to learn to fly fish. Anglers are so desperate for trout fishing in this region that New Mexico stocks trout in their warm water streams in the winter in order to create winter-season, put-and-take trout fishing.

The most popular hole on the San Juan, the Texas Hole, was named after the large number of Texans who visit the river and fish this long, deep pool. Nevertheless, I met nymph-only anglers from all over the country—anglers completely unaware that their sport evolved after debates over the ethics of fishing with nymphs between two early twentieth century, English chalk stream anglers, G. E. M. Skues, a nymph enthusiast, and F. M. Halford, a dry-fly purist. Skues had been a student of Halford, considered the father of dry fly fishing because he wrote the first definitive book on the topic, and he was so concerned about Halford's negative judgments that he fished wet flies in secret for many years. Only after Sir Edward Grey, one of the youngest men to ever win a parliament seat and who later became England's Foreign Secretary, included a chapter on wet fly fishing in his 1899 book, *Fly Fishing*, did Skues assert his views about using nymphs just before a hatch. Nevertheless, he still entitled his book, *Minor Tactics of the Trout Stream*.

For many San Juan Fishermen, nymph fishing isn't a minor, or even a major, tactic—it's the only tactic. I had a conversation with a young man from Wisconsin who hadn't heard of the rivers I named in his state and who was surprised when I added that steelhead are caught in Wisconsin rivers. He didn't know that steehead inhabited Lake Michigan! In fact, he said he never fishes in Wisconsin, but instead fishes only in the West. This was his second trip to the San Juan and he had never cast a dry fly in his life. A guide had taught him how to nymph fish on his first trip to the San Juan, and he'd applied this learning to other western rivers.

The young man from Wisconsin would be glad to know that E. R Hewitt, perhaps the first to design and fish nymphs in this country, considered nymph fishing more difficult than dry fly fishing. He said he could make a man a reasonably good dry fly fisherman in several weeks, but that it would take

New Mexico's San Juan River with Navajo Dam on the right

him a year to produce a good nymph fisherman, claiming that most anglers use the wrong nymph, in the wrong place, with the wrong motion. On the San Juan, however, Hewett's tutoring would be wasted because only imitations of midge pupae and *Baetis* nymphs are useful.

My first visit to San Juan was in August of 2000 with Bob and Tom. We arrived at Albuquerque early Sunday afternoon, left for the river on Federal Hwy. 550 in our rented car, and stopped for a lunch of excellent burritos in the town of Cuba. In the restaurant men's room, a dispenser sold prophylactics that glowed in the dark, but it was empty, hopefully a sign that we'd have a "glowing experience" on the river. We stopped in the supermarket at Bloomfield to buy luncheon meat, cheese, crackers, soda and beer, took a county road off of Federal Hwy. 64 to Abe's Motel and Fly shop, checked in and unpacked our bags, and went to the river in search of an evening hatch.

Bob and his father fished the San Juan in 1994 and Bob caught a 24-inch rainbow and a 22-inch brown. His father also caught some big fish and Bob said, "If my father can catch them, so can just about anybody." I asked Bob, a psychologist, if he'd resolved his Oedipal Conflict. He chuckled and replied, "You've never seen my father fish!" He also added that he lost two huge fish, explaining that because his backing was not securely fastened to the spool, the first fish stripped all of it off the reel and he watched it disappear downstream with his line. As his line floated downstream, an angler accidentally hooked it. Finding himself so attached, he put his rod down, and then, hand-over-hand, pulled in Bob's line with the huge fish still connected. The fish eventually broke off during these maneuvers, but the angler returned Bob's line. Bob told us that returning it was a wasted effort because the second fish also stripped off all his line and backing and, this time, no angler was nearby to retrieve it.

Tom and I asked him why he hadn't knotted the backing to the reel. He declared that his reel spool had a little notch to wrap the backing around before winding it on the reel. We asked why he didn't knot it instead of fastening it to this notch because, obviously, the notch didn't keep the backing securely attached. He replied that he'd been doing it this way for years and never had a problem. We countered that he'd never had a problem because he'd never hooked fish big enough to strip backing off the reel. He agreed, but remarked, "If the backing hadn't come off, the tippet would have broken and the fish lost anyway." We concurred, but asked Bob if it wasn't better to lose a fish than to lose his line and backing. He conceded the point, but joyfully added, "Had I done as you suggested, I wouldn't have this story to tell!"

Used to fishing among hemlocks, maples, and pines, I wasn't sure I'd like fishing in this dry and arid land, but I quickly became enchanted by its stark beauty as I scanned the cliffs along the river and the hills above them. The setting sun made the rocky cliffs to the east burst alive with dazzling reds, grays and rusts, while the shadows on the western cliffs made them appear black. I could visualize the Ancient Navajo making pottery in front of their pit-houses along the riverbanks.

At a spot called "Baetis Bend," where Bob fished on his 1994 visit and landed his biggest brown trout, we watched two anglers float nymph rigs, but there were plenty of fish rising and we hoped to catch them on dry flies. We left just before dark, anxious to fish the next day when our five-day fishing licenses took effect.

The next morning we ate a "Mexican" breakfast in the restaurant connected to Abe's Fly Shop and then went next door to see what flies staff recommended. I never saw so many tiny flies—flies with names as unusual as their colors. Upon close inspection, most were variants of the Brassie, with names such as Desert Storm, Green-Eyed Lady, Orange Larva, Phantom, Pink Panther, Princess, Red Hot, Red Larva, Triple Threat, Chocolate Triple Threat, RS-2, and WD-40. Others were flies I'd heard of, but had rarely used, such as Disco Midge and Midge Emerger. Bob and Tom bought the flies shop staff recommended, but I planned to use the same Brassies I used elsewhere.

We headed to a spot just below the catch-and-release section where Bob lost the two big rainbows on his first trip. The river valley was red in the morning sun and the long shadows made the landscape large and menacing. The cliffs looked like mountains and the narrow washes like giant valleys. Not a cloud tainted the bright blue sky.

Fish were tailing in the backwaters and I made the mistake of trying to catch them on a Griffith's Gnat. Cast after cast over these cruising fish produced no hits. British angler James Dickie once wrote, "The best way of dealing with tailing trout is to look for one which is not." I put on a small nymph and joined Bob and Tom, who were in deeper waters. Bob hooked two nice fish in the same spot where he'd lost his line and backing on his first trip, but all Tom and I got were some short hits in the rapids below Cable Hole, named after a cable over the river.

Browns Versus Rainbows

We returned to the car, eat our lunch, drove downstream, and finished our day at Baetis Bend. I understood how this spot got its name because each time I worked it, I fooled its fish on a #22 Blue-Winged Olive, but I hooked only one brown. Browns are born in the river, but all the rainbows are stocked. The state stocks more than 50,000 three-inch rainbows in the Quality Water, fish that grow to 16 or 17 inches in two years stuffing themselves with tiny midges, resulting in an estimated 20,000 to 25,000 adult fish per mile in the first four miles below the dam. They also stock more than 100,000 three-inch and 50,000 nine-inch rainbows in the "bait water" section that begins about four miles downstream from the dam.

Because fish eggs take forever to hatch in the cold water, mature fish eat most of them before they hatch. In fact, the fly shops sell a variety of egg imitations to use during the spawning season, which occurs in the late fall and early winter for both browns and rainbows. The numerous fishermen who wade through the spawning beds kill any eggs that aren't eaten. In 1996, the Department of Fish and game reported 72,500 anglers days and as many as 300 anglers at one time in the four miles of special regulation water.

In contrast, browns, which make up 80 percent of the trout below Aztec Bridge, successfully spawn in the lower sections of the Quality Water and in the river below this section. Michael Shook writes that lots of browns occupy

Bob, with a fish on in a shallow, flat water stretch of the Quality Water

the Quality Water, but that they're not caught with much regularity. He says that they "hold in different water and require different techniques than most anglers are familiar with." He doesn't say what these techniques are, however, although staff at one fly shop told us anglers from nearly every state come to toss big streamers at spawning browns in October, making it their busiest month of the year. If October is actually their busiest month, I wouldn't want to be there, but my bet is that their promotional efforts have few limits!

We caught nice fish in the late afternoon on small dry flies, with both Tom and Bob landing several browns, until a thunderstorm rolled in and we left. The first thunderhead to arrive was magnificent when silhouetted again the sun, but eventually the whole sky became dark and ominous.

The Value of Studded Wading Boots

On each trip we take together, Bob, who is a careful wader, goads Tom, an aggressive wader, about falling in the river. Tom falls in at least once on each of our annual trips while Bob claims to have never fallen. Whenever Tom slips or slides or actually falls in, Bob calls over, "I never fall in the water." On this trip, however, it was I who never fell in because I had studded wading boots, although I did fall several times walking the muddy-clay banks. Bob fell in at least twice and can no longer brag about his wading prowess.

The Sand Juan has a clay bottom in many section, and besides Tom and Bob, I witnessed a number of anglers fall. The clay simply gave way and their feet slid out from under them. Some were wading when they fell, but others, like Tom, were simply standing and casting. I watched one old timer, into a good fish, pitch face-forward into the river. Somehow, he managed to hold onto his rod and, after helped to his feet by nearby anglers, he found the big fish still hooked to his line. Shivering, he landed the fish to the applause of others. I heard him telling those alongside him that falling in the San Juan was a frequent occurrence and that he kept several changes of clothing in his car.

The Need for a Soft-Action Rod

After breakfast the next morning, we returned to waters just below the catch-and-release area, but this time I ignored the cruising fish in the quiet backwaters and headed downstream to the tailing fish in the long, flat, sandy-bottomed channel on the river's south side. I brought my Orvis Western Series fly rod (a nine-foot rod) rather than the eight-foot Sage rod I'd used the day before because I was worried that the smaller rod couldn't handle a really big fish. I saw no rising fish until I came to the end of the channel. Here, I cast to several different tailing fish and hooked two of them on a #24 midge. Each raced across the flats, reminding me of hooked bonefish in the Florida Keys, but as soon as the loose line had been taken out and the line pulled from the reel, both fish broke off. It was the fault of the unforgiving tip of the stiff rod;

I'd forgotten about the stiffness of Western Series rods!

I returned to using the Sage I purchased in the early 1980s (Generation I Graphite, 8-ft. rod for 5-wt. lines) and I didn't lose another fish on the initial surge during the remainder of the trip. In fact, Bob, using the same model Sage, and Tom, using a soft-action Orvis, also lost few fish once they were hooked. In contrast, I saw lots of anglers losing fish on their first run and wondered if our sport's current fascination with long, high modulas, fast-action rods, rods that throw tighter loops, didn't contribute to this problem.

That afternoon we hiked up to Texas Hole along a dirt road from the lower parking area at Baetis Bend, planning to spend the afternoon fishing our way back and remaining there to fish the evening hatch. We fished near Jack's Hole, noted in Michael Shook's fishing guide, but called Tim's Pool on the river map at Abe's. Perhaps they were neighboring pools. But regardless of its name, we caught many fish toward the tail of the pool in the quiet waters behind a huge boulder on the opposite bank, a spot where guide boats put the rising fish down when they pull into it and instruct clients to float nymphs along the seams of the fast water that run alongside the rock.

Catching fish rising in this protected water required long casts over deep, fast water. The drag-free float was a short one, even when vibrating the rod tip so the line would land in loops, called a "snake cast." Nevertheless, I hooked several fish; more often, however, I hooked the bushes behind me. When Tom arrived from upstream, I turned the water over to him and he responded by quickly catching several fish on a #22 Parachute Adams.

Bob caught two nice fish on a dry fly in the quiet shallow backwaters on our side of Jack's Hole, hooking them behind a small point of land immediately below Tom's back cast. Many fishermen walk through this water or stand in it when casting into faster water in the main channel, never realizing that big fish live by their feet. In the late afternoon, we returned to Baetis Bend and caught fish up to 19 inches on small dry flies until another late afternoon thunderstorm forced us off the river

Nymph Versus Dry Fly

The reader might wonder why we didn't switch to nymphs after witnessing others having better success with them. Being out-fished by anglers using nymph rigs, however, was our usual experience. In fact, when we first started fishing in the West in the early 1980s, we fished primarily with nymphs, placing them below weights and self-made strike indicators, because fighting big trout was an experience new to us.

My companions and I now have years of fishing behind us and although the fight of a strong fish is exciting, we've come to appreciate the early view of British angler F. M. Halford, who emphasized that fly fishing is about fooling fish rather than about catching then. Trout suck in and spit out lots of inedible objects that float by their holding spots and the hesitation of a strike indicator helps to hook them before they can spit out yours. In contrast, when fish come to the surface to take a fly, they think it's real. In addition, when they do so, there's nothing like their strike on the surface!

Imprinted Fish

On the third morning, Tom and I fished below Cable Hole. I put on a midge imitation after I saw a number of fish tailing in the quiet waters along a gravel bar. I stood above the bar and cast downstream to them, nicking one and getting a refusal from another. The three fish then stopped rising and I thought I'd spooked them. Resting the spot, I happened to glance down at my feet, clearly visible in the gin-clear water, and saw three trout feeding on nymphs stirred up by my wading. I first thought that the three fish were the ones I'd just cast to, but I rejected that notion because it defied my experience. After resting the spot, the three fish failed to reappear along the bar. Two other fish were rising about 10 yards below the spot where the first three had risen. I moved downstream to cast to these two. They, too, disappeared after several casts. Looking down, I now saw five trout holding by my feet and realized that my fleeting hypothesis was actually true!

Fish in this stretch had learned to seek out wading fly fishermen and to feed at their feet. Aware of this fact, I looked down at my feet more often and discovered that almost everywhere I went in the upper Quality Water fish followed me around, sometimes as many as a dozen at one time. No wonder the San Juan shuffle, now illegal, was invented here. Fishermen would stir up the water and then dap their nymphs to catch the fish at their feet.

From this time forward, I cast only to fish up and across the stream from me—fish that couldn't learn where I was and come to feed at my feet and leave me casting over empty waters! Nevertheless, the rainbows, that followed me around like newly hatched goslings followed the biologist Konrad Lorenz, were difficult to fool when feeding in waters above me.

At the end of the morning, we compared notes. None of us had hooked a fish using nymphs below strike indicators, while other fishermen around us had done well with this technique. Earlier in the morning, I'd watched a rank beginner, under the watchful eye of a guide, land three fish within his first half hour on the water. We knew we were doing something wrong! I remarked that perhaps the # 20 Brassie I was using was too big. Tom replied that this might be true for me, but he was using a rig recommended by staff in Abe's Fly Shop, a #24 WD-40, with a # 28 Sparkling Midge trailer.

More on Jack's Hole

In 1983, Jack's Hole was named after Jack Samson, former Editor-in-Chief of *Field & Stream*, who grew up in New Mexico fishing the Pecos and Rio Grande Rivers. One October evening in 1999, fishing with Chuck Rizuto, a personal friend and San Juan River guide since the early 1970s, Jack reportedly landed 30 large trout on a #12 Back Wooly Worm in one hour from the deep water and the end of the hole. Nevertheless, I think the story is exaggerated because it takes longer than two minutes to land a big fish.

Jack finds it distasteful to fish with minuscule nymphs below strike indicators, preferring the sudden, exciting strike to a larger fly. He likes to throw weighted, egg sucking leech patterns, on sinking tip lines, into deep, slow-moving channels, or into portions of pools where the water shelves off over a sandy bottom. He lets his flies swing across the current in a dead drift, with the fish hitting them hard just as they complete the swing. I didn't fish in this fashion because I'd taken large fish in other rivers with this technique. Living in Santa Fe, Jack considers the San Juan his home river, but I'd traveled to this desert river to catch large fish on small dry flies and I worked for rising fish whenever I could, which was most of the time.

Because of rain the previous evening, the water was slightly higher. Tom fished Jack's Hole by himself because he was several inches taller than we were and his back cast cleared the bushes on the bank behind him. He fooled 13 fish in the calm waters behind the rock that day, six in the afternoon on a #22 parachute Adams, with a #24 Chocolate Triple Threat trailing behind it (most hit the Adams), and 7 in the evening on a #18 Pale Morning Dun Emerger. His largest fish was just under 20-inches. Bob and I changed the name of the pool from Jack's Hole, to Tom's Spot.

One of Tom's rainbows caught in Jack's Hole

Midges Along the Shoreline

I walked downstream to the flats below Jack's Hole, but fish weren't tailing there today so I went further downstream where fish were taking emerging nymphs in slow waters along the bank. Most ignored my surface fly, but I managed to hook and net three that, unlike the others, occasionally stuck their snouts above water to sip a surface fly. Eventually, I ignored the tailing fish and waited until I saw a head break the surface.

I was fishing my way upstream to the better holding water at a small bend, when a young angler appeared, walked out on the point of land at the bend, and cast a nymph rig into the fast water that caused the nymph to swing into the backwater below. I watched him land three nice rainbows from this water, with the last fish landed the strongest of the three. He placed the fish on his net, returned it, and yelled to me that this was the biggest fish he'd ever caught. I took his remark as an invitation to join him.

I stopped fishing, walked upriver to where he was fishing, and measured the distance he'd marked on his net handle. He thanked me, remarking that he thought the fish was bigger then it measured because it fought so well. He also reported that he'd seen me catch several nice fish and wondered what I was using. When I replied, he remarked that someday he would like to learn to fish with a dry fly—another example of a San Juan fisherman!

The Value of a Guide

In spite of my comments in Chapter One, and humbled by our relatively unsuccessful nymph fishing, I hired a guide for the morning to show us how to nymph-fish the river, remembering the saying, attributed to Ben Franklin, that, "A man who teaches himself has only a fool for a teacher." Between us, we had more than 100 years of fishing experience, but nymph fishing near Cable Hole had made fools of us. We asked the guide to take us to the very section below Cable Hole where we'd been skunked previously.

The guide, Eric Taylor, a young man, had been guiding on the river for two years. He came as a visitor, enjoyed the area, quit his desk job, and stayed to guide for Abe's. He and his roommate, also a guide, rented a small house 20 minutes from the river in Aztec. He rigged us up with the proper equipment, replacing our 10-ft. leaders with 7.5-ft ones, my small weights with tiny split shots, and my tiny flies with tinier ones. I hadn't realized that the barely visible flies sticking to my waders were the flies to imitate, nor did I realize that midges were that small.

We learned from Eric that the key to hooking fish on the flats was mending the line. Although Michael Snook emphasized, in his river guide, the necessity of drag free floatation of the fly, reading about proper presentation and seeing it demonstrated were two different things. Eric didn't throw just one upstream-mend in the line, but constantly flipped loops as the fly floated downstream, and as it floated by, he would throw downstream loops. He said that numerous loops on the water were necessary to keep these tiny flies floating drag-free throughout their float. Although the numerous loops on the water sometimes impeded hook setting, without them there would be no hook in a fish to set! "Tight Lines" was not the catchphrase in this water!

Eric also advised us to focus on a specific fish, visible in the shallow water, rather than blindly casting into runs in the main stem, as many other anglers were doing, and as we had done on the three previous days. He said many fish were caught this way, with the correct imitation, the right number of small weights, and a drag-free float, but he felt the real challenge was catching a specific fish. Consequently, he had us locate and cast to fish that were feeding in the slow moving, flat waters, rather than in the deeper runs and pools. And because the fish were not easily spooked from their feeding lanes, our casts to them were no more than 10 to 15 feet.

Once we knew what was required, we not only caught fish, but we caught specific fish. In fact, floating tiny nymphs to visible trout in the shallow waters below the dam and, later in the day, casting tiny dry flies to rising trout is the chief reason to choose the San Juan over other rivers. Although I've cast nymphs to visible pods of fish in the Green, Bighorn, and Yellowstone rivers, the experience wasn't comparable. In the San Juan many rainbow feed in knee-deep water. Looking for the big ones, short casting to them, and then watching them jump and race across the flats is an experience difficult to duplicate elsewhere. After Eric's tutoring, I landed five big fish, fought and lost three more, and briefly hooked several others, all while casting tiny flies to selected fish. After a while I didn't care if I landed the fish. Donald V. Roberts put the feeling best when he wrote, in *Flyfishing Still Waters*:

> I lift the rod and pull down on the line at the same instant. Everything changes to a blur; events cannot be separated out; nothing is really clear. It is that moment of automatic, non-thinking, total abandonment to the sensations of struggle that makes fly fishing a universal and attractive enigma. It doesn't matter whether I caught the trout. A narration of the final bout is irrelevant, if not a squandering of words. It would reduce the final plot to formula conflict, to competition, to a story requiring resolve.

Tom and Bob each caught over a half a dozen specific fish. Bob also caught the biggest fish of the trip, a rainbow just over 22 inches. He admitted, however, that he'd caught it by following his grandfather's advice, "Never take a nymph imitation from the water." The fish hit the nymph when Bob was walking upstream dragging his line behind him. We took a picture of the fish and Eric asked us to send him a copy, stating that it was "one in a thousand." In his two years of guiding on the river during a year-round angling season, he'd seen only four fish landed that size. Here was an honest professional! Although the San Juan has lots of big rainbows, the majority of anglers catch those less than 20 inches. The beautiful rainbow mounted in the restaurant connected with Abe's Motel is only 21 inches. I know, because I measured it when no one was looking; Bob had said that his 22-inch fish was bigger and I didn't believe him.

I should remark, however, that the need to repeatedly mend line may be unique to the shallow catch-and-release area and the flats just below. Anglers in deeper sections used straight-line nymph techniques and caught many fish, as did Bob, on his first trip to the river in September, and Scott, who fished the river in May. Scott reported that fish moved a considerable distance to

Tom working for visible fish on the flats

suck in his nymph and he didn't dramatically mend his line.

On our ride back to Abe's, I asked Eric if he preferred instructing beginning or experienced anglers. He said he preferred beginners because experienced anglers often resisted his suggestions, thinking that they knew it all. I said that we could understand his feelings because, after all, we knew it all, except for what he taught us!

We asked Eric where we might find good mayfly activity and he suggested the lower end of the Quality Water above the Gravel Hole where the water was warmer. After lunch, we walked along the steep banks in this section, descending to fish the riffles, but only saw small fish rising sporadically and only a few holding in the waters along the bank. This section of the river looked like it would have been less affected by floodwaters before construction of Navajo Dam and I wondered if the Ancient Navajo had lived here, surrounded by cliffs bathed in golden light.

The Ancient Ones

The Clovis-Paleo Indians discovered the plains of New Mexico 10,000 years before the birth of Christ. Their descendants were called the "Anasazi" and they gradually switched from being hunters and gatherers to farmers, building stone and adobe cities up to the 13th century. Their cities remain, but there's no record of Anasazi culture in the United States after the early 1200s. They're believed to be ancestors of today's Pueblo tribes and are often referred to as "Ancestral Pueblo."

The Anasazi hunted and farmed the canyons and mesa tops. They grew in numbers and built great stone dwellings using stone tools. For many years, anthropologists believed they lived an idyllic life in peaceful harmony with the arid but beautiful environment until the Spanish Conquistadors arrived and destroyed their peace. This belief was simply not true! The Anasazi first built on mesa tops, concerned about marauding foragers. When they felt stronger, they built pit houses, fortified by walls, along the rivers, but as marauding groups became stronger, some moved from the river valleys into cliff dwellings.

The pillaging followed a cold period around A. D. 1200 that caused crop loss and famine. The more organized groups moved to fortified dwellings to better defend themselves against looters of stored food. To discourage the more determined looters, homes were built into cliff faces and under great ledges. Eventually, those Anasazi surviving the prolonged inter-group warfare abandoned their cliff dwellings, moved northeast, and built pueblos along Rio Grande River. Others moved to Chaco Canyon, 70 miles south of Farmington, where a warlord group established order and where the Ancestral Pueblo thrived as an advanced civilization between A.D. 900 and 1125.

Chaco Canyon's buildings were not pueblos—that is, independent farming villages—but rather public buildings, warehouses, and palaces within a larger city that encompassed a central precinct of four square miles. The walls of their structures were built by astronomer-priests to align with shadows caused by the solstice of the sun or by lunar standstills. Such an effort requires waiting almost two decades because, in its orbits around the earth, the moon rises each month at different points on the skyline, with the points ranging from north to south during a cycle lasting almost 19 years. The northernmost and southernmost risings are called "lunar standstills," and no other known civilization has aligned building walls with the shadows they cast.

Some anthropologists believe that the 600 room, multistoried rock and flagstone structure at Pueblo Bonito in the canyon, that took many years to build, housed up to 5,000 villagers during the 12th century, but others place the figure for year-round residents at closer to 1,000, claiming that the population increased temporarily during annual pilgrimages from outlying pueblos.

A hierarchical social system undetected in other Anasazi societies is reflected in the communal endeavors at Chaco Canyon. The settlements in the canyon were part of an integrated system of cooperating communities, as roads led to as many as 75 "outliers," which produced and assembled goods for local consumption and for distribution over a 30,000 square mile area.

There is little evidence of warfare at Chaco, which was unfortified, or in the larger realm. Village warfare and raiding may have ceased when grim and oppressive rules were issued from Pueblo Bonito. Order among the pueblos may have been maintained by violence, including human sacrifice and ritual cannibalism. Rock art throughout the southwest depicts warriors with large shields that covered their torsos from thigh to neck.

Some evidence suggests that a group of warrior-cultists, perhaps a group

Quiet backwater channels where stealth and a delicately presented fly are needed and where short-stick nymph fishermen are absent

of Toltecs, displaced after their war with the Aztecs, fled from Mexico to the region, terrorized the local farming populace into submission, and developed a hierarchical social system like the one they had in Mexico. The Mexican cultists may have been the elusive force behind the rise of the Chaco Canyon culture. The canyon was abandoned around A.D. 1125, with some anthropologists asserting that the dwellers left after a major drought, initially relocated along the San Juan River, and then moved south to Mexico.

The Islands on the Upper Flats

On our last evening, we made the mistake of fishing among the islands in the upper flats below the dam, a section Bob had not visited on his previous trip. Actually, I made the mistake because Bob and Tom, unknown to me, had left the stretch after seeing the crowds. The section above the boat ramp was full of anglers, with many casting nymphs in a run called "Kiddy Pool," located just above the boat ramp. The water in the islands of the upper flats was very shallow and almost all the runs were occupied by at least one angler. When exploring this area, I felt like I was on a miniature golf course. Anglers stood in ankle-deep water, bent over and gazing downward, with their rods extending out from their bodies, flipping their lines into shallow water.

The stretch is easily accessed and easily waded, but a difficult one in which to spot feeding fish. I located one small hole, better described as a slight indentation in the river bottom, below a little riffle, but its two occupants moved away each time my yarn indicator drifted over them. I switched to a squeeze-on foam indicator, and then to no indicator at all, but I could interest neither of these fish and, annoyed by my offerings, they left the little hole. I also left the hole and, after winding my way southwest among the numerous small islands, ended back at the boat ramp.

Anglers in the Kiddy Pool were lined up on each side of a small run on the north side of the channel. It looked like the line up on New York's Salmon River during the fall Chinook salmon run. There must have been 20 fishermen in a 15-yard section, many of them elderly because it was easy wading. They could have clasped arms and did a line dance and there was enough yarn floating to knit a sweater for Shaquille O'Neal.

I took a position downstream from the chorus line, where fish were tailing to emerging midges, but occasionally one would gulp down an adult fly from the surface. The anglers ignored the tailing fish and continued to stand side by side, flipping their weighted rigs into the main channel. I targeted the biggest tailing fish immediately downstream from them, planning to drop a pupa imitation just upstream from it that would drift down and, hopefully, be mistaken by the fish for one that rose from the weed bed.

When I cast upstream to these fish, the line of elderly anglers moved in unison downstream and cast their nymph rigs over them. The rule here was the motto of the Three Musketeers, "All for one and one for all," and I was not a Musketeer! Mildly annoyed, I spotted a fish's snout in the slow water on the south bank, where no one was fishing. I moved over to that bank and began casting upstream. The snout appeared again, this time sucking in my fly, but it was only a small fish—my first fish under 12 inches in five days of fishing. As greater numbers of fish began to rise, anglers began to leave the water; the first time I'd ever seen anglers leave with fish rising all around them. After noting my puzzled expression, one remarked, "We don't catch many when they're taking flies on the surface. It's your turn now."

I took four small fish above a sandbar on a midge imitation, with the largest only 14-inches—a good fish on any river but the San Juan. It jumped high in the air, four times in approximately the same place. Tom, who'd come to fetch me, had a good laugh at the expense of this fish, one that jumped upstream, but got nowhere! I did hook a big fish on my next cast, but it got off. I decided it was my last cast and a fitting way to end the trip.

Reflecting On Our Experience

Although the rainbows fought amazingly well for stocked fish, Bob thought the stream-born browns fought better. I caught only one brown and its fight was not so hot. When I got back home, I talked to Scott who'd visited the river in May. He caught no browns, but felt that the Bighorn's stocked rainbows fought better than those in the San Juan, but that the darting runs of rainbows in the San Juan's upper flats couldn't be duplicated elsewhere— that's the experience that would bring me back to this desert river. I can catch bigger rainbows in the Bow and harder fighting rainbows in the Delaware, but I cannot catch them by sight fishing with tiny flies in shallow water.

Looking upstream from Baetis Bend

Perhaps I could have caught the large rainbows in the Green, those that held in the shallow back waters, but ignored our skating Spiders, had I used Eric's multiple-mending technique, but I don't think they would've fought like those inhabiting the San Juan flats.

If you plan on visiting the river, I suggest reading Michael Snook's book, as well as any material you can find on *Baetis* and midge fishing. If you have access to back issues of *Fly Fisherman*, Ed Engle wrote, "Midges for Smutting Risers," in the December 1994, issue and Neal Steek wrote "Autumn Olives" and "*Baetis* Spinners," in the December 1988 and March 1995 issues. You can also critique your line mending skills and use of strike indicators by reviewing Bob Krum's "Water Mends" and Dick Hickson's, "Strike Indicator Tricks" in the September 1993 and July 1994 issues.

Eric Pepper wrote an article on the San Juan that appeared in the September 1993 issue of *Fly Fisherman*. In response to Pepper's article, an angler wrote a cryptic letter to the editor about the river, complaining about the swarms of anglers, the many tired fish, and the rude drift boat guides. Some of the fish did fight poorly, but most fought better than I expected from stocked fish in a river without particularly strong currents. In fact, Tom lost a strong 19-inch rainbow at Jack's Hole that he caught three hours later after a fight equal to its first one. Tom learned it was the same fish when he found two other flies attached to it. The two flies were the Parachute Adams and Sparkle Midge trailer he used in the hole earlier in the day!

Nor did the drift boats really bother us. Several boats stopped in the backwater behind the large white boulder at Jack's Hole, but their occupants cast nymphs into the fast water and left shortly thereafter to anchor downstream, where no wading angler was fishing. The rainbows rose again shortly after the boat left and Tom landed several.

If an angler wants to completely avoid drift boats, he or she can fish above Texas Hole, where they're not allowed, but where lots of wading anglers congregate. There are so many fish in this river that anglers annoyed by those lacking proper etiquette can simply move a short distance away and find equally big fish. Working hard for visible fish creates it own brand of solitude and other nearby anglers go unnoticed.

Since this trip with my angling companions, I've vacationed in the area with my wife and fished the river while she did artwork. I caught a number of fish on dry flies in the tail of Texas Hole while anglers in drift boats continued drifting nymphs through the long pool, rowing up the pools south side and drifting down its north side, like swimmers sharing a lane in a swimming pool. All the anglers in each boat watched me land fish after fish, but none stopped to cast dry flies, content to continue deepwater nymphing.

On one trip, I explored the numerous back channels, using a 7-ft., 3-wt. rod and had the time of my life loosing and landing big fish on this light rod. I also learned that my wife shouldn't accompany me to do artwork on the picnic tables placed at the beginnings of several trails to the river. At one spot, she had to entertain a local weirdo until I returned. In the evening, at the more populated tables at Texas Hole, where a weirdo would be less of a problem, the mosquitoes were so thick that heavy applications of bug spray didn't deter them and when the wind howled, the swarms looked like blowing snow.

Some day I might fish the river in the winter. The canyon receives an average of 325 days of sunshine a year, water releases remain stable, and the river never ices over, making the San Juan pleasant to fish in the early winter when many of its rainbows spawn and its mosquitoes sleep. January temperatures average 43 degrees during the day and 17 degrees at night.

Scott Daniels visited the river for one day in 2008, leaving his wife to enjoy Old Town in Albuquerque. He entered the river at Baetis Bend, where fish began rising at dusk, but darkness came quickly and it hid the opening to the trail back to his car. Alone on the river, he spent an hour pushing apart bushes in an effort to find the trail. He finally decided he'd better work his way through them, but many could not be penetrated, forcing him to return to the river and start again in another section.

Three hours later he came to the road. After walking back to his car, he began the three-hour drive to Albuquerque. His plane was scheduled to leave Albuquerque in the early morning, but he had no cell phone, couldn't find a payphone and, therefore, couldn't alert his wife to his predicament. He didn't get back to his motel until an hour and a half before his flight, to the relief of his worried wife.

Accommodations

There are numerous motels in Farmington and Aztec, about 20 minutes southwest of the river. Some, such as the Anasazi Inn (505-325-4564), where Melody and I stayed on my second trip, have relatively low rates if rooms are booked and paid for well in advance. If you want to be close to the river, Abe's Motel and Fly Shop (505-632-2194) and Rizuto's San Juan River Lodge (505-632-1411) are located in the hamlet of Navajo Dam, but only two places to eat exist there, the restaurant attached to Abe's and the Sportsman's Inn, located up the road behind Abe's.

RV and trailer parking sites are available at both Abe's and the Sportsman's Inn. Campers can stay at Cottonwood Campgrounds, about a quarter of a mile below the quality stretch on the north side of the river. When we were there in August, the campground was deserted, but we saw several anglers fighting fish in waters just above the campground.

Other Activities

As I discussed earlier, the San Juan River was the home of the Ancient Ones, referred to as the Anasazi or Ancestral Pueblo—the first Native Americans to occupy this region. Far downstream from good trout fishing, their artwork can be observed at a large pictograph panel at Lower Butler Wash. Other Native Americans migrated to the region, with the last group arriving around the 1500s. They included the Athapascan, most notably the Apache and Navajo, and the Ute tribes. The Spanish explorers followed and those that settled, with the help of their soldiers, subjugated the Native Americans to their rule and established their own cultural centers.

As a result, the Four Corners has a rich cultural, historical, and geological past. At Four Corners Monument in Ship Rock, New Mexico, four states meet at right angles. Here the angler and his family can stand in Arizona, Colorado, Utah, and New Mexico all at the same time. The Gateway Museum and Visitors Center in Farmington is the information gateway to the Four Corners. Special presentations by local artists and craftspeople, as well as lectures and demonstrations, take place at the center throughout the year.

Other activities include visiting the ancient Native American cities, probing the wonders of the world's only Uranium mining museum, or attending a hot air balloon festival. I know of no place where an angler can combine outstanding fishing with such a diverse range of nearby attractions. Before planning a trip, obtain a copy of *New Mexico Vacation Guide* from the State Department of Tourism and plot out a travel plan. There is so much to see and do in the Four Corners that choices should be made before arrival because one attraction can be easily missed on the way to visit another.

Chapter Ten

Bow River
One Beyond Compare

Melody took my 81-year old mother-in-law, Rose, to Sicily in August of 1997. Her mother, Teresa, came to America with her husband and sisters as a young adult pregnant with Rose. Neither she, nor her husband, ever returned to Sicily, and Rose never visited or corresponded with her relatives who remained there. In the spring of 1997, Melody wrote to the Italian Consulate in New York to ask their help in locating her Sicilian relatives. They, in turn, suggested she write the Mayor of Ragusa, the town from which Theresa had immigrated.

With the help of a friend, who could write in Italian, Melody asked for the mayor's help in locating relatives of Rose who might still live in Ragusa. Time past, with no reply from the mayor, and shortly before her departure for Italy, Melody wrote the mayor again, giving the date of her arrival in Sicily and the name of the hotel where she and Rose would be staying.

After the long trip from Rome to Ragusa, they arrived at their hotel just before bedtime. Shortly after settling in, the front desk called, but the desk clerk didn't speak English. Rose was in bed, so Melody hastily dressed and went down to the lobby where people were milling around.

With the help of several members of an international soccer team, who spoke some English, Melody learned that her relatives were waiting in the lobby. When she introduced herself to the first one who stepped forward, she learned that all the people in the lobby, except for the soccer players, were her relatives—all 37 of them! Most were Guastellas, offspring of Rose's paternal uncle. Although related to Teresa by marriage, the older Guastellas remembered her mother well, and since the mayor's contact, they'd been looking forward to meeting her daughter, Rose, and granddaughter, Melody. Once and Italian always an Italian! Since this trip, Melody has remained in touch with her newly discovered cousins in Sicily, and, as a result, has a much larger family.

What does this story have to do with fishing? Well, I'll tell you. Not even close to being of Italian descent, I decided to fish during the second week of their trip. I'd been impressed by images of the Bow River in the TV mini-series *Lonesome Dove*, and using my charge-card-earned airline miles, I flew to Calgary to fish its famous waters, and perhaps the Crowsnest River, some two hours south of it, discussed in the next chapter.

Big wild browns can be caught in the Bow in the City of Calgary, but I fished below Hwy. 22X, south of the city, where rainbows predominate, descendents of a steelhead strain stocked years ago. Using the *Yellow Pages*, I located the closest fly shop to my motel. It was Country Pleasures, located on Macleod Trail South. My motel, Denny's Restaurant, and Country Pleasures were all on Macleod Trail South, a road that joined Hwy. 2, the Deerfoot Trail, which linked me to the river, making things easy. Country Pleasures turned out to be Jim McLennan's shop. In preparation for my trip, I'd read his article "Bow River Update" in the July 1992 issue of *Fly Fisherman*. He also wrote *Blue Ribbon Bow* in 1987, which I hadn't read, five years after opening Country Pleasures.

At the shop, I bought a five-day Canadian fishing license and the *Bow River Angling Map*, prepared by the Bow River Chapter of Trout Unlimited, which covers the river from Bearspaw Dam, above Calgary, to Carseland, close to 50 miles downstream from the city. I also bought an autographed copy of McLennan's latest book, *Trout Streams of Alberta*, but I didn't read much of it until my trip was over; it's just as well because Jim strongly recommends employing a guide, writing, "Many anglers will continue to struggle with the Bow below Calgary, particularly if they fish it alone. I know of no other stream where up-to-date local help is so necessary." Being alone, I was unwilling to pay for a guide. I'd flown for free, was spending $40 dollars a night for lodging, eating at Denny's, where unlimited soda refills was the practice, and using my own flies. Consequently, the cost of a guide seemed out of proportion to my other costs—it would have been more than the cost of my entire trip!

The first spot McLennan recommended was "Madison Run," reached by driving south on Hwy. 2, the main highway out of town, east on Hwy. 22X, and then south on 168th Street East, a gravel road located next to an abandoned airfield, but, if it wasn't for one lone, dark hanger, I wouldn't have known it was an airfield. Highway 22X, a long, straight, deserted road at that time, ran through sparsely populated plains country and the few small houses

The beginning of the trail down to Madison Run

on the graveled side streets had lonely stretches between them. I assumed they gave these deserted roads street numbers expecting future growth, but such growth looked to be a long way off; they were miles south of the nearest developments. I then took a right on the first road past the deserted hanger, which was no longer 168th street, and traveled along it for what seemed like forever, although the map showed that it was only six kilometers from Hwy. 22X to the river. Upon my arrival at the road's end, I parked, got out, and looked down at the river well below, where I couldn't see a single person anywhere.

Another angler arrived just as I was about to negotiate the steep trail on the bluff. Employed as a public school teacher, he fished the river during the summer months, adding that summers in Calgary were over before you knew it, although the river could be fished during warm spells in other months. We hiked, or should I say carefully edged, down the craggy trial that wound its way down the bluff until it reached the river, more than a half-mile below.

When we arrived at the bottom, the teacher said he was walking about a half-hour upstream to a spot where he could cast to large fish that rose in a deep run along the base of a cliff. The cliff provided shade from the hot sun in the morning, but not in the afternoon, but he still liked the spot. I should have followed him and watched for a while, but he probably wanted solitude because he didn't invite me to join him. In addition, I could see no reason to hike for a half hour when miles of river in front of me were deserted.

After he disappeared upstream, I was alone on this immense river, flowing so deep below the plains that the prairie winds were tamed. Lots of rain had fallen the previous week and the river was high and somewhat discolored. From the Trout Unlimited map, I estimated the flow rate to be about 5,300-cfs, quite high for August, and it made wading difficult. Nevertheless there were lots of spots where I could either cast from the bank or ease in and work my way along the water's edge below them and cast into deeper water.

I worked an Elk Hair Caddis through some riffles with no success. I then worked quieter waters along the near bank and took several small fish. After finishing my packed lunch, I decided to walk upstream to watch the local angler. He said he'd be casting dry flies, but there were no fish rising where

Tom at Madison Run

I'd been fishing. After about 15 minutes of walking, I reached a spot where I could see the river well ahead of me and there was no sign of the angler or of steep cliffs, suggesting that a half hour walk for him was not what it was for me. Reluctantly, I decided to work a nymph downstream.

After fishing through a fine-graveled bottomed section, chocked with long flowing river grass, I reluctantly put a weight above a nymph, attached a strike indicator, and fished upstream, working the troughs between grassy weed beds. About 15 minutes later, my indicator stopped, I set the hook, and a very big fish took off upstream. My drag sang and then went silent. I never saw the fish, but cried out, "That was some fish," but there was no one to hear me for miles.

Somewhat later, the teacher appeared. He'd attracted a number of fish up from the depths with a Stimulator and landed some good ones. They'd begun to rise as he was leaving and he suggested I hike upstream and give the cliff stretch a try. I politely said I might, but knowing how far he'd walked I knew I wouldn't. He also suggested I stay for the evening caddis hatch, so I stayed until dusk, but no hatch occurred. Perhaps the water was too high and discolored, the weather too hot, or I didn't stay long enough, but I had no desire to climb the steep trail after dark, nor did I like driving deserted roads at night with only my headlight beams to guide me.

The next morning, I was at the river by nine o'clock, parked my lunch in the shade of a tree, and began the day with a Woolly-Bugger, working it through several riffles and the pools below them, but I had no hits. I then hiked upstream to the long, weedy, spring-creek-like-run, where I'd lost the

146

big fish the day before. Here, simply lobbing a big weighted Woolly-Bugger upstream and letting it float back down, I fooled several strong rainbows over 18-inches and one close to 20. Things were definitely looking up!

I stopped around noon, ate my lunch, and watched an angler short-sticking adjacent to the power water. He had waded across more than 75 yards of flat water to get to the main channel that swept along the base of a steep cliff, with its blue water sharply contrasting with the gray colored water on the flats. It was a picture-perfect setting and I watched him land three fish. Later, after he left, I tried to wade out to where he'd stood, but couldn't even get close!

Around three o'clock, a drift boat appeared upstream—the first I'd seen all day—and I watched it float down toward me in the glare of the bright sunlight. I felt invaded, a feeling I didn't have when sharing the area with the angler who fished the power water. I considered him "my brother" because he'd navigated the same steep trail I did to get to this magnificent stretch. My restful solitude was broken!

The boat drifted along the base of the cliff on the opposite bank, not just because trout held in its shaded power waters, but also because its occupants intended to stop for a brief break from the hot sun. Just as the guide wedged his boat between the cliff and a large boulder, his client hooked a fish. The fish cleared the surface and its splash resembled that of steelhead in New York's Salmon River. The guide yelled, "Apply more pressure," but his client's rod couldn't have been more bent. The fish took his line so far downstream that the guide reluctantly launched the boat and chased the fish, with the angler still fighting it as the boat disappeared from sight.

I also watched several more drift boats fish through the riffles and the pools I'd unsuccessfully fished earlier in the day, but none took any fish. As one drift boat floated by, I heard the guide remark, "The hot weather and high water has put the fish off feed." The hot sun beat upon me the whole afternoon and by five o'clock I was dehydrated. Luckily, a drift boat floated by and I haled them for a drink; they complied; glad to help a fellow angler in need. Tomorrow, I promised myself I'd pack a 68-once water bottle instead of a 20-once diet coke. Again, I fished until eight o'clock, but I still hadn't witnessed an evening hatch.

The next morning, I stopped at Country Pleasures and listened to two guides, loading two drift boats parked outside the shop, lament about the poor fishing and I felt better. Their drift boats seemed out of place parked in an urban mall next to Honda Preludes and BMWs. On this day, I went to Policeman's Flats, a section accessed off Dunbow Road and 40th Street East. I fished upstream from the fisherman's parking lot, catching only a 13-inch brown on a caddis in the seam along the riffled waters above the flats.

After lunch, I worked a Sofa Pillow along the shoreline above the flats, where a 19-inch rainbow inhaled the large fly as it floated over the pressure wave ahead of a submerged boulder. It immediately took off upstream and

Tom, barely visible across the flats, accessing the power water at Madison Run

jumped, so far above me that I didn't realize it was my fish, except that my line was screaming out at the same time. Only after several upstream runs did the fish turn and dash downstream, where I followed it, worried that it would take out so much line that the hook would work loose.

In the late afternoon, I landed two more rainbows, lobbing weighted tandem nymphs upstream, with one just over 20 inches. It was the first 20-inch river trout I'd ever caught and it took nearly 40 years of fishing to do so. Later, I read in McLennan's book that drift-boat anglers often land a dozen fish over 20-inches in one day on the Bow, but I was satisfied nonetheless; I'd reached another milestone in my fishing career!

Toward dusk, large trout became to rise to hatching *Baetis*, and a rise by a big fish in quiet side waters can create a huge ring of water. My heart racing, I landed two 19-inch browns on a size 18 Adams and lost another, the only large fish I fooled on dry flies during five days of fishing.

On the afternoon of my third day, I fished the Bow at Bankside, a large public park at Hwy. 22X on the river's west bank, where dog owners in Calgary walked their dogs. In the East, I try to avoid geese droppings, but at Bankside I had to watch out for dog poop! I walked carefully downstream for about 15 minutes, and then spent over an hour fruitlessly trying to reach fish cruising in a wide pool below a bend in the river. I waded out as far as possible, but the wind, the distance, and the movement of the fish kept me from reaching these sporadic, but tantalizing rises. The river bottom in the slack water was slippery and each time I carefully waded to where a fish rose, it began rising somewhere else. Frustrated, I walked downstream to where the river narrowed and worked an Olive Woolly-Bugger through pocket waters near the bank, fooling two frightfully strong rainbows in the pressure wave in front of two different submerged boulders. I started downstream to look for more boulders, but two anglers had past me to stakeout spots. I returned upstream, where I fooled a 16-inch brown, but a fish that size was now a letdown, so I called it a day and drove to Denny's to have supper, as well as to quench my thirst.

Capturing the Big One

After a brief trip to Crowsnest River, two hours south of Calgary, I returned to the Bow. The Crowsnest's waters were low and clear, its big fish were hiding, and I figured I'd have better luck back on the Bow. With four days of sunshine, the Bow had dropped to a level where I would feel more comfortable on it. After leaving Pincher Creek early in the morning, I reached Rt. 552 about an hour and a half later, took it east for about 12 miles, and fished the Bow from its south bank east of Highwood River, the major tributary to the Bow south of Calgary, discussed in the next chapter.

After wading across the Highwood, a feat I couldn't have accomplished earlier, and hiking downstream along its east bank, I came to its junction with the Bow, where I was greeted with marvelous looking deep, but riffled power water flowing next to the bank. I cast a streamer into parts of the 50-yard run for about a half hour, but caught nothing, although on subsequent trips I always caught at least one large rainbow from these waters.

I continued working my way downstream, casting a nymph along the bank, until I came to a huge pool, where numerous small trout were feeding on Trico spinners at the pool's tail. Since no large fish were feeding on these

Tom about to net a rainbow just upstream from where I got my three big ones

tiny flies, a fact mentioned by McLennan in his book, I switched to an Adams and hooked a 14-inch rainbow at the head of the pool, but took no other fish from this productive looking water.

After fishing a hopper imitation upstream, I arrived back at a spot where the steep bank was free from bank-side bushes, with open fields behind. Recalling my experience on the lower Madison, where out of boredom, I'd doubled-hauled a #10 Royal Coachman Wulff into mid-stream and saw it sucked under by a giant rainbow, I attached a #8 Orange Simulator to a 1X leader, took a wide stance, and doubled-hauled the fly out into the river's middle. The water was not particularly deep in this long run, a run I'd just worked from the riverbed, casting a hopper upstream along the bank, but had not turned a single fish. In my book, *Capturing Rogue Trout*, I describe in detail what happen in the next hour. In short, on three casts, I hooked and landed three rainbows between 20 and 22 inches, and I did so in the only spot I ever found on the river where I could cast from the bank into mid-stream.

Later in the week, after ascending from Madison Run, I listened to a conversation between two young adults when I was removing my waders. One asked the other what fly he should use, a question that seemed premature since no hatch could be seen this far from the river. The one addressed opened a large fly box and gave the other the largest San Juan Worm I'd ever seen. His fly box had several dozen of them in it. They both tied them on and started down the trail to the river. I mentioned in passing that I was from New York and had just caught a 22-inch trout, the biggest catch of my life. They acknowledged me for my accomplishment and then started down the trail. I called after the one who had chosen the San Juan Worm to use, as he seemed to be the more experienced of the two, "What's the biggest trout you've caught on this river?"

He looked sheepishly at me and said, "A 37-inch brown."

The other angler's face manifested the proud look associated with being the friend of a successful person. Thirty-seven inches, that's probably a 25-pound trout! Angling authors write about catching Bow River fish up to 25-inches, but none ever mentioned any monsters Trout get that size on Utah's Green, who says that can't on the Bow? Guides in Country Pleasures, that's who! After hearing my story, they undoubtedly tell the tale of the gullible nut who believes 37-inch trout inhabit the Bow. Nevertheless, the demeanor of the young man claiming to have caught this fish was more apologetic than braggadocio. In any case, my 22-inch rainbow was big enough for me.

Additional Trips

I've retuned to the Bow every summer since 2001 and each year Calgary extends father and farther into the countryside. Highway 22X is now lined with row houses, as are some of the formerly deserted streets south of 22X. In fact, I doubt if many of the scenes in the TV Mini Series, *Lonesome Dove*, which drew me to the river, could be shot today. Although I've never duplicated my three big fish with three casts, Tom and I have caught a number of trout exceeding 20 inches and Scott Daniels caught his first 20-inch brown when he joined us on our 2008 trip.

We usually catch fish in spurts when they move from the power water onto shelves or gravel bars to feed, interspersed with long periods of fruitless casting. We hook them either on the surface, with Stimulators, or underneath, with large, weighted Woolly Buggers, with Prince Nymph trailers. Mindful of the huge San Juan Worms used by the two young anglers, I tie my Woolly Buggers on 2X, 6XL hooks. In August, when the river is low, and the fishing below average, we fool a number of big fish on a long, wide gravel section adjacent to the power water above Policemen's Flats. Some feed in the knee-deep, fast water, but others rise up from the power water to grab the fly.

On my third trip in August of 2002, I hooked a rainbow that I knew, after it jumped, that I wouldn't land it. It looked like the steelhead we catch in New York's Salmon River. I hooked it casting a #2 bead headed Woolly Bugger upstream, in a long weedy section in Madison Run, and letting it drift back downstream. The fish sucked it in, ran upstream, held in the current, and ran upstream some more. It then ran across the river and up along the opposite bank. By now, I was well into my backing and knew that when it stopped fooling around and ran downstream, "it would be all over but the shouting." It did just that, but it also jumped 25 yards below me and the fly came loose. I sat down and deep belly laughs gushed forth. Why I thought losing a huge fish was comical, I cannot really say; it just was!

On our next trip, I fooled a brown in the slow waters at Policemen's Flats that reminded me of the huge Lake Ontario browns caught every fall in Oak Orchard, one of the lake's tributaries. It took off downstream, rolled on the surface, and the fly came loose. Later in the day, I landed a brown exceeding 20 inches, but it was anticlimactic. Upriver from Policemen's Flats, Tom also lost some monster browns. And I doubted less the angler's story about his huge fish!

Reflecting on my nine trips to the Bow, I've learned that the river's biggest trout don't usually dwell in waters I fish elsewhere. Neither Tom nor I caught many fish from heads and tails of pools, shallow riffles, slack waters at river bends, or swirling waters in eddies. I didn't hook a single large fish casting a nymph across and downstream, nor did I turn any fish floating a grasshopper imitation temptingly along the banks. Maybe their legs needed to move, but what is more likely is that because so much food floats down the river, fish have no need to hug the banks. Nymphs move to shallow waters next to banks to hatch and fish that feed on them follow them there, but fish that feed primarily on other fare, such as aquatic worms, leaches and crustaceans, have no need to leave their holding spots in deep waters because these foodstuffs continually drift by their holding locations.

We also had little luck during the river's "celebrated" evening caddisfly

Tom working an Elk Hair Caddis at the 22X Access as dusk approaches

hatch. We visited the stretch on the east side of Hwy. 22X Bridge, tied on a caddisfly, and waited. About eight-thirty, whether in July or August, browns would sometimes rise to a caddis hatch that neither of us thought was spectacular, but the browns rising to them definitely were! We usually hooked at least one fish approaching 20 inches, but by the time we landed it, the hatch had stopped. One night an angler above us landed a 24-inch brown, also his only fish. Each night it was usually the same; there was just enough time to hook and play one trout, mostly browns, before the small hatch was over.

What amazed me was the amount of browns that sometimes rose in the stretch because I'd fished it during the day a number of times and hooked only one 19-inch rainbow. On many nights, however, especially in August, there was no hatch, at least not at dusk, and we were too tired from fishing during the day to return well after dark to see if a heavier hatch began.

There are spots in the morning where big fish hold along the banks and either grab caddis flies drinking water or tiny *Baetis* that rise sporadically. The task is to find these feeding fish by walking cautiously along the bank until one is seen and then entering the water behind it, waiting for it to rise again, and then casting an imitation of what it's taking into the rise-form, but, if you get impatient and cast before they rise, the fish will spook. One problem, however, is that some of the fish simply quit feeding and return to deep waters, leaving you waiting for a rise that never comes.

Anglers in drift boats, working weighted flies, usually San Juan worms, with prince nymphs or stonefly nymph trailers, through the deepest, fastest waters, out-fished us, but those casting hopper imitations to the banks fared no better. From watching drift boat anglers, we learned that lots of the Bow's

152

biggest rainbows hold behind rocks in the power water, water we could rarely get our flies into with a decent float. Hooking trout on the Bow definitely doesn't involve the finesse required on Silver Creek or on the San Juan.

One drawback of the Bow is that it gets weedy after periods of low spring runoff, which was the case during my second trip with Tom. The winter snows had been unusually light during the past three winters and removing weeds from our flies became a nuisance! A "hundred year storm" scoured the river bottom in 2007, so in both 2007 and 2008, it was weed-free, a situation that left my favorite spot at Madison Run without weed-lined troughs to attract fish. Another problem is the paths made by cows grazing on the river's sloping banks. For example, when faced with a steep bluff upstream from McKinnon Flats, I tried to get around it by hiking a path that went up the bluff, but when it eventually veered from the river, I realized it was made by cows and not by fishermen and that I couldn't access the river upstream!

Lot of anglers float the river to avoid the steep terrain or the walking distances required to access good water. Downriver from Policemen's Flats, the river flows through barren and windswept plains, but it's worn away the land over the years and runs deep below it. It's tree-lined in a many sections, making the river scenic, but difficult to access in all but a few spots.

The Bow River has it all: tree lined banks; long, graveled bottom riffles; long, slick runs; deep, dark pools; swift pocket water; slow-moving, sandy bottomed, grassy sections; steep cliffs; gravel bars; sweeping bends, and wide, flat sections with fine-pebbled bottoms. It's not just a river with big fish; it's a

big river in a notable environment. Both the Bow and Highwood rivers are backdrops in two recent movies, *Open Range*, staring Kevin Costner and Robert Duvall, an excellent movie, and *Broken Trail*, a dull film staring Robert Duvall, who returned to the area to produce and direct it film and the last scene shows him fly fishing the lower Bow.

Note wavy power water on right. Anglers on the far bank caught fish next to it

The Upper Bow

Sandwiched between days on the lower Bow, I took a day on my first trip to Alberta and drove to Canmore to see the beauty of the river above Calgary and to checkout the fishing. Along the way, I passed by the Three Sisters, majestic peaks rising behind the Village of Canmore, enticing each passerby to visit their more majestic relatives in the national parks to the north. The town reminded me of Aspen in its early days, although I'm sure that it, too, will lose its charm with future expansion. Canmore was originally a railroad town linked to the construction of the Canadian Pacific Railroad, but unlike other railroad towns, coal was discovered at the base of nearby Mt. Rundle and the town continued to prosper by supplying coal to the railroads.

The discovery of oil in southern Alberta ended Canmore's reliance on coal. Most of its mines closed in 1922, although one operated until 1979. Over time, Canmore changed from an industrial to a residential community and tourist center. The town was the site of the cross-country ski events at the 1988 Winter Olympic Games. The Canmore Nordic Centre was built and 40 miles of ski trails developed for the games, with just over a mile and a half of terrain lit in the evening. In the summer, mountain bikers use the trails and many bike races are held in the nearby mountains. During September, the annual international Highland Games take place and thousands of musicians, Scottish dancers, and visitors gather to celebrate.

Golden eagles cross Bow Valley near Canmore between late March and mid-May and again in late September through early November. Traveling at speeds close to 70 miles per hour, up to 6,000 eagles pass over the area as they travel between their winter homes in the tropics and their summer nesting grounds in north central Canada. Below Canmore, Tundra swans stop at *Lac des Arcs*, French for "lake of the bows," on their spring and fall migrations. Native Americans used the Douglas fir saplings along the banks of the river for bow making and French trappers named the river, and this small lake, after this practice. The lake was once part of the national park, but it was later deleted in favor of hydroelectric power and mining. Quarrying of

The upper Bow at the Three Sisters

limestone, cement operations, and milling of magnetite continue by the lake to this day.

Trout can be caught downstream from the lake until the first power dam at Seebe. Below Seebe, water releases from a series of power-producing dams create marked fluctuations in river levels downstream to Bearspaw Dam, a water regulation dam just west of Calgary that restores stability to the river, a considerable benefit to trout inhabiting stretches below.

I stumbled upon Canmore's small public park, located along the river, parked my car, and fished upstream. The glacial blue waters flowed swiftly over a fine-pebbled bottom, with no appreciable structure along the bank. In the shallow pools below each riffle, I caught a number of browns about 10 inches, but riffled sections were few and far between. McLennan wrote an article on the upper Bow in the Winter 1999 issue of *Northwest Fly Fishing*, where he reported that the fishing turns off in direct sunlight, but described how to entice large browns out from under bank cover and logjams. Although the stretch I fished was free of structure, the river was stunning and I enjoyed the day. On a second trip to Canmore, Tom and I explored a braided section below the village, but access to productive waters was limited; only anglers in drift boats could work the banks where we explored and I bet that's the case throughout the river's fast-flowing upper waters.

I didn't fish rivers in Banff National Park because I wanted to save the Park for a trip with my wife, although now I can't afford it! The development of Banff was stimulated by the discovery of hot springs. Neolithic men believed that springs connected them with underworld spirits and had healing

Bow River at McKinnon Flats, the only access site between Policeman's Flats and Carseland Weir where you can drive down to the river

powers. Victorian men shared the same beliefs and, later, Franklin D. Roosevelt, in an effort to cure his polio, first visited and later bought Warm Springs, Georgia. Dr. R. G. Brett, Medical Supervisor of the Canadian Pacific Railroad, saw his future in the area's hot springs, left the railroad, and became the Park doctor. Brett constructed a private spa and hospital and attached a hotel to it, piping the hot water, advertised to cure all ills, through a wooden pipeline, insulated with moss, from the Upper Hot Springs to a variety of baths.

Accommodations

All the major hotel chains have accommodations in Alberta, but following Calgary's rapid growth, there are no motel rooms in Calgary, or in nearby Okotoks, for less than $120 per night. On my first trip to Calgary, I stayed at the Econo Lodge South, the closest inexpensive motel to the Bow. When I checked in and mentioned that I was in Canada to fish the Bow, the owner told me she was expecting an angler from Germany who would be making his tenth annual trip to the river. Little did I know that I would also make a number of annual trips.

On our last three trips, we stayed at Okotoks Country Inn (403-938-1999), located in the small town of Okotoks about five miles south of Hwy. 22X. The Alberta Accommodations Guide (800-661-8888) may help anglers to find rooms in Canmore that suit the pocketbook, but I would suggest phoning the Upper Bow Fly Fishing Company (403-760-7668), Green Drake Fly Shop (403-678-9522), Roberts Fly Shop (403-932-5885), or Banff Fishing

The Bow below Highwood River, with the type of banks that make accessing the river difficult in all but a few spots (Tom Royster Photo)

Unlimited (403-678-9522) and ask where budget-minded anglers stay.

There are numerous campgrounds within the national and provincial parks and four campgrounds along the Bow below Canmore, They are: the Bow River, Three Sisters, *Lac des Arcs*, and Bow Valley campgrounds. All campgrounds, both within and without the park, are operated on a first come first serve basis. Information about campgrounds in Banff and Jasper national parks can be obtained by calling 403-762-1550 and 403-852-6176, respectively. If I were going to camp near the upper Bow, I would make motel reservations and then cancel them if I found an unoccupied campsite.

Other Activities

A modern Canadian city, Calgary has many activities to choose from. These can include trips to: the zoo, a Chinese culture center, several outdoor gardens, a speedway, museums, several large shopping centers, an Imax Theater, and Stampede Park, where the world's largest rodeo is held every summer. St. George's Island is home to the Calgary Zoo, Botanical Gardens, and Prehistoric Park. The zoo is Canada's largest and one of North America's top ten. The Prehistoric Park is a recreation of a Mesozoic landscape and is accessed by a suspension bridge across the Bow. Almost every building near the city's center is modern and, for this reason, the city was the setting for the movie *Superman III*.

Alberta's rivers fish best in mid-July, but over 250,000 visitors flock to Calgary for the Calgary Stampede, held each year during the first two weeks of this month and hotel rates sky rocket. In addition to many festivities, the Stampede includes rodeo contests and chuck wagon races. To get a seat at these events, make reservations well in advance by calling the Stampede ticket offices (800-661-1767). About 10 miles south of town, off McCloud Trail, sits the Heritage Park Historical Village (403-268-8500), a 60-acre theme park replicating life on the old Canadian frontier. At least 150 restored buildings were transported to the park from small frontier towns. The turn-off to the park is marked by a large maroon steam engine.

Nevertheless, many visitors skip these urban offerings to spend time in the national or provincial parks northwest of Calgary. If planning to do so, I'd recommend purchasing a copy of Graeme Pole's *Canadian Rockies: An Altitude Super Guide.*

Chapter Eleven
Castle, Crowsnest, Highwood and Oldman Rivers
The Best in the Canadian Rockies

Canadian anglers support artificial-lures-only regulations in their rivers, restrictive harvests of trout, and catch-and-release fishing, with almost 90 percent of fish released outside of designated no-kill areas. Trout are stocked only in lakes and the harvest of wild trout in streams typically limited to two fish, with the season either closed or regulations switched to catch-and-release during spawning. Because the fish are wild, the rivers fairly fertile, and the regulations followed, relatively small streams produce relatively large trout.

Before presenting these wonderful rivers, let me state that all are subject to significant runoff each spring, changing their riverbeds from year to year, rivers where Fred Evert's observations, written over 55 years ago in his book, *Fun with Trout,* clearly apply.

> It is with streams, the lifeblood of trouting fun, that evolution is the most rapid and visible. From year to year, yes, sometimes from day to day, our streams change. Our favorite pool today is gone tomorrow and where no pools existed before, new ones are formed. While the stream may flow here one day, it may flow over there the next.

Nevertheless, except during major droughts, the same numbers of fish usually inhabit them; they've just changed locations. Many stretches of the rivers presented are accessed by rarely oiled gravel roads. As a result, your car is completely covered by the dust kicked up by the first car traveling in the opposite direction. In order to see, you need to keep about a mile behind any car ahead of you. Our car was so dirty by the end of our trip that Tom thought we should wash it even though it was a rental car!

Crowsnest River

I first fished Crowsnest River on my 1997 trip to Bow River. I'd read an article about this small, mountain-valley river located in Crowsnest Pass, between Alberta and British Columbia. The river was noted for excellent hatches and hard fighting rainbows. From Lundbreck Falls upstream to East Hillcrest Bridge is a long stretch of water where year-round, catch-and-release fishing is permitted. Above East Hillcrest Bridge, bait is allowed and two fish over 12 inches can be kept. Below Lundbreck Falls, down to Oldman Reservoir, two sections have a slot-limit and a two-fish harvest. One trout must be longer than 18 inches and the other shorter than 12, or both must be shorter. Bait is banned and the season is closed on one stretched and catch-and-release regulations enforced during certain months on the other.

One morning. I left Calgary and took scenic Hwy. 22 to Crowsnest Pass, a two-hour drive southeast of Calgary. When I arrived at the river, about ten o'clock in the morning, it started to drizzle. I'd been fishing the Bow under a bright sun for four days and enthusiastically welcomed the light rainfall and overcast skies. Unfamiliar with the regulations at the time, I fished upstream from East Hillcrest Bridge, where I fooled a number of small trout on a Tiny-Blue Olive. Big fish inhabited the stretch, as a boy with worms caught two

Southern Alberta's Crowsnest River

from a deep pool where I'd unsuccessfully worked a nymph about an hour earlier. Nevertheless, I wanted to try a different spot.

I'd read that the river's biggest fish occupy waters below Lundbreck Falls, where brown trout join the fishery. I headed to this spot, hoping to fish before the rain picked up. Below the falls, the river, in a series of step pools, flowed through a canyon of barren and jagged rock walls. This August, these pools were shallow and I suspected that the river's big fish had moved elsewhere. Nevertheless, I fished several pools, but turned no fish.

For reasons I couldn't put my finger on, I found myself uncomfortable with the surrealistic quality of the terrain. The chiseled rock walls lining the river lacked greenery; they looked liked the creation of a dynamite man. I left the river, checked in at my motel, ate an early dinner at the family restaurant next door, and spent the evening reading McLennan's book. I learned that the section below Lundbreck Falls had been subject to a "mitigation" project to improve fish holding lies as compensation for the 30 miles of river lost to Oldman Reservoir.

McLennan stated, "Each time I stop the truck and look down the road at the twenty-four rock structures in the Horseshoe Bend, I'm stricken by the artificiality of it all and I can't help thinking that they overdid it. But when I'm standing down in one of those man-made pools, catching more fish than I deserve, my vision narrows until I see nothing but trout, and my opinion softens a little."

When the Crowsnest flows well, and flies are hatching, large rainbows can be caught in this relatively small river, but following both floods and drought conditions, there are less large fish for several years. Whether they

The Crowsnest gives up some big trout for such a small river

drop down into the reservoir or succumb to the heat is unknown. With the exception of one year, when the river was exceptionally low, Tom and I have fished the Crowsnest on each of our annual summer trips to Alberta since 2001. Although I've hooked only one fish exceeding 20 inches, those between 15 and 17 put up an exceptional fight. In both 2007 and 2008, however, the fishing was poor and both Tom and I caught only small fish so we concentrated our efforts on other rivers in the area.

Castle River

During our first few trips to Alberta, we stayed in Crowsnest Pass to be close to Crowsnest River, but after fishing other nearby waters, we switched to Pincher Creek, closer to the stretch of Castle River that we usually fish, a stretch just above where the river enters Oldman Reservoir. Large fish occasionally visit the river from that body of water. It also contains large bull trout in its deeper pools, as do most of southern Alberta's streams.

We first fished the river from lands owned by the Mennonites who, though and intermediary, give us permission to do so. The go-between was a restaurant owner in Pincher Creek who we befriended. Tom asked a middle-aged, female waiter in the restaurant if she knew of any good fishing spots, a question I would've never asked her, and she replied that she didn't, but the owner did, and she would get him! It pays to ask "stupid" questions!

In 2005, we fooled lots of cutbows and rainbows up to 17 inches in different pools next to the property. On subsequent trips, we fished the same waters by hiking downstream from a nearby bridge. The Province owns water rights to the high water mark, allowing anglers access to all Alberta streams, as long as private property is not crossed to reach them.

In 2007, both Tom and Scot caught at least 10 rainbows between 13 and 15 inches in one pool on dry flies, while I'd fished upstream from the bridge, in waters where we'd caught a number of good fish in 2006, but I fooled only two small cutthroats and turned one rainbow. Frustrated, I hiked downstream to see how Tom and Scott were doing. No longer getting any strikes, they

Castle River above Route 507

turned the pool over to me and went further downstream. I rested the waters for a bit, after which I managed to fool one 14-inch rainbow, but that was the last fish from the pool; it pays to be in the right place at the right time!

In 2008 the water was quite low in the Mennonite stretch, so Tom hiked upstream from the bridge. Nevertheless, I went downstream to the "productive pool," but it, and the good pools both above and below it, had changed significantly, with one almost completely filled after the spring flush. I fooled only two 14-inch rainbows in these waters.

Since it was approaching our meeting time, I hiked back to the car. Tom hadn't arrived yet, so I fished the first pool upstream from the bridge. After some time had past, I begin to worry about Tom. I walked upstream along the dried-up riverbed, where irregular stones made walking difficult, until I could see the last pool we usually fish. Nevertheless, I couldn't see Tom and wondered if he'd fallen and been hurt. Consequently, I walked further upstream to look for him.

After about 15 minutes, I saw him well upstream, standing and casting in water we'd never fished. Realizing he wasn't injured, I sat down on a boulder to rest. Not long after, Tom joined me and excitedly remarked, "What a beautiful day, and what beautiful water. I caught about a half dozen fish from the gin-clear waters, but even if I hadn't, you couldn't ask for better water or a better day! This is what fly fishing is all about." Robert Haig Brown, an eloquent writer, described Tom's feelings when he wrote, in his book, *Fisherman's Spring*:

Tom fishing a deep pool on the Oldman that holds a big bull trout

I could not say exactly what it is I expect from a day's fishing now as I start out, only that it is something very much more than fish, something more even than good fishing. It can be almost anything about a day on the water, in combinations of things or in single isolated things. The only certainty is that it will be there if one is looking for it.

Miles of water on the Castle are accessible above the last bridge on Rt. 507. We walked a not-so-well-worn trail, which parallels the river well away from it, for about a mile upstream and then worked our way through high grasses and trees until we reached the river and then fished upstream. Downstream from the Rt. 507 Bridge, we've taken a gravel road that leads to a rodeo grounds, parked by the river near it, and fished downstream. In one pool in this stretch, a huge bull trout chased a 12-inch rainbow I'd hooked and I instinctually pulled the rainbow from the water. If I'd left it in, maybe I would've hooked the bull trout!

The head waters of the Castle, its South and West branches, and Carbondale River can be reached by traveling Rt. 507 to Rt. 774 and then taking a gravel through the mountains, providing scenic views, as well as access to rivers lined with dark-green spruce, some at well-spaced public campsites along their banks in Beauvais Lake Provincial Park. In 2006, when water in the Castle was at normal levels, we parked in an unoccupied campsite and caught beautiful cutthroats up to 16-inches, all while yelling "Yo Bear," so any bears along the way wouldn't be surprised!

Oldman River in the "Gap" below the Forestry Trunk Road

Oldman River

The Oldman River is the largest tributary to Oldman Reservoir. Because the river can be accessed where it flows under Hwy. 22, about 45 minutes north of Lundbreck, we usually fish it on our way to and from Calgary. We first fished it below the Hwy. 22 Bridge, taking a gravel road on the river's north side that leads to a gravel pit, where you can park and walk down to the river. In most stretches of the lower river, the banks are too high and too steep to hike down. Slab rock step pools characterized this section and although we caught some fish, we didn't much like it.

We next accessed it by taking the road on the south side of the Hwy. 22 Bridge, paved for a short distance and then graveled, that parallels private lands until it reaches a section called the "Gap," pictured on the previous page. The short stretch in the Gap is superb when strong winds aren't blowing. We then continue to the Forestry Trunk Road, where both Racehorse Creek, a "cast and dash" river at this time of year, and the Oldman's upper waters can be assessed. The Livingston River, which flows south next to the Forestry Trunk Road for some distance, joins the Oldman just after it flows down from the mountains in the west, offering the angler two side-by-side choices to catch native cutthroat, cutbows, and an occasional brook trout, descendents of those stocked years ago. In fact, I caught a strange looking brook trout that I later learned was a brook trout/cutthroat hybrid.

Both the Oldman and Livingston rivers above the Trunk Road are marvelous cutthroat streams, but like most of the cutthroat in these mountain streams, they don't get very active until the afternoon.

We now primarily fish the lower Oldman, accessing it from private

Oldman River above the Trunk Road

property, leaving the owner a bottle of wine as we depart as thanks for his generosity. Nevertheless, we sometimes see another angler in this stretch who took the gravel road on the north side, found a spot where he could cross the fence line, and walked down to the river from bluff-like banks that are less steep than average.

How we got permission to fish the Oldman is a story worth telling. We were removing our waders after an afternoon on the Castle when a car arrived. Its driver parked near our car, got out, and walked over to us. He was about to fish the river and wondered how we'd done. Tom related that we'd fooled some fish in waters just above the bridge, but did better in a pool about a half-mile upstream. Tom and he chatted and Tom asked him if he fished the Oldman. He replied that he did and added that he also fished the Castle and, therefore, knew Tom was honest about where to fish. For this reason, and because we visit the area for just a few days each year, he told us who might give us permission to fish the lower Oldman, but added, "But don't tell the owner I suggested it!"

We thanked him, got into our car, and left him the river to fish. When we got to the highway, however, we saw a pickup truck following us, with its driver signaling us to stop, so we pulled off the road, The driver stopped behind us, came up to our car, and said. "I forgot to give you fellows some flies that should work well on the Oldman." He also gave us his business card. He and a friend operated "Trout Bums", a guide service in the area, and said he'd appreciate a reference.

In the stretch of the Oldman that we fish, there're some deep holes that hold huge bull trout. We've seen them reject the big streamers we've thrown at them, but we've hooked some large rainbows and cutthroats that we wouldn't have hooked otherwise. We rarely fish for these huge fish, however, because, as mentioned in Chapter Seven, it's not much fun slinging the large streamers required to capture their attention.

The upper Oldman, but it could easily be the upper waters of any Trunk Road stream.

In 2007, the Forestry Trunk Road was closed because of exceptionally dry conditions and fear of fires. As a result, we couldn't fish the upper river and, therefore, fished only its lower waters, although the fishing wasn't nearly as good as when the water was higher.

Highwood River

The Highwood is the major tributary to the Bow below Calgary and we've fished the Bow where the Highwood joins it and I always catch at least one large rainbow in that location. Nevertheless, the

Highwood doesn't come into its own until above the hamlet of Longview. The river along Rt. 541, above Longview, has a number of official angler access sites, but until you get above the Indian Reserve in Edan Valley, only a mountain goat can get down to the river from them.

We fish the river several miles below the Forestry Trunk Road at two picnic/campgrounds in Don Getty Wildland Provincial Park, where access is easy and where Tom and I have landed several 19 rainbows and fooled some larger ones. My first lost fish screamed downstream and broke off and my second leaped in the air and my fly popped out. Most of the rainbows are visitors from the Bow that remain after spawning. You can fish a stretch and not turn a single rainbow; another 100 yards upstream, however, and you may hook one, but then catch only cutthroat for the next hour, after which you fool another rainbow when your mind-set is on smaller fish. In the evening, the bigger cutthroats rise to flies and the rainbows become inactive.

On one trip to the Highwood, we were rigging up in one of the parks when two pick-up trucks arrived, with full cabs and people in the truck beds. About 15 people emerged from the trucks, walked down to the river, and started wading across a wide section at the tail of the pool where we were about to fish. Most wore sandals, including an elderly woman, well into her 80s, assisted by several younger women, although she managed quite well by herself. We asked the last to cross where they were headed and he replied, "We're accompanying our grandmother to the top off Sacred Mountain, where she has come to pray since she was a child." They were Native Americans from Eden Valley and Mount Burke, with a height of 8,333 feet, was the mountain they were about to ascend!

Alberta's cutthroat don't come as easily to the dry fly as they do in the

Highwood River below the Trunk Road (note the large river bed)

pebble-bottomed Elk River, a British Columbia river flowing on the west side of the Rockies, not far below Crowsnest Pass. We first heard about the Elk from Scott's daughter, Durae, who fishes it with a Tarantula, a big, bushy fly with rubber legs. In certain sections of the lower river, heavily fished by those drifting platoon boats, but easily waded, cutthroat school-up and hold off the main current. Once they're located, they'll rise from the bottom and engulf the Tarantula when it floats over them.

Although the fight of cutthroats in the Elk cannot compare with those in the Oldman, hooking over a dozen cutthroat, between 11 and 17 inches, in a day's fishing can renew one's self confidence after slow periods on other rivers. Unfortunately, the Elk has become a popular destination and British Columbia has increased the cost of a non-resident fishing license to the point where my companions and I no longer fish this beautiful river.

If the cost of a license is of no concern, I'd suggest fishing Michel River in British Columbia, on the east slope of the Rockies, easily accessed off a gravel road not far from the last town in Crowsnest Pass when traveling west. Although the Michel is a much smaller river than the Elk or, for that matter, than any other river discussed in this chapter, we caught cutthroat up to 18 inches when we fished it before the price increase.

On a trip with his wife, Tom fished several rivers in British Columbia situated north of the Elk, one of which is the St. Mary's, located near Kimberly, the highest city in the Rockies and called the "Bavarian City of the Rockies." Bavarian style buildings line its main street and every hour tower bells "yodel" instead of chime. Most anglers fish below St Mary's Lake, but Tom took a mountain road into lumber company lands above the lake, only to learn on his return that he was supposed to have a two-way radio so he could

British Columbia's Elk River below Fernie (Tom Royster Photo)

communicate with the lumber trucks that "haul-ass" on the back roads.

If planning a trip to the Canadian Rockies, I suggest buying Barry Mitchell's *Alberta's Trout Highway: Fishing the Forestry Trunk Road* (Barry Mitchell Publications, Red Deer, Alberta). Barry is a long-winded guy, but he describes in honest detail each river. Other books include Jim McLennan's *Trout Streams of Alberta* (Johnson Gorman, Red Deer, Alberta) and Jeff Mironuck's, *Angling in the Shadows of the Canadian Rockies* (Sandhill Book Marketing, Kelowna, B.C.), but neither book does justice to the areas smaller streams, many of which hold some surprisingly large cutthroat.

Barry Mitchell has fished every mile of water off the Forestry Trunk Road, from Waterton Park to Grande Prairie, a distance of about 435 miles.

British Columbia's Michel

Jim McLennan was one of the first guides hired by Russell Thornberry, a transplanted Texan, who introduced guiding and outfitting to the Bow by starting the Bow River Company in the 1970s. Jim later bought the company from Thornberry, but then sold it to fellow guide Peter Chenier to raise funds to start his fly shop, Country Pleasures.

Jim sold Country Pleasures, so I didn't expect to see him again. Nevertheless, on one of our annual visits to the thrift shop in Okotoks to buy martini glasses, we saw him instructing student-anglers on the Sheep River, a tributary of the Highwood. It upper waters are spawning grounds for bull trout, but it's a mediocre trout stream.

Chapter Twelve
River Itchen and its Chalk Stream Neighbors
Waters Steeped in Tradition

A marvelous opportunity presented itself during the summer of 1982; I had a chance to spend seven weeks in England, with most of my living expenses paid for by my traveling companion's employers. Armed with P. J. Wades "Trout Fishing on the Test and Itchen," which appeared, God only knows why, in an issue of *Gourmet* that I'd flipped through in my doctor's waiting room, I took my annual month vacation and a month leave of absence from work and, with their permission, uprooted my two daughters from our home in New Paltz, New York.

We first visited Paris and then took the ferry across the channel to England, rented a car, and drove to Winchester, where we stayed in a quaint hotel for several days until moving to a rented house in a Winchester suburb. In early September, I enrolled Kalay in the secondary school in Winchester and Kaylin in the primary school in the suburb of Weston. As a result, I spent seven weeks in Hampshire, a county in Southeastern England, near the storied River Itchen, in the early fall of 1982.

Some readers might question why I'd write about a river I visited more than 25 years ago. After all, the river must have changed in the intervening years and my knowledge of it now outdated. Significant changes in 25 years—that's a distinctly American way of thinking. As I mentioned in Chapter Ten, my late mother-in-law, Rose, went to Ragusa, Sicily, more than 150 years after her father was born, and all his offspring, and their offspring, still lived there, many in the same houses.

The River Itchen, and its surroundings, has a timeless quality and should I return to it today I'm certain it would look exactly as it did then. Black coots would be resting on their green nests, standing high in the reeds along its banks; cranes would be rustling through the reeds; water birds would be searching for tidbits in the shallows under the trees; swans would be swimming gracefully in its wider sections, occasionally dipping their bright orange beaks into the floating weeds; and large brown trout, England's native trout, would be holding between the water grasses in its deeper runs.

In fact, the river would look much the same as it did when King Alfred, in his defense of England against the Danes, first established fortified towns, called burghs (and later boroughs), with Winchester being one of them. These towns would later become the principal cities of Southern England and Winchester would become England's first capital.

From ancient times until the present, the river experienced only three minor changes. Godfrey de Lucy, Bishop of Winchester, toward the end of the 12th century, created a 200-acre reservoir on River Alre, one of two small upstream tributaries to the river, to drive a number of water mills, but it primarily replaced neighboring marshland. The Bishop also completed minor channeling to make the river navigable for barges carrying products from the mills. In the early 19th century, docks were built at Southampton, extending the river about a mile south into Southampton water.

It's a short river, less than 30 miles long from its origin in the chalk hills at Kilmeston, made by the seas of the Cretaceous Age a hundred million years ago, to its tidal salt estuary below Southampton. Between its old milldams, it's a narrow river, no more than 40 or 50 feet wide in many stretches, and, as it winds its way through Winchester, it braids into several channels that flow against the foundations of the town's red brick buildings. A marvelous walkway parallels the largest channel and trout are sometimes seen swimming among the waving water plants in the river below it. Even after hours of rain, the river still runs clean.

Because nearly ten million gallons of water are pumped from the river each day at the Pumping Station at Otterbourne, a small village south of Winchester, the lower stretches of the river look similar to the upper ones. Consequently, it's a small stream, as streams go, from the town of Mansbridge, near its mouth, to its headwaters at Itchen Stoke, where River Candover and River Alre join it. Because the Itchen becomes three times the size where these three steams meet, I call the spot "The Three Beginnings," after Noreen O'Dell, who described the river from its mouth to the "Three Ends" in her descriptive little pamphlet, *The River Itchen*.

There is an intimacy to the river not found on most North American streams. But as small as the river is, it's played a major role in the affairs of the nation that grew up around it. Ancient civilizations lived along the Itchen, called "Yeanan" on early maps, long before Roman legions explored its inlet from the sea in 43 A. D. The Romans traveled upriver and built a fortification they called Clausentum, after Emperor Claudius who ordered the invasion of Britain. Clausentum served as a port for Winchester for more than four centuries.

After the Romans departed, the warlord Cerdic arrived in 495, with his Saxon soldiers, killed or drove off the locals, and established his headquarters near the river's edge. The Vikings followed, but King Arthur temporarily stopped them. Later, King Alfred, the youngest son of King Ethelwulf, rallying the common man behind him, stopped invading Danes and ended King Guthrie's dream of a Danish empire in Britain. Nevertheless, the Danes, along with their northern neighbors, raided coastal towns and villages after England's unity dissolved under King Ethelred, the Redeless (meaning "plotter" or "traitor"). In addition, King Sweyn Forkbeard, of Denmark, sailed up the Itchen to take revenge on England for Ethelred's purge of Danes in York, a population that included Forkbeard's sister. He and Olaf of Norway established camps on opposite shores at the river's mouth in 994. Later, Edward the Confessor, followed by William the Conqueror, used the harbor as a resting place.

No, the river won't have changed much in 25 years! In fact, I'd bet I'd find young children fishing from the same worn spots on the banks of a millpond where I found children fishing 25 years ago. But now it would be the son's of the fathers. Landowners on some sections of the Itchen, unlike other rivers in England, still let local children fish, although few trout inhabited the stretches they were fishing. On other England rivers, huge stretches are owned by private fishing clubs, or by large landowners who, working through a middleman, called a water-bailiff, rent out sections to pay-to-fish clients. These rivers are heavily stocked.

Arrangements could be made (and still can) to fish some stretches of the Itchen and its trout were wild (and still are) and, because they're wild, they're less of them and the river not heavily fished. In addition, it had no river keepers to regularly cut the river's rapidly growing water plants or to build wooded river platforms on which mayflies could crawl on the undersides to lay eggs and thereby limit the consumption of mayfly eggs by predator insects, such as caddisfly nymphs. Until the local River Authority decided to use tax money to cut the river's plants, which didn't appear to be that often, the river remained chocked with water plants in many sections. As a result, flows were not maintained through channels, the channels disappeared, and some trout disappeared along with them; I'm sure it looks the same today.

The river was fertile, with both stream-born insects and freshwater shrimp available to fatten up the trout, and those that found a good feeding lane grew large and wily—not as large as those in the painstakingly managed rivers, like the Test, where trout were selectively bred for fast growth and came freely to the dry fly, but large enough to excite most fishermen.

Nevertheless, the children I saw on the river didn't care, like most children the world over, ignorance is bliss and they fished anyway, many still dressed in the uniforms they wore to school. If they got lucky and a trout rose, they tossed brightly colored flies, as well as worms, into the rise-form. If one rose elsewhere in the pond, they ran over to the spot and cast again. When their enthusiasm gave way to their hunger, they stopped to eat whatever they had left over from lunch, after which they engaged in ruff and tumble play and much chasing of each other around the pond. Eventually, they calmed down and settled on rock skipping, with fishing forgotten.

Trips to Southampton

After getting the girls off to school, I drove to Southampton, where I did research in the library of South Hampton University in preparation for a book a colleague and I would later publish. Each morning, I was usually the first to enter the university library and I quickly learned to wear a warm sweater and to find a sheltered corner in which to work, as it's the English custom to open all the windows in the morning to air out the building. Both my grandmothers and my mother engaged in this practice, but I'd forgotten it. Although still technically summer, the nights were cool and it took some time for the building to warm up after the windows were closed later in the morning. I found it difficult to take notes when shivering! I also found it difficult to pass by the numerous shelves of history books without stopping to read some. In one stop, I learned that Shakespeare had taken considerable liberties with history when he wrote his famous play *Macbeth*, a play most of us studied in high school.

In reality, neither Macbeth, King of the Scotts, nor Lady Macbeth, who compulsively washed her hands in the play, ever felt any guilt about Duncan's slaying. Duncan's reigned as King of Scotland was marked by disastrous wars and internal strife. It ended in 1040 when Macbeth, the great steward of Ross and Moray, encouraged by his many followers, assassinated Duncan and became king, after which Scotland flourished.

Later, Macbeth learned that Duncan's widow was both penniless and homeless, ejected from her home by her son who, in keeping with the existing law of primogeniture, had inherited his father's estate. Macbeth, feeling responsible for the widow's fate, sheltered her in his own estate. In addition, he changed the Scotland law to one where wives inherited their husband's belongings. Only later, did he become romantically involved with the widow.

Ironically, it was Duncan's son, Malcolm Canmore, who, sympathetic with British interests, drove Macbeth and his soldiers into the Scottish marshlands and slewed them, followed by Anglicization of the ancient Celtic culture. Nevertheless, shortly after Canmore became King Malcolm III, and married an English princess, William the Conqueror invaded his lowlands and annexed Scotland to England.

The guilt and endless hand washing by Lady Macbeth were figments of Shakespeare's imagination; a sign of the prejudice English residents harbored again the Scotts at the time of his writings. Shakespeare based his work on *Chronicles of England, Scotland, and Wales*, written in 1577 by a British chronicler. The history was slanted due to the long conflict between England and Scotland, perhaps stimulated by a Scottish march into England. One hundred years after Macbeth's death, during weak King Stephan's reign, the Scotts, in return for William the Conqueror's earlier invasion, massacred England residents and enslaved its women. Macbeth left a legacy, however, more valuable to women than Shakespeare's play—his inheritance law was adopted by England, and later by the United States.

Walks Along the River

On days when I didn't have a car, I walked down the gentle hill from our house into the historic town of Winchester. Each day, I sat for a moment in the Winchester Cathedral that dwarfed the nearby buildings. This majestic and spacious building expressed, for me, the universal importance of religion in our lives and the cosmic imagination of men who had mastered the lost Roman art of vaulting great spaces in stone.

After a brief period, I left the church and walked along River Itchen, letting my mind assimilate and integrate my library readings with my past knowledge. Other, much more famous writers had done the same thing. Perhaps the first was Izaak Walton, the 17th century writer of biographies, most noted for his book on fishing.

Walton strolled along the riverbanks during his declining years, but fished the river heavily early in life, using live mayflies attached to a small hook. In fact, his book, *The Compleat Angler*, written in 1653, provides instruction on where to find the right flies and how to tie an artificial, although I'm told that the fly fishing sections in his early editions were contributed by Thomas Barker, an expert cook and a fine fishing writer in his own right. In a supplement to the fifth edition, the English poet, Charles Cotton, wrote, "With a light and gentle rod, Walton cast one of twelve mayfly imitations that was made to angle with on top of the water. He worked his way downstream, with the sun before him, and, hopefully with the wind at his back."

Walton is buried in Winchester Cathedral, as is Jane Austin, whose books I read at night after the girls went to bed. There's a window dedicated to Walton in the church and one small detail of it shows him reading peacefully by the Itchen, with St. Catherine Hill in the background and his fishing tackle beside him, and quoting from his favorite text *Study to be Quiet*. Another detail shows him at the River Dove, saying grace over he and his companion's streamside lunch.

Jane Austin died at the age of 41 and a marble stone marks her burial place. On the stone is written, "The benevolence of her heart, the sweetness of her temper and the extraordinary endowments of her mind obtained the regard of all who knew her and the warmest love of her intimate connections."

A British chalk steam winds it way through open countryside

Charlotte Yonge, England's first notable woman novelist to write under her own name, completed 160 novels when living in Otterbourne, where her father was the Squire of Otterbourne Manor. During the Victorian period, it was not proper for ladies to earn a living by writing, particularly the writing of novels, since all novels, regardless of their topic, were considered "racy." George Elliot (Mary Ann Evans), an even more famous British novelist, was thought to be a man. Yonge escaped criticism because she donated all her earnings to church and mission work. Later, her success contributed to new ideas about the role of women in society.

Benjamin Franklin, as chief representative of the American colonies, and later as an agent for Pennsylvania, lived in England for a number of years before the American Revolution. As a young adult, he'd worked in two of London's foremost printing houses, where he made a name for himself. Franklin was often a guest of Jonathan Shipley, Bishop of St. Asaph, who had a summer home in Twyford, where it's believed Franklin started his autobiography. The historian who wrote the preface to a modern reprint of Franklin's book asserted that he worked on his autobiography for several hours each day during his summer visit with Shipley in 1771. In the evening, with his host's family gathered around him, Franklin read aloud what he'd written about his boyhood and early career in America.

Other biographers believe that Franklin related tales of his past in evening conversations at Shipley's home and was encouraged by his audience to put them into writing. In either case, in August of 1771, he started his autobiography in the form of a letter to his son. Noreen O'Dell, in her pamphlet on River Itchen, referred to Franklin as a "famous son." This reference is quite a compliment, considering he was a Bostonian who strongly supported the colonial cause.

Anthony Trollope, who attended Winchester College a four-year high school, for three years in his youth, and who played along the river, based his first novel, *The Warden*, on a newspaper attack on a Winchester charity. The novel was the first in a monumental series of chronicle novels, called the "Barchester Series," that depicted the problems of villagers in a fictitious town. It was the first of 60 books he would pen. His second series of novels, the "Palliser Series," about politics and government, were adapted for television in the 1970s, nearly 100 years after his death

Lord Edward Gray, who not only wrote a splendid book on fly fishing, but also several about his career in public service and one on birds, strolled along the river, as well as fished it, even when his vision became so poor he could hardly see. As his vision deteriorated, he gave up the use of dry flies, and eventually of wet flies, and in the year before his death in 1933, resorted to worms, a method he hadn't used since his early childhood in Northern England.

In an introspective letter to a friend, he wrote, "I cannot see whether I put my worm into the water or onto the banks. With my ducks I can at any rate feel when they take it out of my hand, and distinguish some of them when they are very close."

Lord Gray had fished the river in his youth and had fond memories of it. After his father died, Gray, like Anthony Trollope, attended Winchester College, his first private school experience and one to which he never fully adjusted. He took solace in fishing the Itchen each day in a half-mile section known as "Old Barge," a private stretch where anglers paid a small daily, or annual fee, for fishing privileges. He fished both during his lunch hour and after school, throwing three wet flies, as he did as a lad in the North Country, with his whippy, double-handed, 13-foot fly rod.

Gray caught only one keeper trout during his first spring at the school. He rarely fished during productive periods in June and July because the evening hatch began close to his eight o'clock bedtime. In his second year, he watched Mr. Hammon, an early authority on River Itchen, working a fly on the surface to rising trout. Gray bought some flies from Hammon and copied his technique of presenting them. Hammon's flies were not tied with a divided wing, as are today's dry flies, but they could be made to float.

Gray also met several other renowned anglers in the Old Barge stretch, most notably George Selwyn Marryat. Marryat, the namesake of a current fly reel manufacturer, enjoyed instructing others and Gray watched him fish and listened to his impromptu streamside lectures.

Gray's catch of trout exceeding the limit of three quarters of a pound increased over his four years at Winchester College, catching 76 legal-size trout in his final year. His biggest fish, fooled by a Gray Quill Gnat, was three and one quarter pounds. Lord Gray reports that fishing the Itchen was good preparation for life, writing, "To get used to hard work and to expect little is the best of training."

Other great writers who walked along the River Itchen's banks included: Alexander Pope, the great satirical poet of the early 18th century; John Keats, the gifted early 19th century poet and leading figure in the romantic movement; and Rudyard Kipling, the late 19th and early 20th century author and Nobel laureate, regarded as England's greatest short story writer,

Pope went to school in Twyford, a village below St. Catherine's Hill, six miles south of Winchester, but had to leave because he wrote a satire on his teachers. Keats, like myself, walked along the river in the fall and was so taken with the beauty of the surrounding countryside, that he wrote his brother George that the "Dian skies, and their clouds, the soft twilight, the warm stubble plain, struck me so much on my Sunday walks that I composed upon it." The *Ode to Autumn* was the poem he composed.

Many angling writers, to numerous to mention, fished for trout from the banks of River Itchen. Frederick M. Halford, author of *Floating Flies and How to Dress Them*, and the leading authority on dry-fly fishing for three decades, established the doctrine of exact mimicry of the natural mayfly on Itchen waters. Shortly after, G. E. M. Skues, considered the father of nymph fishing, used a dry fly he called "Tup's Indispensable" because it was tied from the fur of a ram, or tup. The fish refused the fly, but when the poorly tied fly sunk, the fish eagerly took it and nymph fishing was born.

Skues, familiar with the shape of nymphs, concluded that the Tup's Indispensable was shaped more like a nymph than conventional dry flies and tied the pattern with hen hackle so it would sink. Later, he tied flies to directly

River Itchen

imitate nymphs. Although Skues is most noted for his work on nymphs, he also wrote on other angling topics. Perhaps his book with the most intriguing title was *Side-Lines, Side Lights, and Reflections*.

The most significant figure in my life to walk the banks of the Itchen was my friend Tom Royster, who has published nothing, but who is a great storyteller nonetheless. He visited the river 10 years before I did and remembers it flowing through channels that passed through the weathered brick walls of Winchester's buildings and under the road where King Alfred's statue watches over the city. Tom's first wife was an airline stewardess and they flew free to London and toured the surrounding area. Tom remembers wishing he'd brought his rod when he saw big trout foraging for food in the Itchen.

The River North of Winchester

Narrow foot trails border the river along its entire length, but I usually walked the section north of Winchester, where the "Worthies" were located. Each of the small hamlets along the river's east side were "Worthies": Headbourne Worthy, King's Worthy, Abbot's Worthy, and Martyr Worthy. I asked several villagers why they were called "Worthies," but the only answer I got was "They always have been." I suspect, however, that each village was once a petty kingdom during the Anglo-Saxon period. The village farmer who demonstrated loyalty to the settlement leader, usually a Saxon King, was considered a "moot-worthy," "fold-worthy," or "fryd worthy" man, a man worthy of a place in the justice court, the sheep fold, and the tribal militia, that answered the King's summons in time of war.

A small brook flows into the Itchen from Headbourne Worthy, passing under drooping willows, as it encircles the old church of St. Swithun, isolating it on an island in an enchanting wooded section. St. Swithun, bishop of the Saxon Cathedral in Winchester, was made a saint because of his great humility and longstanding efforts to help the poor. The old stones in the church's thick and sturdy walls and its small windows, some of which were colored, revealed that the church was first built by early Saxons and that I was walking where these early invaders had walked a 1,000 years ago.

Further on, I passed exquisite stone houses, with thatched roofs and stately gates, through which I could glimpse old trees and carefully kept gardens. From the banks at Martha's Worthy, I saw the distinctive spire of Easton Church sitting on a rise, the usual site of a Saxon church, but its rounded end and south door revealed that, like the great Winchester Cathedral, it was rebuilt during the reign of William the Conqueror. At Chilland, north of Martyr Worthy, on the Avington Estate, sat a little village church that may be England's best example of a Georgian church, a church built after the Norman influence.

The river then swept around a bend to Itchen Abbas, the village where

Charles Kingsley, 19th century novelist and journalist, and leader of Christian Socialism, spent his time-off from his parish commitments at Eversley. A quaint church, Itchen Abbas Church, sits on the river's banks in a setting of beech woods and green meadows. John Hughes, whose only distinction was being the last horse thief to be hanged in England, is buried in the church grounds.

I crossed the river on a footbridge near a 13th century fulling mill, located just below a large watercress bed, and walked into Old Alresford, where the red brick church of St. Mary stands on a rise and overlooks other watercress beds. Watercress has been grown for years near Alresford Pond, Bishop Godfrey de Lucy's reservoir over the River Alre. The spring water is ideal for growing this plant, used as a garnish the world over.

The milling, fulling, and tanning industries, which utilized the reservoir's waterpower, no longer exist and the reservoir is only a quarter of its original size. Nevertheless, I could still walk across the Bishop's "Great Weir" because it became part of a road that travels north of New Alresford.

Another church, the Church of St John the Baptist, a large imposing Norman structure, also sits in the town, as does the Swan Hotel, a once busy stopping place built in the 1700s, when the town was booming. There were so many churches in the villages along to the river that I wondered where their members came from.

From Winchester to the "Three Beginnings" was a long walk. When I visited this area again, I drove to Ovington, parked my car near the Bush Inn,

The River Itchen's upper reaches

and walked upstream. I usually ate a ploughman's lunch at the inn, (bread, cheese, and a drink) before I walked upstream, taking a gravel path across a bridge and then down the center of an island that split the river in two. Here, I sat and looked for trout, hoping one would reveal itself in a barely perceptible ripple, or perhaps even rise to a damselfly fluttering about.

More often, however, I saw moorhens drifting in an out of the weeds, mallard families up-ending themselves to feed, and stately swans drifting with the current. Once in a while, I might even see a water shrew sliding into the stream in search of food.

At the end of the path, the two channels merged and the trail continued upstream to Itchen Stoke. If still early, I walked further up River Alre to the villages of Alresford and Bishop's Sutton, the latter once owned by Harold of Wessex, but after his defeat by William the Conqueror, in the great Battle of Hastings, it passed down to King Stephan, son of William the Conqueror's daughter and one of England's weakest kings. Stephan gave it to his clerical brother, Henrie de Boise, the Bishop of Winchester at the time. The Village of Bishop's Sutton was listed in the Doomsday Book, but it was noted earlier in 17th century records. The Doomsday Book was the written record of a survey ordered by William the Conqueror to register the country's landed wealth so he could determine the revenues due him.

I could also walk further up the Itchen to Cheriton, the site of a decisive battle in the Civil War. With 10,000 soldiers to a side, the Roundheads and the King's Men fought on a foggy morning in 1644. The Royalists hoped to prevent the Parliamentarians from advancing further west, but a better tactician led the latter. When the King's Men charged down a narrow lane, Sir William Walker's more disciplined soldiers trapped and slaughtered them. The mounds east of the village are said to cover the bodies of the 2,000 fallen soldiers.

The south flowing River Candover, passes by the Buried Church of St. Nicolas, an underground crypt of a by-gone place of worship, the village church at Clinton Candover, and the richly filed Northington Church, built by the noted Ashburton family.

Everything along the paths was "old." I don't think a building had been constructed along them in hundreds of years; that's what made the stretch, and others like it along the river, so charming. It was like stepping back in time. I didn't need the Hollowdeck on the Star Ship Enterprise to create a mediaeval setting; I could just walk along River Itchen.

The river in its upper stretches was chocked with plants with novel names like Crawfoot, Mare's Tail, Ranunculus, and Starwort. Even if I'd brought my fly rod, any hooked fish would've darted into these water plants. If my tippet didn't break, I would have to break the fish off, perhaps hurting them in the process because I couldn't wade into the river to pull them free from the plants. Wading into a finely pebbled, sandy bottom river, like the Itchen, just isn't done.

Wading was not considered gentlemanly on southern England's chalk streams because it stirred up silt that spoiled the river for downstream anglers. Spotting fish and casting from the bank is the only acceptable way to fish English chalk streams. I also didn't want to cast for fish in this stretch because, sooner or later, my back-cast would catch in the tall nettles behind me, requiring me to push through countless prickles to free it from them. But, more importantly, the river was not yet ready to fish.

The summer months had been hot and dry, warming the river well above its year-round temperature of about 57 degrees, fish had become sluggish, and no flies were hatching. To effectively float a nymph through one of these narrow troughs would actually require dapping the fly and my 8-foot rod was much too short for this task. The early chalk stream anglers used long rods to dap their wet flies. In early October, I would fish the caddis hatch that occurs during this month.

Pay to Fish Waters

Southern England embraces diverse counties, such as flat Essex, lush Hertfordshire, rural Buckinghamshire and Oxfordshire, rolling Wiltshire, wooded Hampshire and Surrey, hilly Sussex, and "Garden" Kent. Visits to these counties took us by other famous English Chalk Streams. When visiting the Salisbury Cathedral, I watched large trout holding in the following nearby rivers: Wlye and Wiltshire Avon, draining areas to the north, Hampshire Avon, running south to the English Channel, and the Test, running through nearby Stockbridge. When we visited the Roman Baths, at the Town of Bath, I saw them in the headwaters of the River Avon.

The area around the hot water springs at Bath, which the Romans channeled into elaborate tiled baths, were first settled by King Bladud, an Iron Age ruler, who named the spot Kaerbadum, In addition to baths, Bladud built a temple to honor the Moon God, Minerva. Springs, particularly hot springs, were focal points of worship; gateways to the spirits that resided underground; places for rejuvenation, where secret powers replenished life. Later, the Romans built *Aquae Salis* over Bladud's more primitive structures, but the Saxons later destroyed many of their works.

I saw trout in several less famous streams, two of which Izaak Walton undoubtedly fished. The first, River Meon, flowed through Hampshire's East Meon, where Izaak Walton Inn sits on Main Street. The second, River Dove, in Staffordshire, flowed out of Axe Edge, near Buxton, and traveled south for 45 miles to its lowland rendezvous with River Trent. In the tiny hamlet of Milldale, sat the Viators (meaning Traveler or Wayfarer) Bridge, and old packhorse bridge that crossed the River Dove. A character in Walton's *Compleat Angler* described the bridge as being "not two fingers broad."

In beautiful Arum Valley, below the South Downs chalk hills, which rise close to 1,000 feet in height, I visited a private hatchery, where trout were raised to giant sizes before being stocked in the headwaters of a stream that fed River Arum. The huge trout they put into this little stream were way out of proportion to the stream's size. In contrast to wild fish, they sought no cover and swam leisurely away when I leaned over a fence and poked them with a long stick. They were so tame I could have "guddled" them, the 19th century practice of scooping trout up with your hands.

Since most of England's rivers have restricted access, only wealthy British gentlemen can afford to fish them. Selected sections of these rivers contain wild trout, such as Wiltshire Avon, managed for years by river keeper Frank Sawyer, whose observations of nymph behavior are recorded in his book, *Nymphs and the Trout*, but others sections are put-and-take fisheries.

I was not a bit envious to learn that the annual catch of the Houghton Club, a club founded in 1822, whose several dozen members own 16 miles of stocked water on River Test, was a 1.000 pounds of fish, weighing one and one half pounds or larger. Theodore Gordon once wrote, "I would not care to fish in a well-stocked preserve, and as for catching trout that I had bred and raised, I fear that such sport would possess few attractions for me."

In Stockbridge, I found a spot where I could pay to fish the River Test. The price was reasonable and huge fish could be seen in its clear waters, but fishing behind an ivy covered inn and walking along a manicured lawn, lined with flower beds and barbered shrubs and dotted with strategically placed ceramic lawn benches, didn't appeal to me, even though they claimed the fish were wild. Almost everything is manicured in Southern England. Even the forests are free from natural debris.

There was another reason I didn't want to pay to fish. In contrast to our encouragement of catch-and-release angling, anglers fishing in managed pay-to-fish rivers were required to keep the fish they caught, even though it cost a pretty penny to raise them to the large sizes stocked. In the United States, raising a trout through its second year cost more than five dollars. The big stocked trout, in the most primitive pay-to-fish stream I found, were fattened-up for at least three years before their release, although the cost was well covered by the fee.

Keeping the fish is based on the view that stocked trout are weakened by struggles with anglers and, therefore, vulnerable to disease. As a result, returning them places remaining fish at risk. Pay-to-fish stretches also limit the number of fish caught to two or three. I visualized myself paying $40 to fish for an afternoon and having to quit fishing after 20 minutes, the time it might take me to land two or three of these big, stupid fish. Twenty minutes on a river is hardly enough time to free my mind of its accumulated worries, one of the main reasons I fish.

The Last Two Weeks in October

I'd decided early on that I would rather fish the River Itchen in the fall, when it turned cool, than to pay to fish other rivers. The River Itchen is also a " pay-to fish-river," but the fish are wild and not stocked and the land along it owned by individuals rather than by fishing clubs. It would be tough fishing, but trying to catch wild trout from the waters where the "fathers" of fly fishing caught them and where they could be returned after being caught would be a worthwhile effort.

Unfortunately, Nature played a dirty trick on me and it rained steadily during the last two weeks in October, the river swelled over its banks, and I never got to wet a line before our stay in England was over. Winchester was so wet during that October that the cathedral suspended its subterranean tours.

Angler on River Itchen—the only one I saw during my visit

The great church has been waterlogged in places ever since first constructed, but sections were now dripping wet. I did, however, finish the research for my book

Perhaps I should blame St. Swithun for the rainy weather. Swithun, born in Wessex, was chaplain to West Saxon King Egbert. Shortly thereafter, the king selected Swithun as tutor of his son, Ethelwulf. When Ethelwulf succeeded his father as King, he appointed Swithun as Bishop of Saxon Church in Winchester. When Bishop Swithun died in 862, he ordered his body buried in the churchyard, a sign of his great humility, as bishops were traditionally interned inside their churches.

Over a 30-year period, St. Swithun's successors, bishops Ethelwald and Elphege, reconstructed Saxon Cathedral and in 971, the cathedral was consecrated, with St. Swithun's name placed alongside that of the Holy Trinity, St. Peter, and St. Paul. Saint Swithun's grave was reopened and his remains transferred to the cathedral. In response, the heavens wept for 40 days and England's weather has been rainy ever since.

A Chance Meeting with an Icon

One day in September, I ran into William Humphrey, author of the classic short story about an aging angler after a large aging trout, entitled, "My Moby Dick." He and his wife were in Winchester to spend a week fishing River Itchen and to write about this experience for *Sports Illustrated*. I mentioned that, as a charter subscriber to this magazine, I'd yet to see an article on fly fishing grace its pages. Nevertheless, Humphrey had been commissioned to do the piece and assured me it would appear. I told him I'd enjoyed reading "My Moby Dick," as well as his satirical piece on sex, called *The Spawning Run*, where he described Britain's famous chalk streams, but never fished them.

After returning from England, I anxiously awaited the arrival of each issue of *Sports Illustrated*. Humphrey's piece finally appeared seven months later in the May issue. I read the article, entitled "The Rivers of Thou Shalt Not," with great interest and I'm happy to say that the hard rains probably saved me from a humbling experience. Humphrey reported that he and his wife caught only one small trout between them fishing a private stretch of River Itchen at Easton Village, across the river from King's Worthy. They also were invited to fish the Test on Houghton Club waters in Stockbridge, where Humphrey wrote that an invitation to fish was "like being presented privately to the queen." Unfortunately, St. Swithun saw to it that they were rained out.

Nevertheless, Humphrey is a marvelous writer. His story was entertaining, the catching of fish incidental to the storyline, and the angling codes on southern England's chalk streams came to life. Perhaps that's all that really matters. I can't imagine other outdoor magazines publishing an article about a week's effort to catch one small fish. Actually, Humphrey did well on the Test when staying at a friend's cottage on the river. He landed a two pound rainbow on his first cast and lost one about five pounds after a long fight. On the lower Test, he landed the largest trout of his life, a seven and one half pound rainbow. He was fishing near the river's mouth for the elusive Atlantic salmon, casting downstream with a salmon fly, and the big rainbow took it on the swing.

Accommodations

During the week we were waiting for our house, we stayed in Wykeham Arms (+44-1962-853834), an ancient inn close to the cathedral and to Winchester College. I enjoyed its large bar decorated with an odd collection of old sports equipment and pewter mugs. The room prices were reasonable, but if cheaper accommodations are desired, the more modern Hotel Marcue Wessex (+44-1962-861611) has rooms that view the cathedral. Both hotels have restaurants, but we found English restaurant food distasteful and preferred to eat in a "Carvery," a large pub that serves roast beef, turkey, or pork, with roasted potatoes and fresh vegetables. For lunch, I always ate the ploughman's lunch in a local pub.

The trout season in England runs from April 1 to October 29 and the salmon season from March 1 to September 28. A rod license is needed, available at fishing tackle stores, hotels, and post offices, or you can write the Environmental Agency, South West Region, Manley House, Kestrel Way, Exeter, Devon EX2 7LQ, United Kingdom (+ 44-1329-444000). This will allow you to fish in the counties of Avon, Cornwall, Devon, Dorset, Somerset, Wiltshire, and Hampshire.

Other Activities

Touring the British Isles can be an "other" activity, but I prefer to familiarize myself with one small area rather than traveling aimlessly around larger ones. When not watching trout in River Itchen, I enjoyed hiking along Hampshire's many walking tails, some of which were Roman roads where legionaries marched to keep order during Caesar's reign. Many Roman roads, used later by Saxons, were renamed with Saxon names, like Watling Street and Fosse Way. Although I enjoy wilderness trails, there was nothing wild about the Hampshire countryside; it was a groomed and peaceful place. The mountain ranges had long ago crumbled to form the loam of its fields. The hillsides, once thick with tangled bushes and scrubs, had been nibbled away by generations of horned sheep, goats and pigs.

Unlike the Bronze Age men, who left ancient monuments and elaborate gravesites, or the Romans, who left stonewalls and statues, generations of farmers, first the Saxons and then the Celts, turned Southern England's countryside into a gentle, domesticated, and peaceful place. In fact, I've never felt more peaceful than when on an evening walk through the region's fields and along its hedgerows. Although I never got to fish any of the quiet rivers that flowed through this tranquil land, the images of them, and of the regal trout they contained, remain fixed in my mind.

Index of Waters

Racehorse Creek—164
Red Creek—93
Red Deer River—4
Rio Grande—126
River Alre—170
River Avon—180
River Candover—170
River Dove—180
River Itchen—
River Meon—180
River Test—181
River Trent—180
River Wiltshire Avon—180
River Wlye Avon—180
Roaring Fork River—43
Rock Creek—104
Ruby River—104
Ruedi Reservoir—39
Sacramento River—12
Salmon River—66
Salmon River, Middle Fork—69
Salmon River, Yankee Fork —68
Salt River—123
San Juan River—125
Seeley Lake—112
Shoshone River, North Fork—37
Shoshone River, South Fork—37
Silver Creek—59
Slough Creek—29

Snake River (Wyoming)—116
Snake River, Buffalo Fork—117
Snake River, Henry's Fork—123
Snake River, South Fork—123
Soda Butte Creek—31
Spotted Bear River—109
St. Joe River—113
St. Mary's River—167
Swan Lake—112
Swan River—112
Taylor Park Reservoir—46
Taylor River—45
Thompson River—113
Tongue River—89
Trail Creek—72
Trapper's Lake—50
Trinity River—17
Tuolumne River—10
Webber River—102
White River—47
Yaak River—108
Yampa River—93
Yellow Breeches River—60
Yellowstone River (Black Canyon)—29
Yellowstone River (Buffalo Ford)—26
Yellowstone River (Paradise Valley)—34

About the Author

John Mordock has been fly fishing since his youth, schooled by his father, uncle and grandfather. His first real trout adventure was a pack trip into California's High Sierra with his uncle and cousins. He also fished for trout in Wisconsin and Michigan rivers while canoeing them on weekends and vacations. In the summer, he spent several weeks each year in the Boundary Waters Canoe Area along the Minnesota/Canada border, where he learned to catch fish on streamers and popping bugs.

After completion of his graduate work at the University of Hawaii in 1966, where he surfed waves with many of that sport's early icons, he moved to Pennsylvania, but didn't fish any Pocono Mountain streams until after he moved in 1969 to New York's Shawangunk Mountains, a small mountain range east of the Catskills. John has fished in the Catskills for over 35 years and he relates his experiences on its waters in his guidebook, *A Fly Fisherman's Guide to Catskill Coldwater Streams and Ponds: Their Histories, Their Fish, and Techniques to Catch Them*, published in 2008, an outgrowth of his chapters on Catskill rivers in his earlier book, *Northeast, Trout, Salmon and Steelhead Streams: Every River Has a Story*.

Over the years, John has subscribed to many outdoor publications and has painfully learned that many angling writers describe experiences that he does not share. They write about catching large trout in waters John has fished and never turned a single fish approaching the sizes of those they claim to catch. In fact, both electo-fishing studies and angler surveys on some of the waters support John's experiences. Many writers also exaggerated the numbers of trout caught and recommended ways to catch big trout that John hasn't found particularly effective. As a result, in 2008, he published *Capturing Rogue Trout: Strategies of a Third Generation Fly Fisherman* in an effort to set the record straight about catching trophy trout. This book is a similar attempt to present the truth about major rivers that attract scores of fishermen each year.

While John can't claim he was a writer before he was a fisherman, he was a writer before he published his first fishing book. In 1975, he published *The Other Children: An Introduction to Exceptionality*, a textbook used in over 200 universities that might be the only textbook ever published by an author outside of academia. He has also published a dozen other books, most recently *Common Phrases and Where They Come From*, now in its second edition, and *Managing for Outcomes*.

John has been a member of the Catskill Mountain Chapter of Trout Unlimited since the early 1970s and feels privileged to have "rubbed shoulders" with a number of fly fishing icons, including Art Flick, Wes Drake, J. Michael Migel, and Ray Smith.